GENDER

JAMES C. NEELY, M.D.

THE MYTH OF EQUALITY

SIMON AND SCHUSTER   NEW YORK

PUBLISHED BY SIMON AND SCHUSTER
A DIVISION OF GULF & WESTERN CORPORATION
SIMON & SCHUSTER BUILDING
ROCKEFELLER CENTER
1230 AVENUE OF THE AMERICAS
NEW YORK, NEW YORK 10020
SIMON AND SCHUSTER AND COLOPHON ARE TRADEMARKS OF
SIMON & SCHUSTER
DESIGNED BY EVE METZ
MANUFACTURED IN THE UNITED STATES OF AMERICA

1   3   5   7   9   10   8   6   4   2

LIBRARY OF CONGRESS CATALOGING IN PUBLICATION DATA
NEELY, JAMES C.
GENDER.
INCLUDES BIBLIOGRAPHICAL REFERENCES AND INDEX.
1. SEX ROLE.   2. SEX DIFFERENCES (PSYCHOLOGY)
3. INTERPERSONAL RELATIONS.   4. LOVE.   I. TITLE.
HQ1075.N43   305.3   81-9075
ISBN 0-671-41542-5   AACR2

Portions of this book have appeared in slightly different form in *Columbia* in 1978 and in *Esquire* in 1979.

The author gratefully acknowledges the following permissions and sources:
AUDEN, W. H. Excerpt from "In Memory of W. B. Yeats" by W. H. Auden, from *The Collected Poems of W. H. Auden* edited by Edward Mendelson. Copyright 1940, renewed 1968 by W. H. Auden. Reprinted by permission of Random House, Inc.
BRAZELTON, T. BERRY. Excerpted from the book *Infants and Mothers:*
(continued on page 305)

PATTI AND ME

CONTENTS

Do not deny yourselves to one another. . . . Then throw off falsehood; speak the truth to each other, for all of us are the parts of one body.

—*Saint Paul*
Corinthians 7:5; Ephesians 4:25

PREFACE

THIS BOOK AROSE in me as the result of the terrible, the unnatural differences that have come between the sexes in recent years. These differences have been tearing our families, our very social fabric apart. It is therefore quintessentially a book about healing and the inevitable, the forgotten antidote of love. To appreciate this is to follow the necessary progress of our life as male and female from birth to death, and to know the substrate on which our sex is based. The method becomes that of the process of a natural life's journey, with crucial scientific stops along the way to explore the basis on which our ultimate completion depends. In the end we grow together in love.

What everyone who writes a book discovers is that no one person ever writes a book. It is the work of many, many people. And just as the surgeon depends on those about him for assistance with surgery, so does the author for his book. It happens that the persons who surround this book are mostly women. I am indebted to them in both a negative and positive way. Regrettably the learning process sometimes depends on painful misinformation and wrongdoing. My debt to the negative, therefore, is greater by far than to the positive, and I would gladly acclaim each name were it not that the greater half would feel it an aspersion on their person, rather than the character weakness in me it likely has been.

The ones who never lost faith and kept me to it know who they are. But Ceil, Molly, Jean, Donna, Terrie, Heather, and Patti were closest to the firing line. Bless them. Without a daughter and a wife—Heather and Patti—I wouldn't trust any man who ever wrote a book like this. I knew love, devotion, and nourishment galore from them and from all these remarkable women. Nor need there be a special accolade for my painstaking editor, Barbara Grossman, for a place has already been set aside for her in heaven where I am not likely soon to meet her.

I thank my son Christopher for reminding me all over again of the dignity and courage it takes to grow into manhood, and my sainted father at the other end for the example of his death. There were two magazine men—Byron and Rob—who latched onto me and gave me my first cover story, a distant numinous kind of man's love, but an essential inspiration for this book. There was Jamshed who listened and encouraged and then went back to help in Iran.

Finally, a special ineffable debt of gratitude to my confreres in medicine. They will recognize themselves and their work here and will understand that, for the sake of narration and bringing our message to all, I had to avoid our traditional scientific format. The ideas are theirs, not mine. What I have done is to attempt to say it my way. In a day and age when the jackals are circling closer and closer to an honored profession, I want the world to know that those who night and day ask their fellow beings how they feel and really mean it are still of the highest calling.

If this book somewhere helps one man and one woman understand themselves and each other a little bit better, it will have served its purpose. After all, that's where all knowledge began. And there's no reason it can't again.

ONE

SEXUAL
DESTINATIONS

The Angel that presided o'er my birth
Said, 'Little creature formed of joy and mirth
Go, love without the help of anything on earth.'
— *William Blake*
The Notebook

SHE HAS BEEN IN CHILDBED for over twelve hours. The sweat and agony of it is beyond her worst dreams all these nine months and the girlhood years before. She is certain she will die, at the very least that now she knows what death is like. This baby is to be hers and hers alone. It is the product, carefully planned, of an agreeable weekend liaison with an attractive man, a stud, as the avant women in northern California delight to call him. But it is to be her experience alone. A woman's growth experience. All hers.

Throughout gestation this woman had made a point to her midwife friend that this child would be raised without the horrible stigma of the sexual differences of our society. There would be no baby blue or pink discriminations, no skirt or pants differential, no toy pistols for one kind and soft panda bears to cuddle for another. The child-to-be's name—Robin—had been carefully chosen for its neutrality so it could be easily interchangeable and equally applicable to either sex. And now, at last, the moment of accouchement was at hand. She had worked so long and hard for this. There would be none of the confusion of the mating dance. It would be natural, no episiotomy, at home with a good friend in attendance. It would be perfect. Nature's way.

Now the head pops out beautifully controlled as the midwife with the skill of the queen's obstetrician gently protects against a vaginal tear and proceeds to rotate the shoulders through one by one. The rest of the child follows and suddenly a mother is crying again uncontrolled, eyes glazed in wonderment as she screams, "What is it? What is it?" It is her soul speaking, her very soul, as she looks down across her sweated bosom, across her now-flattened abdomen, across her mound of Venus to the wax-coated, stool-splattered, bloodied baby who is now complaining bitterly at entering this cold world. She asks the question women have asked since the dawn of time. She asks the question echoing down through all the centuries. She asks

14

the gut question—the first words that come to her, the first her child is privileged to hear in this world from mother, "What is it?" And the excited reply comes back quickly from the midwife, "It's a boy!" And crying, "O Lord," with joy, she takes him to her breast without a thought. And in that act of love another destiny is sealed. Nature has spoken to us again.

But are we listening? In just a few hours this woman's primal expression, her screams and cries, will be forgotten and relegated to the realm of cerebration where she can once again control her world and that of her son by the thought processes of the higher brain. The process of nature, of which she is so much a part and in which she has just demonstrated herself to be so inherently successful, will be isolated as a lived experience in independent growth and dissociated from the sexuality that is her and her son's very birthright, indeed their raison d'être.

Nature, at least until very recently, has made no manifest point of psychology. Hers (and note we always use the feminine form in referring to nature) is largely a matter of demonstrable processes that occur again and again and again with predictable regularity and character. And so we must go back to the stud farm in northern California to look for origins that may have been lost to the higher nature of the participants in Robin's conception. For it is there we will find an astounding, more than just coincidental, germinal male and female pattern, one that seems to begin as far back as our gametes, her ovum and his sperm, and that will recur at higher levels throughout life, and that may give some clue to the inevitability of our sexual essence. Nature does not care a hoot in hell if the mother available is nut shucking and emotionally constipated, if the father has the nerve endings of Sherman's statuary horse. Something immensely beautiful and more fundamental to each of their natures is taking place within them and apparently unbeknown to them.

We know that Robin's mother has produced and readied within her womb one perfect egg, probably no more and assuredly no less. The process of ovulation is singular and goes as far back as the perfection given a mother at her own birth. For she was born with a full complement of eggs that will not decrease or increase in number until they can be brought to fruition, one at a time, twelve to fifty years later. In a sense, then, she has been born whole because all the eggs she will ever need to reproduce have been endowed her at birth. Robin's father was not endowed with so wholesale a complement of germ cells that had only to be differentiated in time. He was born with the potential for a diffuse and wasteful apparatus, which, once it got going, manufactured a quantity item in grapeshot fashion and very inefficiently allowed for the mass production of millions of spermatozoa (sixty to one hundred fifty millions per cubic centimeter) in the hope that, imperfect as many of them were bound to be, there would be the one perfected sperm the female would find suitable to allow through her egg cell membrane. (Woody Allen, in his genius, has not lost sight of the tragicomic aspects of this scenario in his magnificent *Everything You Always Wanted to Know about Sex but Were Afraid to Ask.*) Along with his fellow sperms, this chosen one is in a state of nervous prostration in the bowels of a huge cannon just now agitating to ejaculate him and his comrades to almost certain death, for only one of the membership will survive, and even he will most likely lose his identity in the appointed task. It is kamikaze stuff. The sperms are hilariously dressed as circus performers. And so it is to our apparent misfortune that the male is somewhat distant or peripheral (not to say extraneous) to the reproductive process. The man sleeping with a pregnant woman feels the quickening inside her with excitement, but at a distance. His excitement is as much as anything else an excitement for her. The fetal kicks she feels he senses as part of her, even, indeed, as she feels them herself as integral and natural to herself. It is his child all right, but it is his child by proxy, because the child seems to him part of nature and nature is on her side. A chasm exists that never can be closed, try as we may. Even with modern natural birth techniques, which through the method of Lamaze training attempt to involve the father as a "coach" in the childbirth process, he feels distant and artificially employed. Attending such classes, one is struck by the conscious effort the men have to put out in order to participate and how naturally the women are involved. When the sexes are divided into groups, the women are found to discuss matters concerning babies, the men, often the ball scores.

William Carlos Williams, the father of modern poetry, and for years a successful obstetrician in Rutherford, New Jersey, was most proud till the day he died that he had delivered more babies (over 3,-000) than poems into this world. In the opening of his brilliant novel *White Mule*, the doctor speaks of woman, her strength, her incomparable courage and value. The scene is all for women. A midwife delivers a multiparous mother of a baby girl. "She entered, as Venus from the sea, dripping." There follows the blood, the urine, the sweat, the cleansing, the humor, the exhaustion of the birth chamber. The midwife says to the little girl, "Open your legs now I'll rub some of the oil in there. You'll open them glad enough one of these days, if you're not sorry for it. So, in all them creases. How it sticks. It's like lard. I wonder why they have that on them for. It's a hard thing to be born a girl." When the child is all cleaned and dressed and taken out to be shown to the father, "There seemed to be a spot of blood upon it. He looked and a cold dread started through his arms. . . . Then he sat on the edge of the disheveled sofa where, in a blanket, he had slept that night—and waited. He was a good waiter. Almost time to go to work." It is a magnificent passage, showing what it means to think and feel the wonder of woman's work and the unfathomed distance from it of man. Ironically, it could not have been written by a woman—unless she were a doctor.

And so, in the current argot, men and women would seem from the outset to be hopelessly out of sync. Robin's father and mother have extrapolated this confusion to the limit, both performing a biological service for the other to satisfy themselves momentarily and perpetuate the species, making no attempt to bridge the dark gap that stretches out painfully between them. And yet the desire is there and always has been there. The two split reeds so beautifully described by Plato have always sought to come together to become whole again. The late Margaret Mead showed clearly that polygamy is almost unheard of in ancient cultures; it doesn't seem to work, and again and again men and women seek each other out individually to complete their lives. But how in the world can this be done today?

Human nature does provide an answer, although not animal nature, for it is uniquely given to human beings to reach out beyond themselves in a way that distinguishes them from all the other animals. Jesus said it most simply in his famous parable of the woman at the well, "God is spirit." But it was the poet, Williams, who put it best for us today when he said, "Only Love stares death down." And it is this ageless human quality alone that can bridge our gap. Love. And we must not flinch from exploring it. Equally, we can't ignore the scientific knowledge, hard and soft, physiological and psychological, on which that love is based. We must have it all.

Life is graciously seasoned with a kindly sort of disillusionment and all our organ systems have a merciful periodicity. For the heart's systole there is always diastole, for inspiration there is expiration, for the nervous system an obligatory latency period before the next stimulus, for the skeletal structure the bones are motionless when the musculature rests, and our pancreas at ease between meals. The ebb and flow of sexual impulses are together one of the most successful indices to the state of our health, both individual and social. The sick or injured lose their sexual desire before all else. An animal dying will die systematically, losing bones and breath and gut and heartbeat and finally the nervous system at the very end and thus, almost cruelly, it will be aware of what's happening till the last. But the least necessary system to individual health and survival, the reproductive system, will cease functioning first. As if put on ice, there will be an atrophy of disuse. One sees this again and again in human disease. In concentration camps it has been well documented. In the wilds of nature, as with the endangered African gorilla, there seems to be a loss of sexual interest when species, for whatever reason, become diminished. There is almost an involutional melancholia that turns animal nature in upon itself in such cases and makes individual members wander off and seek shelter by themselves. The gorilla will nest alone at regular intervals separated widely from the possibility of a mate and even be annoyed when one such approaches to suggest the possibility of companionship.

But if sex is the first to go in ill health, it is also conversely the best indicator we have of health and a healthy society because of its dynamic dependence on the integrity of all the other systems. When we are feeling well, we are feeling well in our sex. The birth rate goes down in the doldrums of a depression, and when the boys return from war the birthrate goes sky high. Don't let your meatloaf, soldiers like to say upon discharge. It was Alfred Kinsey who showed long ago that those people who start sexual activity early tend to be those who continue it late and those with the healthiest and most wholesome sex life. Certainly the heartiest. And if there is anything that psychiatry has shed bright beams of light upon, it is the importance of infantile sexuality to our adult responses. It is not too much to say that those children—for whatever sad accident of birth, inculcation, or acquisition—who are not properly indoctrinated to infantile sex are likely to be maimed for life, and spending time in adult life talking about it from a couch is likely to serve no more than a palliative function. Few enlightened psychiatrists claim to cure anything, and even to modify sexuality that has been unnaturally indoctrinated is a Sisyphean exercise.

A favorite parlor game is to ask who are the three greatest people of the twentieth century. Invariably, two names, Churchill and Gandhi, are mentioned, and the third is usually up for grabs. When Sigmund Freud's name comes up the rejoinder often is, "Most influential, yes, but not one of the greatest." But it is impossible to get at infantile sexuality without Freud. I remember once asking my father, who was born in 1900 and grew up with this century, what people thought at that time of Sigmund Freud, and he quickly replied, "We thought he was a crackpot." The word "Freudian" now may be found in any dictionary. It is a household word and pervades our life.

A baby first discovers its genitalia at age five months when its hand coordination becomes sufficient for personal exploration. The baby

19

boy, if we follow Freud, discovers in himself the presence of a handle. The baby girl recognizes in herself its absence. This differentiation is more pronounced and progresses to complete gender differentiation at about age two when boys become sure of their identity as boys and girls know they are girls. Prior to the genital phase the child has passed through phases of oral fixation and anal fixation, during which the feeding impulses and bowel impulses have provided erotic enjoyment and gratification, both of which persist in various guises into adulthood. All of this is in the natural order of things and should receive the dignity and respect of parental, most particularly motherly care. Above all, it should be fun for all concerned—and natural.

Freud goes to the myths of Oedipus and Electra to name the problems that now begin to confront the little boy and little girl respectively. Oedipus, whose parents were unknown to him, in fulfillment of an oracular prophecy, inadvertently kills his father, Laius, and marries his mother Jocasta. These two horrors remain undiscovered by all until, after many years, Thebes being afflicted with famine and pestilence, the oracle is consulted again and reveals the double crime. At once Jocasta puts an end to her life by hanging. As for Oedipus, in the words of Sophocles: "Tearing from Jocasta's robe the clasps, all chased with gold, with which she had decked herself, he with them struck the pupils of his eyes with words like these, 'Because they had not seen what ills he suffered, and what ills he did, they in the dark should look in time to come . . .' "

From this myth, Freud developed his theory of a boy's fear of castration by the father because of his competitive love for the mother, however natural that love might be. In order to achieve a healthy emotional development, the boy has the problem of putting the father's anger and the mother's love in a balanced perspective, not clinging too much to the latter and not feeling an overwhelming competitive force in the former, and thus not being doomed, as was blinded Oedipus, to eternal guilt in the process.

In another myth Electra's mother, Clytemnestra, has been false to her absent husband, Agamemnon, and along with her paramour plots to kill him. Clytemnestra and Aegisthus thus kill Agamemnon in his bath just before the banquet scheduled to celebrate his return. Electra, who feels that her mother has killed her father out of jealousy of her own love for him, conspires with her brother Orestes to kill her mother, and they, in turn, slay both Agisthus and Clytemnestra.

Here Freud sees the little girl's problem as a perception that the mother and daughter are vying for the father's love. The girl senses the absence of her genitalia as evidence that her mother has already taken something away from her, castrated her, and her desire is to take revenge for the love for her father her mother has competed for or destroyed. To do this Electra acquires the help, by devious female means, of the male member, Orestes, and avenges her loss. Once again the little girl has the problem of putting the father's love and the mother's ire in balanced perspective for a healthy emotional development, not clinging too much to the former and not feeling an overwhelming competitive force in the latter. The major difference between the development of the boy and the girl is that the natural sex difference the boy senses in his mother makes it easier for him to leave her, whereas the girl feels a natural pull to remain as part of her in their similar feminine role.

All of this, of course, requires, as Coleridge once said of good poetry, "a willing suspension of disbelief." (Which, of course, does not make good poetry any the less helpful or instructive.) For those who would look for proof in this theory—or proof for the very myths themselves—it will be a long time between drinks. One has to accept this as a creative clinical metaphor and not as fact. The diploma in medicine is awarded for proficiency in the Art and Science of Medicine. It is to be noted that art comes first. And this is because medicine, whatever special discipline thereof, is forever citing large numbers of cases—five thousand breast cancers, ten thousand schizophrenics, twenty thousand smokers. But when it comes down to individual cases, a doctor has to be a clinician dealing with individual idiosyncrasies. The great actor Peter Ustinov, writing in his wonderful autobiography, *Dear Me*, has this sage advice about generalities and the sexes: "The relationships between the sexes are so inextricably fouled up by wits, cynics, wiseacres, philosophers, psychologists, psychiatrists, and finally Woman's Lib, that it takes the best part of a lifetime to find out that the general has no bearing whatever on the particular. Those who maintain the link exists are like explorers who lose heart in the face of a natural barrier, and never penetrate into the hinterland where people are people, and not merely slaves to a physical apparatus which has slanted minds into channels dictated by convention." As often as not we can throw out all the data and start from scratch to deal with one person, but guidelines such as Freud's do get us started. In any event, Freud has been the shibboleth from which all others have felt the urge to separate, of whom there have been many. And still the father figure, the crackpot, remains.

Anybody born in the Western world in the lasty fifty years has been born to worship science and scientific methodology. We split the atom and walk the moon and control fertility and eliminate smallpox, thanks to science. With science, we grow up thinking, go fact and formula and statistics—all things we can learn as true and real and reliable. Many premeds (as I myself did) take chemistry and physics and biology to get into medical school because you can get a good grade by giving specific answers in quantitative chemical analysis, or by memorizing Newton's laws, or the course of the twelve cranial nerves. The whole image is one of precision and accuracy, immutable facts you can hang your hat on. And contrariwise, the message you get about art is that it is arbitrary, subjective, wishy-washy, and nothing tangible that will last or that you can depend on with any consistency. The fact is most people have art and science just backward in their minds, for it is science that constantly changes, and art that can possibly remain forever unchanged.

If you study a Rodin sculpture, listen to a Wagnerian overture, view an impressionist painting by Monet, you are likely to be partaking of a masterpiece. One of the characteristics of a masterpiece is its reproducibility in time of the same creative impulse it originally contained. Thus, generation after generation turns to *Hamlet* to see the same tragic enigma and, despite the modernization of sets or change in actors, the human residue remains. Shakespeare's words touch the same spot in our souls, transcending time. Not only is this true with the generations, but it is true for ourselves. We can return again and again at different times in our life and see more and more in any masterpiece, which nevertheless still exudes its original charm and energy. J. D. Salinger's classic, *Catcher in the Rye*, is hilarious at fifteen, nostalgic at twenty-five, sad at thirty-five, human at forty-five, loveable at fifty-five, and magnificently entertaining literature at sixty-five. There is an artistic impulse at the core that one can predict and always return to enjoy.

But this is not so of science. Science is born to be changed and altered by trial and error. Negative information is just as useful to the scientific mind as are positive findings, for the one merely makes the other possible. There is no shame in being wrong, only shame in not following the proper method. The difference between science and art is that the scientist is working in a milieu he knows is tentative and the artist in one that may be permanent. Dr. William Carlos Williams describes in his autobiography how early on in medicine he realized that scientific knowledge was endless and inexhaustible, but that with artistic knowledge he could grasp something definite, a poem could sometimes make time stand still. In jest he used to say (with reference to Proust), "Art kills time," because a finite experience was possible in poetry but not in science. Some people have even carried this one step farther to claim that any intense emotional experience, say an orgasm, does indeed make all time stand still, but with the process of thought we are invariably in a cerebral dynamic state and hence forever changing. This would liken art to emotional expression and science to cerebration, which, although true, is true in the broadest sense only, for in the higher metaphysical flights of science, great scientists have necessarily always entered the spiritual. Albert Einstein wrote: "Everyone who is seriously involved in the pursuit of science becomes convinced that a spirit is manifest in the laws of the Universe—a spirit vastly superior to that of man, and one in the face of which we with our modest powers must feel humble.

In this way the pursuit of science leads to a religious feeling of a special sort." As we review some of the latest scientific findings today we must bear in mind how topical and susceptible to change they are apt to be. Science for all its wonder is not the ceiling of the Sistine chapel.

The point we are about, then, is to isolate the gender characteristics that seem to be basic to the male and female selves. These needs take the form of certain congenital and certain acquired characteristics that the wisdom of the ages confirm as integral to our respective souls, as needs inseparably a part of ourselves, not only for our individual selves but for each other, together, as one. This means ambivalence, yes; this means unclear lines of solution, yes; this means no pat answers, yes; all of which require the fantastic tolerance and understanding of a selfless nature filled with what we humans uniquely understand as love. For in the last analysis, to see the problem highlighted is to begin to answer it and enjoy it. We all have this psychobiological destiny, which takes the form of a life's journey, and which provides signposts and roadblocks all along the way. We can enter the flow of that journey or leave it at any point, and at various rhythmic phases for each along the way, but we deny it only at the peril of madness.

TWO

SEPARATE, NOT EQUAL

But this by sure experiment we know
That living creatures from corruption grow.
—Ovid
Metamorphoses

THERE ARE TWO SEXUAL PHENOMENA that distinguish the human female from her animal counterpart. One is the ability to achieve orgasm, the second to have sexual intercourse at any time. Nature provides estrous cycles for all female animals, a time when they are available for sex, and long periods when sex is unacceptable. But all the animal evidence available indicates orgasm is characteristic only of the human female. There is no such analogue in the male of any species, human or otherwise. The male is available for sex at any time, and orgasm accompanies the ejaculatory impulse in both humans and animals. This is really all we know, or need to know. Nevertheless, inordinate amounts of scientific literature are currently being produced to explore and account for the differences between the sexes. As the blush fades from the rose of early marriage a young couple comes face to face with what increasingly seem innate sexual differences. It is best we now honor the scientific literature and explore some of its findings.

The extruded egg, caressed by the fimbria of the tubes, has been carefully ushered from the ovary to rest in the warm vascular cushion of the protective uterine lining. There it will have to wait, perhaps die waiting, in order to be differentiated into male or female as the result of the male's specificity. Two adult female sex chromosomes (XX) are all the mother provides and thus the half component she donates to fertilization will necessarily always be female in her ovum. But the adult male (XY) has both a female (X) and a male (Y) sex chromosome and in splitting up to form donor sperms will provide female-carrying sperms and male-carrying sperms in about equal proportions.

It is important to pause and realize how firmly based we are in our female nature since there is a predominance of three to one female sex chromosomes between XX woman and XY man. We do not have to study Amazon woman or go back to Nefertiti's matriarchy to establish the primacy of female sexuality. We don't even need the silvery moonlight of alchemy. It is our natural state. We have it and live it every day within ourselves. Let no one doubt that female is the foundation, the fundamental sex of humankind, for in order to make a male, you simply add a Y to the female configuration. Observed another way, a male is simply a differentiated female—a fact intuited and enjoyed to the hilt by many a poet.

It is hard to get at the destiny of one bolus of sperm without, again, the clinical assistance of Woody Allen. But there it is. The poor wriggling creature deposited on the vaginal mucosa, required to traverse the cervical os, finds its slithering way through a dark passage into the uterine cavern, to flagellate helplessly there for seventy-two hours and generally give up dead exhausted. It is Gilgamesh all over again, earning the princess, the tasks of Hercules revisited. But despite all our temptations to misgivings, the male component at conception takes on certain undeniable characteristics. The sperms are competitive for the egg. As in the flight of the queen bee, it seems that the longest and strongest win the prize. The deformed or injured or immotile or inadequate haven't a chance and will succumb to those who can make the grade. Once they do, the ovum, which has been waiting, sedentary, with its exclusively female sex gene, seems to exercise choice in preferentially allowing only one sperm to enter its outer membrane to the exclusion of all others. Microscopy has shown that a number of sperms may cluster around a ripe egg, but only one is permitted access. And in that moment of access the sex of the zygote, the fertilized egg, is sealed by the addition of a Y or an X to what is already and always will be a firm female substratum.

The fetus, Robin, will persist in its female form for five weeks. It is only at that time that the chromosomal message of masculinity begins to take effect by differentiating the gonads into testicles, which, in turn, produce testosterone and convert the female substratum into male form. Should the gonads of a fetus be removed at this point, the basic female configuration of the embryo will be retained and, though castrated, will nevertheless persist in her female characteristics. There is likewise a curious confirmation of this fundamental sexuality in our adult hormonal distribution. If you remove the male hormone, testosterone, the male becomes strikingly feminine in the sense that his breasts enlarge, his voice achieves a higher pitch, his skin softens, he assumes a female hair distribution, and so forth. This is because his suppressed female hormone, estrogen, takes over. But if you castrate the female, you do not render her masculine to the same extent, only less feminine, for she has little or no circulating testosterone and only shows the effects of diminished estrogen. Her voice will not achieve a much lower pitch, her muscle mass will not thicken, and her skin will not markedly harden, though hair may alter somewhat.

What is to be learned or acknowledged from all this? What now seems so natural to us has been widely accepted by biologists for only the past twenty years. It is, and the point needs reemphasizing, that a male is merely a differentiated female, that our nature is basically feminine, and that it is only by the addition of something to the feminine that a male is produced, whereas subtracting from feminine forms produces nothing especially different. This biological phenomenon leads to a certain inherent vital firmness and superiority in the female and to a certain brittleness and vulnerability in the male, which is reflected statistically in his higher infant mortality rate at birth from congenital inadequacies.

Let us all begin again and keep clearly in mind that there is a predominance of three to one female sex chromosomes between XX woman and XY man. Thus, in a theater audience half filled with men and half with women bear in mind the chromosomal content is nevertheless 75 percent female and only 25 percent male. It is important also to observe that a Y is nothing more than a truncated X, or an X with one limb completely removed, giving the male Y chromosome one quarter less effective chromosomal mass. This genetic deficiency has an overall bearing on the vulnerability of the newborn male and the health of the male sex generally throughout life. But it is the XX or the XY of the conceptus that acts on the primitive cells of the promordial gonadal ridge to determine whether ovaries or testes will develop from that embryonic structure. After this initial template is established, the sexual differentiation into two distinct dimorphic sexes is strictly a hormonal phenomenon. Most particularly, it is the work of the male hormone, androgen (androgen and testosterone are the same), secreted by the developing testes.

Androgen has its effect on the young fetus in two main areas, the genitalia and the brain. If androgen from the fetal testes is present, genital masculinization will invariably take place. This effect must occur within a very short period of exposure, usually at five weeks of fetal life, because both before and after that period of time the masculinization effect is lost and the fetus remains forever a female. This crucial time for fetal sexual differentiation by androgen action is species specific. In the total absence of primitive testes and fetal androgen, female differentiation will always result. Similarly in the absence of ovaries and fetal estrogen the morphology will remain female, though nonfunctional in any reproductive sense. Furthermore, if you castrate a male fetus during the crucial period or use female chemical antagonists (such as estrogen) you render the fetus forever female. And if you subject a known female fetus to androgens during the crucial period you render that fetus male. So in both a positive and a negative experimental way we can confirm the key differentiating effect of androgens on fetal development of the sexes.

The evidence is now overwhelming that all mammalian species undergo brain differentiation into male and female as the result of androgen action in fetal development. The site of this action is on a poorly understood structure deep in our midbrain called the hypothalamus, sometimes referred to as the seat of our emotions. It had long been known that steroid hormones (for example, cortisone, estrogen, androgen) have the capacity to organize, at least in functional terms, the neural circuits that regulate neuroendocrine function in adults. But only recently has it been shown that male sex hormone is changed to estrogen in the brain and in this process of conversion a masculinization of the brain takes place that is manifested by certain changes in the hypothalamus. Most biologists now feel this is the site of brain sex differentiation.

29

The precise mechanism of action of androgen on the hypothalamus may be threefold. It is known that hormone action on nerves involves an interaction between the hormone and a cell. Once these cells are activated on their surface, the message is transmitted to the cell nucleus, the tiny brain of each cell. These cell receptors thus receive their initial conditioning in fetal life, although the message must be renewed throughout life.

Secondly androgen may act at the level of the neurotransmitters. Neurotransmitters are certain chemical proteins that occur when nerve end impulses are called upon to activate gland functions. Serotonin, dopamine, norepinephrine (a form of adrenalin) are good examples of such transmitters. If, for example, you masculinize a female rat by giving androgens you will block dopamine and eliminate her ovulatory cycle. And if you take that same masculinized female rat and selectively destroy the serotonin neurons you can induce ovulation once again. All of which is good proof of the intimate relationship of these neurotransmitters to sexual functioning. The hypothalamus is rich in such neurotransmitter activity.

Yet a third and most convincing explanation is that actual morphological (anatomical) changes in neuron connections can be demonstrated in the anterior hypothalamus with neonatal exposure to androgens. Until recently it was believed that the male and female brain were precisely the same and showed no differences in anatomy. But these were gross similarities only. Now the electron miscroscope has revealed that there are in the amount of space between nerve endings differences in the hypothalamus. The tiny arborizations at the filamentous endings of nerves are called dendrites, and these have been shown to be in more abundance, less diffusely organized, and more centrally located in the hypothalamus of male hamsters. Androgen-treated female fetuses resemble males, whereas castrated males show a diffuse or female dendritic pattern. And in the male canary, who sings alone, the hypothalamic nuclear concentration is again manifest. But females, initially with a diffuse dendritic pattern, can be masculinized to the point of singing, at which time the male nuclear configuration is noted.

Androgenization of the rodent brain does dramatically enlarge the hypothalamus, the front area of which has recently been designated the sex center because of its apparent ability to differentiate the brain into two sexes. The female normally has fewer neurons within this center than the male, but with hormone therapy her volume increases to reach his. Contrariwise, the castrated male readily regresses to the smaller female neural complement. And not only is this a time-related phenomena, but a hormonal dose-related phenomena. Because it can be shown that females exhibit all degrees of acyclic activity depending upon the amount of androgen present in the hypothalamus, where gonad-regulating hormones are released.

We can summarize this by saying that fetal androgen (or its lack) exercises an organizing influence on the hypothalamic brain that renders it male or female. The effect of androgen is to order a steady acyclic state, the male pattern of instructing the pituitary master gland to release a steady flow of gonad-developing hormone. The absence of this results in a hypothalamus organized to instruct the pituitary to mediate a cyclic, or female pattern of gonadotrophin release. In most mammalian species this directive is for life, but reversal experiments can be conducted that confirm these findings, resulting in a cyclic sex hormone pattern in genetic males and an acyclic pattern in genetic females.

The most fascinating result of these exciting new findings in the hypothalamus are the sex-specific behavioral traits as manifested in copulation and social behavior. For example, laboratory animals, such as hamsters, rabbits, mice, guinea pigs, show specific reflexive movements and patterns to encourage or facilitate sex. In females this is called lordosis (rolling over on the back) in preparation to being mounted. This can be eliminated by removing the hypothalamus or replacing it by androgen influences during the critical period of fetal development. Masculinized female guinea pigs show no such female lordosis. They display normal male attitudes toward normal females. And fetally feminized males exhibit lordosis and all the other traits of normal female response. Although among lower orders of mammals there is very little mating activity that is not directly sexual, as we progress beyond these usual laboratory animals to primates we can see social behavior that is sex-specific. Male rhesus monkeys threaten, initiate, and engage in mock battles and rough-and-tumble play. They frequently attempt to mount. The females withdraw more frequently, are much more domesticated, docile, and less aggressive and inquisitive. And these traits are both readily reversed by cross-hormone administration at the appropriate time.

Although it can be argued that animals are not humans, it is also clear that experimental confirmation of these findings in humans is unthinkable and totally out of the question, but that nevertheless we are left with an immense burden of biological proof. The possibility that an inherent brain differentiation exists in mammals is overwhelming, and at the very least cannot be empirically denied. The predictability of the process of sexual differentiation is so consistent as to suggest verification. In fact, certain endocrine disease processes in humans duplicate very closely animal experiments and these clinically corroborate the experimental evidence. This is probably as close as we are ever going to be able to get to any definite proof of inherent sex differences.

Hypothalamic tumors, for example, interfere with sexual function by altering the message release of pituitary hormones (gonadotrophic hormones) that stimulate the ovary and testes to activity and release of estrogen and testosterone respectively. With complete destruction of the normal hypothalamus in disease, there is an almost immediate cessation of libido and potency in both sexes, and depending upon the extent of the hypothalamic tumor involvement, one sees a commensurate loss in degree of gonadotrophic dysfunction. As opposed to other pituitary hormones, which require this releasing factor from the hypothalamus, the pituitary hormone of lactation, prolactin, is inhibited by the hypothalamus. When a nursing mother has "let down" as her suckling baby first stimulates her breast, the hypothalamus goes into a reflex shutdown, disinhibiting the pituitary, and prolactin flows from that gland to stimulate breast tissue to more milk production. When the hypothalamus is destroyed by tumor, galactorrhea (constant milk production) is one of the easily detectable presenting symptoms from overstimulated breasts. An elevated prolactin blood level, therefore, is diagnostic of a hypothalamic tumor that is interfering with sex life. In this way, sex-regulated activity has been shown repeatedly to originate in the hypothalamus.

There is a congenital condition (Turner's Syndrome) in which the fetus develops without the male Y chromosome, an XO fetus. Like the castrated male fetus, these babies differentiate anatomically as infertile females. Despite the fact that they are aberrant males, they develop without either male or female gonads and hence experience no fetal gonadal hormones. Specifically, the influence of fetal androgen and estrogen is absent. Nevertheless, they appear anatomically female and are reared as such, and in spite of all the terrible ambivalent handicaps of their condition, these women are highly maternal and make superior adoptive mothers. In testing they score as more highly feminine than do normal girls and adult women, which some have attributed to the total absence of the very small amount of androgen ordinarily produced by the normal ovary. In any event, the aberrations of Turner's Syndrome prove at the very least that wholesome genetic sex alone does not determine psychological sex, as if the hypothalamus possessed some innate difference related to the undifferentiated X chromosome. Incidentally, Turner Syndrome females, who are really male misfits, have a notably low emotional and psychosexual disturbance rate, as if they have no trouble with their sexual identity and know just who they are, despite their XO genetic makeup and absence of hormones.

Yet a third corroborating condition is called the adrenogenital syndrome. The overgrowth of the adrenal glands in female fetuses may cause masculinization of the genitalia because of androgen secretion originating in the adrenal gland. Even when these cases are recognized at birth to be essentially female, are surgically corrected and then reared as girls, they consistently display a shift toward male behavior and away from female. Though these girls show no problem with their core gender, that is, they know they are girls, they overwhelmingly prefer boys' toys and guns to girls' play and toys. They are less interested in jewelry and hairdos and more active in sports

33

and outdoor activities. They fantasize less about romance and prefer careers to marriage. A similar result, but more pronounced, may be seen when habitually aborting women are administered progesterone early in pregnancy to retain the fetus. Progentins undergo metabolic degradation to androgens, giving the young fetus an androgenized effect. In these cases, despite hormonal withdrawal at birth, the altered female offspring persists, as in the adrenogenital syndrome, with the same masculine proclivities.

What can one reasonably conclude from this? First, it should be clearly acknowledged that there is a primacy of cultural influences in all human beings that cannot be denied, and postnatal conditioning, as we shall see, has universal bearing on sexual inclinations, probably much more so than biological inculcation. Second, not only are obvious differences present in our bodies and our hormones, but all the available evidence supports the view that male and female brains are differently organized to receive this culturalization process. It is the midbrain hypothalamus that seems to be the organ that receives this differentiation and acts as a sex-governing body throughout life. Aside from the greater influence of family and parents and social pressures, the newborn mind at birth is not some hypothetical blank or empty state, a tabula rasa, susceptible to any and all sexual manipulations, as if we were all born switch hitters. The brain produces sexually appropriate behavior patterns and is geared to respond most readily to its opposite number in that process. The differing functions of male and female brains are innate biological distinctions that can be modified, but not eliminated, by society.

For those looking for hard workaday scientific data, however, to substantiate the innate differences of the sexes there is one well-documented area, that of muscle endowment. Little boys are consistently born with a greater measurable muscle mass that they must learn to cope with, a hard fact with immense implications for all our lives. This establishes the growth curve for little girls at a lower level than that for boys, a curve that has for years been available as standard reference in all pediatric textbooks. This muscle mass also gives little boys certain characteristics, observed again and again in clinical studies, that distinguish them in a general way from girls. Male infants show themselves to be more actively motor, more hyperkinetic, more curious, more "penetrating." Females tend to be more docile, loving soft things, and are much more successfully composed. This is not just a social conditioning phenomenon, but seems to be a response to the burden of the muscle activity given at birth that makes little boys more motor. This motor activity also makes them more interested in objects than in people, more skilled at gross movements, more rough-and-tumble, more inclined to play with objects other than toys, more exploratory, more inventive, more easily distracted by novel possibilities. As infants, girls are measurably less distracted by sights and sounds, less spacially visual, better in fine coordination and manual dexterity, better at rapid choices, more attentive to sounds and people, more socially responsive. All these early activities have great bearing on our adulthood and can largely be traced to our different muscle endowment. It is a hard fact of our innate sexual lives that goes back into all of history and has not been sufficiently emphasized in recent years.

In keeping with the spirit of the times, however, we do well to remember from the bottom up all the peripheral exceptions to any male-female generalizations. Thus in Dr. T. Berry Brazelton's popular book, *Infants and Mothers*, he distinguishes three types of babies relative to their activity quotient, active, average, and quiet. It happens that the examples given for the first two are males, and the third a little girl, but Dr. Brazelton hastens to add, "Even though such quiet, watchful inactivity may be more appropriate to a girl than to a boy baby, it need not be sex-determined. I have seen many little boys with this same makeup who are sturdily masculine as they develop." Methinks the doctor protests too much.

In a classic study entitled, *Motor Performance and Growth*, Harold E. Jones showed clearly, over thirty years ago, that boys are consistently stronger at grip, pull, and thrust measurements for all age groups. Not only is this true early, but the male hormone of puberty has a muscle-building effect that potentiates the male's already greater endowment and leaves the female far behind. We now know that certain countries in Eastern Europe have tacitly recognized this problem by administering anabolic (protein-building) hormones, male hormones, to their female athletes. But those feminists who have said, "we will leave the pole vault to the men," have taken a more realistic view of innate muscular potential, man's ability to clear the high bar.

Two other things happen to the female that enhance the gross motor differences described above. One is that the epiphyseal ends of their bones, the growth ends, consistently close down and complete their growth earlier than those of the male. Viewed one way, this gives her the advantage of completing her growth earlier than the boy, at least of knowing that's all the farther she is going to go, whereas he often awkwardly goes on and on and where he'll stop nobody knows. This is reflected in part in the old saw that "girls grow up faster than boys." Then, too, the hormones of her lunar cycle cause fatty deposits and fluid retention that further tend to potentiate her muscle imbalance relative to the male in the early teens. But that gets ahead of our story.

In the zeitgeist it is all too easy to become a Cassandra about the God-given male superiority of muscle endowment, because feats of strength and daring do catch the imaginative fancy of childhood and enable one to grasp the gold ring on the merry-go-round. But great benefits, which she has always put to good use, accrue to the young female as the result of this lack. She doesn't waste as much energy in painful physical trial and error. Teachers note that she doesn't fidget as much in school, is more content to sit and patiently work things through. She has a natural compensatory inclination to words and verbal skills that she can perfect to great advantage (how many women there are in publishing!) and a natural gravitation to the necessity of relatedness, socializing, in order to get what she wants. It may be years before her male contemporary sees the importance of these things that she comes to in a much more natural way. He will have to work terribly hard to make up for this later on, and she, meanwhile, can build her musculature by the simple expedient of exercise, which more and more girls are conscientiously doing.

In an article for *Columbia* magazine in 1978 entitled, "Why Men Dominate Women," one of our leading anthropologists, Marvin Harris, carefully begins with ancient civilizations and traces the muscle problem right down to our current gender disarray. He shows clearly how necessary for survival it was to have the naturally best coordinated and strongest become the warriors and protect the tribe against enemies of all kinds, and how the other essential activity, obtaining food, was divided between shooting game, a coordination and strength feat, and gathering mineral-rich berries. It takes little imagination to see that this was not a prejudicial decision, and that, especially when you add the uncontrolled matter of childbirth and rearing, the division of chores between men and women assumed a rather natural distribution relative to natural endowment. Richard Leakey, in *Origins*, puts it this way:

If our cultural expression of sex roles were totally unbridled by basic biological patterns and influences, we should expect to see a more even balance between male and female-dominated societies. It would surely be somewhat remarkable if all the social and economic systems that have ever been invented were to have led to male social dominance simply through cultural conditioning, as the extreme environmentalists suggest.

Leakey shows clearly that when *Homo erectus* began migrating from Africa to the colder realms of Europe he needed meat, which had to come from the slaughter of large animals, a job the men generally were better equipped to perform. Meat then became the spoils of any conflict and a source of power in the tribal bargaining, and the men were the natural purveyors of such power. He shows, conversely, in rare societies, such as the Hadza of Tanzania or the Paliyans of India, where aggressive behavior or migratory propensities are minimal, the men and women enjoy equal opportunities. They eat little meat, derive most of their food from plants, and have almost no political currency. Also, they are among the most backward and stagnant people in the world.

37

From fetal life to remote old age (women live on the average seven years longer than men) the female of the species is infinitely better suited by her constitution to withstand the rigors of life. The incidence of spontaneous abortion of males in early pregnancy is fully one-third greater than of females. Congenital malformations occur (at a ratio of two to one) more frequently in males. Hernias, for example, often a life-threatening condition in the newborn, are five times more common in baby boys. There are absolutely more female babies born than male babies (51 percent to 49 percent) and the infant mortality rate for baby boys is considerably higher. Lung disease is higher in boys. Crib deaths during the first year of life are higher in baby boys. When the baby loses its material immunological endowment at six months, boys become much more susceptible to infection than girls. Mortality rates from blood poisoning and meningitis are six times higher in boys. Even after the advent of antibiotics, which have greatly reduced infectious diseases, there was an increase in the disparity of female survival relative to male, further suggesting the higher resistance potential in the female. The immune proteins that combat such diseases are felt to reside on the X chromosome, half of which is missing in the male offspring. Hence it takes longer for his immune mechanism to respond and to progress to maturity. Another advantage the female has is the pairing of like chromosomes (XX) so that if there is one bad locus on one X the other matching pair from the good X can dominate or mask or attenuate the bad effect on the other. This is called heterozygosity and obviously is absent in the XY male, where, if there is a bad gene on either chromosome, it cannot be overridden or neutralized by its opposite matching partner. This leads to certain sex-linked diseases, such as hemophilia, in which the bad gene in the female is successfully masked but becomes manifest in the male. She remains a carrier by virtue of her heterozygosity, but the male offspring become bleeders, as in the old royal families of Europe.

In adulthood there are only a few disease processes more common in women than in men. Gallbladder and liver disease, such as hepatitis, are more common in women. And diseases related to the immune body system, such as arthritis and lupus and erythema nodosum, so-called connective tissue or collagen diseases, are more common in women. This is thought to be related to the increased immune burden of the X-dominated chromosome configuration which, it is estimated, gives them a 5 percent greater genic mass than men. But in all other commonly shared disease categories, men for all of life are more vulnerable to disease. The incidence of diseases of stress, such as hypertension, peptic ulcer, and coronary thrombosis, are much higher in men. Cancer of the lung, brain, gastrointestinal tract, and skin are higher in men. Arteriosclerotic disease, occupational diseases such as asbestosis, bone and muscle cancer, traumatic disabilities, infectious diseases are infinitely higher in men. Certain X-specific diseases, which women are relatively immune to, occur commonly in men. They include drug-induced anemias, diabetes, clotting disorders, hypoparathyroidism, rickets, protein deficiency states, to mention a few. The old expression has it that it is hard to be born a woman, but all recent studies tell us it's probably a good bit harder to be born a man.

Anthropological evidence of innate male and female differences has long been noted. As we come up the phylogenetic order from lower animals to primates, developmental learning becomes more sophisticated and sexually differentiated. Lower animals are programmed in fetal life, as we have seen, for sex-specific behavior. There is no conditioning that can change this postnatally. But in primates, rhesus monkeys for example, much of their sex activity and sex-specific activity must be acquired as a juvenile learning experience, although organization of the fetal brain facilitates or inhibits such activity. For example, female rhesus monkeys can learn *de novo* adult copulation, but males cannot unless continued in childhood. Also, females with destroyed brain cortices will continue to function sexually, but male monkeys so altered will not be able to copulate. The higher brain centers seem necessary to successful male sex, but not to female, and this is borne out in human clinical states. Men with cortical brain lesions lose their potency, women do not lose their capacity.

A comatose female has been known to conceive and deliver a normal child. A woman may conceive even if repelled, uncooperative, half-starved or "unconscious" in the modern sense. A carnival performer, a high dive expert, conceived once between acts, continued to perform for nine months of pregnancy while at the same time she lost weight to maintain her image, delivered a normal baby, and then died of starvation. A normal man can perform sexual intercourse only under conditions that allow his brain enough leeway to permit erection, intromission, and ejaculation. No unconscious man has ever become a father, except again in the current use of that term by which we mean unaware or unfeeling. It seems that the male's sexual success is relatively more contingent upon learning and is much more vulnerable to mislearning than in the female, which may account for some of the attractiveness of older men. On the contrary, when sexual activity is mislearned, the male sex is much more susceptible to extremes, bizarre and sick sexual aberrations such as sadism, masochism, transsexuality. Cadaverous sex, necrophilia, has never been reported in a woman. A woman rarely rapes a man. It is noteworthy as well that homosexuality occurs ten times more frequently in men than in women.

None of this of course has to do with the profound psychological or emotional commitment necessary to sex, which is immense, unique, and of overriding importance in human beings and will be discussed later. What is obvious and is now emphasized is woman's relative hardiness and intrinsic advantage for the sex act. She can make love any time whether she wants to or not. A man can't. She has an almost unlimited capacity for orgasm, whereas the male undergoes a mandatory postcoital latency. She can do it without thinking and a man cannot. She can space out and have intercourse without feeling, and man cannot. Though her emotional pleasure may be more easily inhibited, her functional capacity is not, and, contrary to the male, she is not as susceptible to extreme sexual malfunction. Because of all this, it is easier for her, anatomically and physiologically, to whore.

The innate biological superiority of the human female is a scientific fact of nature, and this will not change in any way until after the hormones of puberty pour forth. What disrupts us now in our late industrial age is that brawn as such has progressively become less necessary to any sexual division of labor, a division that has come to seem more and more artificial, for not only can woman control her sex cycle, but mechanization can allow anybody to perform the same tasks with equivalent skills. Unfortunately, this leads us to extrapolate back with magnificent retrospectoscope to say one sex was always oppressed or punished or exploited, when the more accurate truth is that people lived life the best they could and dealt with a historical imperative. In his classic *The Decline of the West,* the great German philosopher, Oswald Spengler, describes the inevitable rise and fall of all cultures relative to the division of sexual labor. In ancient cultures the separation, as above, is great. The distinctions always become less and less with increasing culturization and finally, when functional homogeneity is achieved, the end is at hand. The process is predictable and has occurred repeatedly in all cultural disintegrations of the past, according to Spengler. His book was written in 1912.

Might we not pause and say to ourselves once more, *Vive la différence?*

THREE

THE ANTIDOTE
OF LOVE

The feminine is rooted deeper in the earth and it is immediately involved in the grand cyclic rhythms of Nature. The masculine is freer, more animal, more mobile as to sensation and understanding as well as more awake and more tense.

—Oswald Spengler
The Decline of the West

On HIS DEATHBED, asked if he were prepared to die, the late James Thurber replied, "Yes, because you can't fool little girls the way you used to be able to!"

You can be sure, in addition to acknowledging his own diminished potential, Thurber was making a sane sociological observation about something about which he had considerable misgiving, or at the very least ambivalence, allowing his wonderful release in humor. Again, it is the philosopher Spengler who puts the problem beautifully:

In man and woman the two kinds of history are fighting for power. Woman is strong and wholly what she is, and she experiences the Man and the Sons only in relation to herself and her ordained role. In the masculine being, on the contrary, there is a certain contradiction; he is this man, and he is something else besides, which woman neither understands nor admits, which she feels as robbery and violence upon that which to her is holiest. This secret and fundamental war of the sexes has gone on ever since there were sexes, and will continue—silent, bitter, unforgiving, pitiless—while they continue. In it, too, there are policies, battles, alliances, treaties, treasons. Race-feeling of love and hate, which originated in depths of world-yearning and primary instincts of directedness, prevail between the sexes—and with a still more uncanny potency than in the other history that takes place between man and man. There are love-lyrics and war-lyrics, love-dances and weapon dances. There are two kinds of tragedy—Othello and Macbeth. But nothing in the political world even begins to compare with the abysses of a Clytemnestra.

In the twenty years since Thurber's death, feminists have carried the message of liberation to us with such thumping sobriety that the Western world cries out for some perspective with Thurber's sense of balance. Above all, we need his reminder that we are all in this life together and need each other terribly. As with generations, so with the sexes—the similarities are eventually much greater than the differences and we are all headed for the same place, a fact we might lose sight of in the adversary atmosphere many young women are now creating. And, baby, them polar fields can be mighty cold. Ask the man who owns one.

Psychiatrists again and again come up with an undeniable emotional residue in the extreme or militant feminist, namely, an unfortunate or unsatisfactory relationship with the male of the species that derives originally from the young girl's relationship to her father. Between the ages of six and twelve a girl learns a sense of her own worth to men from her father's image of her. At this time, above all, she needs his social companionship, a developed sense of sharing with a mature member of the opposite sex that she will emphasize and enjoy in her nature all the rest of her life. This is part of her, part of her need. The young boy, although needing the father's example of how to enter the world, is much more apt to emphasize individualism and be a loner developing his own skills to strike out on his own. The father's support need not be as immediate.

My daughter, when very young, used to come to me with her girlfriends and say, "We don't like ourselves." I was nonplussed. This was an astonishing thing to me, that three little girls had agreed they didn't like themselves and were reporting it to me. My son might be seething, furious with his own stupidity, upset with the world, disappointed, enraged—but it never occurred to him to complain that he didn't like himself. Erica Jong allows in *Fear of Flying* that men don't understand that all women feel they are basically unattractive, but my wife, of course, easily understood how my daughter felt in such moments and as mercifully as possible absolved me from causing any long-term psychopathology. She would explain my daughter's feelings beautifully: It was simply a matter of needing worthy reassurance and not being available to the state of love at that time; every woman knew that.

If the young girl is denied the esteem and social grace in her sex that she seeks from her father she begins, often prematurely, to seek it elsewhere. Many fathers of later militant women have been shown to be either ill or frequently absent. An overwhelming number of

45

these fathers have been alcoholics whose emotional affect and pre-dictability to the young girl is ineffectual. And so she feels forced to seek the company of men elsewhere. She will do this almost any way she can to discover her worth as a social self, which, unfortunately, often leads to time-honored means and one of the greatest disasters of womanhood—precarious, premature, promiscuous sexuality. When she does this, she often invests her whole youthful idealistic self in a man she thinks she loves, and when this fails and she is, in her words, "fucked over" by him, she is more than heartsore—she feels irrevocably damaged in her substance. So what was already a poor sexual self-image derived from a negligent father, has now be-come, in her feeling, a total loss of esteem. She undergoes what I call A → Z reasoning for all men everywhere, and she no longer is willing to risk making the distinctions necessary to distinguish between good, better, or bad men and so seeks the more comfortable com-pany of women. As often as not she becomes organically anorgasmic for men. This happens with sufficient frequency as to represent a clinical syndrome to psychiatrists. In most of these women they note an extreme intelligence that even further separates them from their feeling or feminine nature, but allows them to match wits with, even outwit men. This merely dissociates her more from her self and po-tentiates the emotional problem. One thing above all else is true. If a woman has ever had a good relationship with a man, be it father or lover or both, she is not ever likely to become a militant feminist, and she will make distinctions, as she must, between men. The rela-tionship of a father to his young daughter, his love for her, mani-fested especially in shared companionship of a socializing nature, has a direct and immense bearing on our modern society, and specifically the feminist movement within it today.

The young girl making her first forays into the real world leads forth from what she has gathered from her mother to be the strong bastion of femininity. In her life, this is and will always be a solid core to which she can retreat, a core that the young boy is not as directly or naturally privy to. My mother used to say to us children, "There is not much that happens to a woman that can't be made better by combing her hair." As a boy I couldn't imagine what magic accrued from combing your hair. For a man it takes his own eight-year-old daughter to make him realize that the retreat to a lavender bubble bath, or a shopping spree that delivers a soft yellow knit sweater, or baking cookies on Sunday afternoon can really change the world around her for a woman. Girls know this and feel this balm when quite young. If for some reason this core feminine self is not nurtured by maternal example, a whole protective cocoon is denied her that is her birthright and much of her natural charm and beauty. It is natural, then, that the mother-daughter bond is a strong one and an enduring one, and one that is broken eventually (as indeed it must be in adulthood for a healthy woman!) with almost invariable trauma. Mother and daughter growing up are feminine souls together in their firm bastion, scheming against the cruel world and comforting each other in a very natural way. Any maternal disruption or denial of her own feminine self at this stage will be a misrepresentation to her daughter of the women's role in her natural life journey. If the mother uses this bond to convey only the unspeakable doldrums and denials of marriage, the drudgery of homemaking, the mess of diapers and dishes, the unspeakable pain of childbirth, the young girl sees all this as something to be avoided. Often such mothers produce asexual, anhydrous spinsters. But if that same mother explains the pros and cons of marriage and the ambivalence of human relations with up-beat emphasis on the joys and glory of love and relatedness and bringing new life into our world, she will have produced a blossoming woman.

Not long ago my daughter had her menarche, a time of life about age fourteen which, despite all parental preparation, a father anticipates with trepidation. One evening she excused herself from the living room and returned *to me* to describe *to me* a "vaginal discharge" that was dark and different in color. When I explained to her what this was her only comment was, "It's no big deal, you know." And then, in the astonishing way of children, there was a long pause, and then she quietly said, "Daddy, how do you know when you are in love?" I can't imagine a more gratifying response any father could

47

ever hope for from a daughter sharing her first menses. Needless to say, I felt my grandiloquent response inadequate to the circumstances and enlisted the help of my wife (my daughter's stepmother), and together they went off into their world of women and got it all straightened out. It was beautiful, particularly to an outsider like myself. Yet I was pleased she had first come to me with her problem.

Though conscience is largely developed in early childhood, consciousness is primarily evoked between the ages of six and twelve. It is interesting that conscience is formed during a period of relative sexual intensity and consciousness during the years of childhood when sexuality is relatively dormant and the difference between the sexes naturally deemphasized. Consciousness is a word that has been so bruited about in recent years it has almost become a cliché and has been grossly misunderstood and misrepresented. Since it will come up again and again the meaning needs clarification.

Consciousness is not I.Q., not an A.B. or M.A. or Ph.D. or M.D. Consciousness is not intelligence, it is not cerebration or the intellect or the power of the mind. Consciousness is a self-identifying awareness of other people. It is an intimate awareness of one's own feelings that leads to an understanding that can be thoughtfully translated into the needs of others. Being can get along without consciousness, but consciousness cannot get along without being! Thus it does not need pure intelligence as a prime requisite, nor does it necessarily exclude this. But to say that somebody is stupid, that is, unlettered or unschooled, does not necessarily render them unconscious, just as conversely the high groves of academe, brilliant with accomplishment, preserve some of the most unconscious specimens available. A conscious person is somebody who has effectively integrated mind and body and thereby becomes almost naturally unselfish. Such people seem instinctively to know life is not achieved by grabbing for all you can get, but rather being sensitive to others' feelings because you know those same feelings within yourself. It follows that one gains a life only by giving it away, the message of Christ.

In considering the development of consciousness in the six to twelve year old, one must give particular attention to the congenital temperament, especially to the extremes of introversion and extroversion that allow a person relative access to body sensations. Although we acknowledge different sized breasts, different sized stomachs, different lungs and livers and arm lengths, we are loath to accept the empirical fact that some people have limited access to feeling capacity. Such people are congenitally tilted toward the introverted end of the mind-body equation and achieve consciousness, as here defined, with the greatest difficulty, because their approach to the world limits their feeling-access at all times—whereas the extrovert opens arms to welcome all feelings, good and bad, in the learning process. Often it is on this introverted emotional template that the seeds of later militant sexism are sown, mistreatment compounding once again what is already a congenitally tenuous emotional system.

It may be well to digress now and expand a little on what I think one day soon will be viewed as the true, modern, tragic personality type. I refer to the congenital introvert, who suffers from a poorly understood and not really correctable constitutional disposition common to both sexes. The example of ex-President Nixon comes easily to mind and into ready focus when you understand this phenomenon. Henry Kissinger has stated that only a dramatist will ever capture the likes of this man, but I think it is much simpler if one is aware that such a person is born with only a limited emotional access. He or she can be likened to one of those Swiss fortresses of hewn rock that guard the narrow alpine passes, in which here and there one can see man-made peepholes projecting from the fortress which allow the occupants to spy on the world. In the same way, for the introvert, the outside light and seething world experience is allowed to enter only in very small aliquots, to be processed thoroughly and slowly mid all the turbulence within. The introvert has all the internal equipment, in fact cerebral equipment galore, for this thoroughgoing process, but the reduction and depotentiation of all sensation takes place at the point of entrance, shutting out worldly sensations, both good and bad. The introvert sees the emotional world through slits, as a slit lamp for visualizing the eye will come down to a very tiny and limited focal point of light access. Hence, from early on in life, such people have a slowly developing and limiting emotional experience that (and this is the modern tragedy) has little if anything to do with intelligence, the quality on which our modern world places such a premium for success. Introversion has nothing to do with intelligence, but it most assuredly does have to do with feeling tone as internalized in all its abundance and then processed by the sensitized intellect.

Nixon is a brilliant man. But one born, as was Nixon, with this congenital limitation, can function for years with involuted thought to the exclusion of thought-feelings. In the ex-president's case this led to an almost intuitive overcompensation for this deficiency, for example, when he made his famous broadcast, looking at you squarely from the tube, coming through with all apparent sincerity, even to pointing out his wife's cloth coat and his dog Checkers, and with the inevitable rim of perspiration beading his upper lip. Nixon is always forcing something he knows he *should* be feeling, but does not really feel, or feels in a limited way only. It probably came as a sincere shock that the people turned against him over Watergate, because he had never experienced the feelings that this mess evoked in most people's hearts. Those who say that Nixon's introversion is a rarity in politics are close to the truth of his enigma, for his politics is a compensation, or at least an attempt to compensate, for introversion. But it must be clearly understood that this is an inborn condition of limited emotional, not cerebral, access that stunts the total growth and stems from a tragic flaw. Psychiatrists will tell you it is next to impossible to break open this *festung Swisse* to a feeling world. It is not, as some people are so quick to insist, merely Tricky Dick at work, lying and cheating again. It is unfortunate Dick, working in an industrial world that craves feelings but rewards the intellect, and working with a nature that is poorly inured by birth, inculcation, or acquisition to the feelings we all basically share and live by. Unfortunately, most people who are healthily inured to feelings cannot achieve what Nixon did, because the pain of accomplishment is far too great for the sensitive. And this, I fear, is the tragedy at the heart of the crisis in our political leadership. Could we make room today for an Abraham Lincoln? What happened to Adlai Stevenson? Has not external approbation come to exclude the inner feelings of fullness of such sensitive men? Here is how the novelist, Nina Schneider, expresses a wife's view of the Nixonian phenomenon:

She nodded, wondering how conscious he was of communicating no S-E-X. Were his little power plays and boyish intrusions tricks for making her tense? That was glamorizing him into higher consciousness and rascality than he had. Had he always had them and she not allowed herself to be conscious of them? Or had she been as afraid of having to act as Adam was to feel?

It was not that he was stupid. By no means. By inclination and career he had specialized his mind to take in and put out limitless amounts of precise information. He was an authority in his field. When he spoke he sounded firm and confident. But on personal matters he was silent or vague. By overdoing precision he had relieved himself of the necessity, and Ariadne of the possibility, of trying to express the inexpressible.

At the other extreme, open-ended extroversion, we pay the price of a Howard Cosell on Monday night or Bella Abzug on Saturday afternoon, people who wear their uninhibited hearts on their sleeves, relentlessly murdering the King's English with whatever mixture of metaphor or hyperbole occurs at the moment of feeling. No cliché, no destruction with faint half truth, no tawdry barroom brawl can stay these "circumlocutory purveyors" of life. We are expressing what we feel! Alas, we needn't embrace the extreme edges of the bell-shaped curve of personal character variability. There is a happy medium between introversion and extroversion. Excellence may be predicated on eccentricity, but so indeed is mediocrity.

Just as the young girl has her problems of socialization between ages six and twelve, so the young boy has his own which are apparently sex-linked. Above all, from the father he needs a hero to worship. This comes through not only in the pictures of Reggie Jackson he hangs above his bed, the crossed hockey sticks on the wall, the magazine cutouts of Eric Heiden or Roger Staubach, but in the temporary denial of the feminine as worthy of his own aspirations. No matter that male ballet dancers are exceptional athletes or that Nadia Comaneci is beautifully muscular doing her free-style floor performance, these and the like are not encouraged to take root in his mind as especially or distinctively masculine. "Of arms and the man I sing," writes Virgil as he begins to relate the heroic deeds of Aeneas, the defeated Trojan, but nevertheless founder of ancient Rome. It is the archetypal war hero, Aeneas or Ulysses or Hector or Achilles, that fires the imagination of the young boy. The world of manly deeds now lies before him and he longs for models he can worship. No matter that the dark side of his curiosity runs to Godzilla or the Incredible Hulk, his concern is being brave enough to enter this manly world of achievement. In this he is very lonely because in the normal course of his development he has by now left the protective aura of mother. Much more so than his sister he feels emotionally alone and left alone to achieve on his own meritorious endeavor. The monkey is on his back and he feels it. Unlike his sister, he has no feminine base to return to to lick his wounds. He can't just comb his hair, he can't resort to "well, I can always be a mother." In his own mind his underpinnings are very weak, what he does is lonely and therefore heroic, because it is his daring risk against the cruel world. In this he needs a father to show him the way. If it is the mother's role to give him unquestioned, unselfish, full-bodied natural love at all times when he is hurting in need, it is the father's role to make fine distinctions in his love that specify and reward achievements while leading the boy into the mature world of rules and regulations. And this is the stuff of heroism. Watching a group of schoolgirls play softball you can be sure the rules will be changed and reassessed and readjusted all afternoon. "Making the rules up as you go along," is strictly OK. Watching a group of boys organize a softball game is the schoolboy analogue, where endless procedural detail is argued and stamped out well in advance of the game. When at long last the game begins, a boy tries to become a hero within the limits set forth beforehand. And though he may

argue like hell a close call, the fact is he doesn't change the game because when he's out he's really out. Thus the boy, all alone, in this
way learns early to swallow a bitter pill. If the girl, however, is pained
by this same process she has recourse always to her natural achievement of womanhood, whereas the boy feels his whole worth is bound
up in winning or losing, above all, in how well he played today. In
this his father is the guide, whether it be in the way he handles the
gas station attendant who slops excess gasoline over his car, or the
store clerk that intentionally shortchanges him, or a patient who has
died that day on the operating table because of his inept clumsy
hands—in all this, in adversity and in triumphant success, how the
father handles himself will be the model for the son to study and
learn and imbibe as the essential heroics in living. Father's example,
positive and negative, relates son to the world, which in time will include the world of women as well. For the moment, however, he is
even more asexual than his sister, who knows she is a woman-to-be,
whereas he is struggling with father to become a man. Not until he
becomes that man in his own eyes will he want to return to woman.
Not until he is a man will woman really want him, and this explains
why young girls naturally find older boys more interesting. Any neglect or absentee landlording of this paternal responsibility will not
only screw the boy up for life among men, but for his return to
women as well. My oldest son when very young taught me the hero
lesson in a most remarkable, most painful way.

Christopher's first-grade teachers were always "complaining" that
my son was "very verbal." I accepted the pejorative connotations of
this observation and painfully recalled my own childhood during
which, at some point, I had been reprimanded in class and required
to write "I interrupt proceedings" one thousand times. One evening
while watching television it became evident that this six-year-old boy
had an uncommon ability to parrot back dialogue, especially commercial patter. I thought I would try him on some Shakespeare, and,
lo and behold, he gave me back almost exactly word for word what I
gave him through several long soliloquies. A year later I discovered
he could read these same kinds of passages himself. He would then

hand you the page and you could "hear him." This process took a long twenty minutes, to get, say, a Caliban or a Prospero passage of twenty or thirty lines from *The Tempest* approximately 85 percent accurate. Ah, but there's the rub! For you see it was necessary for Daddy to sit there and wade endlessly through "For we are such stuff as dreams are made on" jolly long after my genuine tears had dried, in order to bring the boy to a flowering 100 percent accuracy. Needless to say my enthusiasm for this waned and, although clamors still came regularly from his school, I said "Fuck that noise" and let it go. Then one day Christopher, now age eight, came home with that inscrutable smile of the Cheshire cat. He wouldn't speak to me at all until bedtime when, as was our custom, we always set aside a time for what he called "important talk." This was a time of day he valued to talk about such things as R2D2 and the real origin of life on earth and elsewhere. In one such profound session he named his dog for good—"Earthling." On this particular evening, however, there was a true moment of epiphany when he suddenly blurted out from the darkness of his bed where he was all carefully tucked in by me for sleep, "Daddy I discovered myself today!" Upon inquiry it evolved he had been chosen that day out of eight hundred odd students to be on stage as the sole straight man in a show for the local visiting version of Captain Kangaroo. When I asked him why he enjoyed it so much, he smiled from ear to ear, and declared, "Daddy, I want to be *seen!*" It was as if the world had heard him.

I don't have to tell you that for months he had been surreptitiously readying himself for this acting role behind my back, and that thereafter I enrolled him almost immediately in acting classes that eventuated in a dossier which over several years included legitimate theater productions of *Horatio, Street Scene, Waiting for Godot, Peter Pan* (he was Peter), *The Tempest,* and others too numerous to recall, all by age thirteen. I do not downplay the burden of this to a father who, having been a stage door Johnny in rainy downtown San Francisco at midnight the night before, must get up early to do surgery the next day. Nor those numerous occasions when he has been employed for two minutes in the last act to help carry on a candlelit funeral pyre from which he comes out waving fifty dollar bills, smiling so wide that his ears are wet. Union pay, man.

But through it all came one clear and unforgettable lesson. Again and again I saw him make terrible errors, again and again I watched him return disappointed in himself after failed auditions, again and again febrile or sick with a cold so that I shuddered to see them string him up and go soaring through the Palais de la Legion d'Honneur theater as Peter Pan when I knew he had vomited (I held his head) all of his lunch. What I'm sure had happened in this young life is that he had come to grips with deadly fear, and cast it aside as not worthy of his attention. This was not the reckless abandon of some misguided gung ho war hero charging the pill box to almost certain death and coming away with a lucky medal, but the concerted achievement of one who cared desperately about his goals and had reckoned the relatively meager pain to him that they entailed. And it was he at age twelve who led me to Faulkner's magnificent Nobel acceptance speech and brought it all home.

He must teach himself that the basest of all things is to be afraid; and, teaching himself that, forget it forever, leaving no room in his workshop for anything but the old verities and truths of the heart, the old universal truths lacking which any story is ephemeral and doomed—love and honor and pity and pride and compassion and sacrifice. Until he does so he labors under a curse. He writes not of love but of lust, of defeats in which nobody loses anything of value, of victories without hope, and, worst of all, without pity or compassion. His griefs grieve on no universal bones, leaving no scars. He writes not of the heart but of the glands . . .

It is such stuff that children are made of and will teach you if only you will see.

Perhaps the hardest thing for a mother to do is to let her children go, but that is precisely what they need. A boy, more so than a girl, breaks the bond to mother more naturally (but, as we have seen, with greater earlier trauma), and so by the age of six or eight he wants to be out exploring on his own. If the boy's mother is a smothering mother and will not permit him to leave the fold, his attitude toward the opposite sex may be jeopardized later on for all other women, because she has limited his emotional development. "Do as I say, not as I do" becomes that child's burdensome watchword, an almost impossible row for him to hoe. In the case of Mary Pinkney ("Pinky") MacArthur, the mother of General Douglas MacArthur, however, all of her maternal dreams were abundantly fulfilled. She kept Douglas in dresses and curls till he was eight, saw him, a sickly adolescent, through the rigors of overcoming physical and mental handicaps to enter West Point, and remained there with him for four years, living in a hotel near the Point, having tea and a stroll with him each afternoon before dinner. At one point she unpretentiously wrote him the following poem:

> Remember the world will be quick with its blame
> If shadow or shame ever darken your name.
> Like mother, like son, in saying so true
> The World will judge largely of mother by you. . . .
> Be sure it will say, when it's verdict you've won
> She reaps as she sowed: "This man is her son!"

Pinky MacArthur, in the words of William Manchester, "was a complex woman, being both meek and tough, petulant and sentimental, charming and emotional. Under her mannered, pretty exterior she was cool, practical, and absolutely determined that her children would not only match but surpass the achievements of her father-in-law and her husband. Americans of a later generation may find it hard to fathom a woman could realize her ambitions through the exploits of her men, particularly when they wore a uniform she hated in her youth. Nevertheless it remains true that in her own complicated way Mary Pinkney MacArthur was resolved to defeat the Yankees on a battleground of her own choosing, with her own weapons, under a flag she alone could see."

It's fair to say that Pinky MacArthur achieved every external thing and more than she had ever dreamed of through her son. And yet, contrary to her expectations, she is not really remembered through him. Instead, he is remembered for himself. Such astonishing personal aberrations as the discovery that General MacArthur first married when he was almost fifty, and had his only child by a second wife when almost sixty are what lead us back to questions about the true warmth and wisdom and worth of Pinky as what we now call a real woman. Because the fact is that Pinky MacArthur was a smothering mother who *never* let her son go. We shouldn't be surprised that Douglas turned out to be a macho man who had psychosexual problems with female relationships well into middle age. While chief of staff in Washington at age fifty he kept a concubine in a Washington hotel and forbade her to leave her rooms at any time lest she be unavailable to him. Exquisitely beautiful, with braids down her back as far as her buttocks, she nevertheless had a chorus girl mentality. Douglas provided her with everything, including a poodle, an enormous wardrobe, and black lace lingerie for daily occasions, which he surreptitiously indulged in ad libitum. It was an act of defiance against a mother who had raised a perfect son. He achieved (and still holds) the highest grade-point average in West Point history. He won seventeen silver stars for gallantry in the First World War! (My father won one and was a hometown hero.) He was one of the youngest and brightest generals in the history of the United States Army. Handsome, a perfectionist, brilliant in every way, he was a mother's dream. And yet not until he was relieved of that mother's yoke when she died could he begin to have (at age sixty-two) enduring happiness with a wife and family.

Some such men, of course, never leave this motherfold, some have a higher than expected incidence of homosexuality, but frequently such men become reactionary womanizers and actually exhibit deep disrespect for the opposite sex by using women in a superficial and demeaning way. Thus, we have in them the analogue of the militant feminist in the male whose maternal relationship was improperly directed. As often as not such a man has had one or two bad affairs with women and, rather than risk the inevitable pain that love and relatedness in any relationship entails, he subsumes all women under the whore or bitch category and uses them accordingly. But here once again, just as in the girl's development with her careless father, we have a defect arising from a too careful and overbearing mother. The upshot in both cases is aberrant image of self-worth, almost a mirror image, as it relates to the role model available in the opposite sex at a young age when consciousness is being developed within the child. And it is equally true for a man that, if he has ever known the incomparable love of a good woman, he is never likely to settle for less.

One of the terrible things that happens in life is that inadequate parents tend to produce inadequate children (and so on, ad infinitum) and render unto society problems that are essentially insoluble by the time they are presented. It is this that we should be trying to get at during this early stage before the die is cast, to interrupt this vicious cycle, so that we may not be put off from the each others we are soon to need so badly. Because by the time we are old enough to indulge our sexual differences that attitudinal die has long since been cast. At best we are overcome by the process, too poorly equipped with self-identifying awareness to understand each other's needs. And our parents are the only ones who can help do this for us by proper preparation. The Darwinian point has been made that the sexists of our society, those who for one reason or another have chosen to forego the opposite sex, will in time by virtue of their lack of reproductive activity merely destroy themselves by natural selection. But all evidence points to the fact that sexism is an acquired characteristic, not congenitally predisposed, and so for us who care to change things our inculcation is all. For given even the slightest chance, the sexes will plunge eagerly into puberty together, be it on the "American Bandstand" or, as I managed once, in the open back of a rumble seat in the Hudson Tunnel at night. And I'll bet you can even top that.

For years the reknowned psychiatrist Carl Jung had a wonderful amanuensis, Jolande Jacobi. She wrote, in her remarkable autobiographical account of her own analysis, *The Way of Individuation*,

"The difference in the sexes at first is so great as to seem almost insurmountable." The words to be emphasized here are "at first," since the heavy burden of reproducing the race, and all its attendant confusion, has always fallen to the young. This is because the natural business of perpetuating our species requires work and often hard labor. We are, of course, called to this responsibility at a time when, intellectually and emotionally, in the mature sense, we are least equiped to do so. But uneven nature (perhaps with good reason) has not yet evolved human integration that far. Nature makes sure for the race that the younger the woman the better she is at labor—a phenomenon honored in jungle law and Greek myths as well as in modern obstetrical circles. Late teenage girls breeze through pregnancy. But the male/female fallout arises just at this time. Because when we are old enough to indulge our sexual differences our emotional templates are long since stamped. We are overcome by the process, too poorly equipped with our own awareness to understand each other's needs, the essential cornerstone of every human relationship. T. S. Eliot puts the painful process of learning this way:

> *In order to arrive at what you do not know*
> *You must go by a way which is the way of ignorance*
> *In order to possess what you do not possess*
> *You must go by the way of dispossession.*

All that we have learned so far about the differences between little boys and little girls comes to naught, comes to us as idle theory, at this time of getting together. Midge Decter states clearly in *The New Chastity* that young women and men come together for wholly different psychobiological and social needs, deriving perhaps from infantile social conditioning, but they are not the least concerned with such at the time of the required coupling. The young man feels his sex as a specific discomfort, a localized immense tension and drive, with uncontrollability at the damndest times. It gets in his way. He is a cub bear attempting to masturbate with boxing gloves on—silly, awkward, uncontrolled. He wants her very specifically for

59

release, and he painfully learns discipline in risking himself in this often frustrating way.

Young men at this time, seem always to be carrying a prostate as big as a baked Idaho potato. They are, as we know, as potent at eighteen as they will ever be, and can sometimes continue intercourse repetitively without cessation, or perhaps after only a brief latency. Above all, they are easily aroused in a matter of seconds by the female sex stimulus. Perhaps some of their male infantile urge to novelty, visual-spatial curiosity, instinctive aggressiveness come to the fore, a sudden chthonic force with a very short fuse. It is hard, if not impossible, for a young woman to understand this burden and the force, the suddenness, of this desire. All she is likely to do is accept it, maybe pity it. The man does not comprehend why, if she intentionally dresses, looks, smells, and feels stimulating, he shouldn't be immediately stimulated. The trigger phenomenon that a man possesses is almost inconceivable to a young woman, whose sexual reaction time is much more of an acquired taste than an intrinsic conditioned response. Lace panties to the young woman are something that have to be washed and worn so they feel and become part of you, but to the male they are an erotic object of arousal. He will squirm (I still do) to spy up a skirt at underthings with which she is merely adorning herself to enhance her beauty and sense of physical worthiness. In doing this, not only is his innate curiosity for angles and nuance challenged, but his muscular coordination called upon to participate in and complement his imagination. His imagination draws him ever closer to the stimulus and catalyzes what is already likely to be his erected state. The masturbatory fantasies of Bo Derek on the cover of *Playboy*, the prospect that Cheryl Tiegs may drop her towel or Farrah Fawcett reveal the inner aspect of her upper thigh are sudden and wild experiences that promise immediate relief from the burden of manhood. In a matter of seconds, say thirty, a young man may be brought from a state of dormancy to shooting off sperm, millions of them, in all directions. The name of one pornographic movie is *Heavy Load*, and believe me that is just how a man feels it. He feels it specifically in his genitals, in his seeds,

and in the deep hot fullness of his perineum where his prostatic potato yearns for release as he walks down the street. The sooner the
better is the message his brain keeps getting.

For him, a woman is not just the cause of his fireworks, she is the
promise of release, the easing of his specific tension that borders on
pain, and he feels that her intention is to live up to his desire. His
initial desire, then, the driving force in him, is physiological, but not
so strong is that tension that, in order to achieve completion, he can't
be persuaded to do almost anything—including love. But the young
girl wants her sex for another reason entirely. In general, she has not
lived at the constant sexual level of tension that he has. Her problem
is, her desire is, she wants to wake up. In her fantasy life she has been
up the mountain, but not yet with the apparent numinous intensity
observable in men. She is, in the phrase of one woman who has been
there, Dr. Jacobi, more "diffusely aware." What she sees in boys
with envy and admiration is a sparkling intensity of sexual and psychosexual energy and experience. To think "he can get it on like that
and I can't" is what draws her to him. "You Light up My Life,"
Debby Boone sings, and every teenage girl knows she is talking about
this apparent sexual awareness the young man has and can visit upon
her dark unawareness. "You Are the Sunshine of My Life," she
sings, because she feels him as brightening up her sexuality and her
whole being. So beginning with this diffusion of sensuality, she seeks
out the male for his apparent bright and numinous sexual imagery.
This means that she brings to the love equation, with her desire, a
physiological feeling tone much more related to the conduct of her
entire self, not just her genitals, though that is surely part of it.

"Diffuse awareness" brings down the wrath of the feminists because it is not understood how very beautiful and not the least pejorative this description is. At one obvious basic level it derives from
the multiplicity of erogenous areas in the female genitalia and
breasts, and the internal, hence not specifically tangible, placement
of her vital reproductive self. At another psychobiological level it
means she must seek her specificity external to herself, which she
senses, in her oft-expressed words at this age, as "I want to wake up."

61

And so this diffusion creates that need for help in discovering her specificity through a man's apparent awareness, and hers becomes a process, much more so than a man's, of socializing a totality of existence. The late Kaiser Wilhelm, of all people, once said in retirement, "To judge the success of any ruler you must look to see how the women of that country have found their society." The late, great comedian Lenny Bruce put it laconically this way, "If a man and a woman were marooned on a desert island, the woman would immediately look for a place to put her clothes and a man to put his dick."

What brings a young man and a young woman together, then, is this fantastic steam engine in trousers and her unreprehensible, curiously wet urge to get a piece of that action. The Fonz, John Travolta, John McEnroe, and all manner of wide receivers for the Dallas Cowboys would, from a distance, seem to fill the bill for her. But, as every barnyard watcher knows, up close there are few self-respecting hens who merely squat down for a rooster before socializing his worth. Thus the clash of the mating dance begins full tilt and the frenzy goes on throughout life in one sublimated form or another. That hen wants to see the rooster strut and crow his magnificence, and demonstrate his worth by a thoroughly exhausting chase around the barn in which he surely is equipped, by her lights, to outdistance and overcome her. In this way she begins to feel and share and test this fantastic steam engine energy. It is a process to her of socialization and mental participation, while firing his imaginative capacities and enhancing the fireworks yet to come. It is precoital play at the corner deli. It is "we'd be so good at the game." What these instinctively female barriers do to the male is enhance what are his already immense imaginative fancies about her and envision her, as a matter of psychosexual energy, as a necessary part of himself that must against all odds be completed. For this he will climb every mountain, ford every stream, learn to dance like John Travolta, even promise to go to work every day to support a family. Thus, he becomes for her a manageable social animal, one that she feels she can take on to enhance her own self-image and self-worth, while not being destroyed in the process by his animalistic (but wildly exciting) nature. Man then becomes socialized to succeed with woman, and woman sexualized to succeed with herself. Again and again as years go by they will reflect back on their early endeavors together. Sophie will observe, "I didn't know anything about sex until I met George," and George will observe, "I didn't know anything about women until I lived with Sophie."

Carl Jung called man's magnetic love for woman a function of the animated feminine part of himself which Jung named the anima. The anima in the psychologically normal male acts to project itself on the female because of her attraction to him. Without the anima, it should be noted, the job often might not get done, because it is this quality that enables the man to endow his love object with attributes he needs and wants to complete himself. From this arise two most important concepts for man and woman getting together, one very tough assignment for each. As the man tends through the propensities of his anima (more marked in creative people) to project his grandiloquent thoughts and feelings upon his beloved, he may in his subjectivity be attributing all sorts of qualities to her that simply don't exist and are farthest from the truth about her. An extreme example of this is the chorus girl syndrome where the paste areolar sequins and G-strings become the very person. We know that ballerinas are frequently asexual, even amenstrual, and in order to maintain their svelte image often suffer from anorexia nervosa (compulsive vomiting and refusal of all food). On stage, however, they captivate the male anima. William Butler Yeats, the great Irish poet, put man's problem this way in "Among School Children":

> O body swayed to music, O brightening glance,
> How can we know the dancer from the dance?

And so it is the male's job by careful introspection and confirmation of his fancies to get his anima in proper perspective and use it beautifully and realistically to get her straight. The man who whistles at a woman is still whistling through his anima. For all he knows, beneath her pointy breasts she may be suicidal. When young men (and older men like me) go to the ballet, we must concentrate on the performance, not the panties. When someone like Norman Mailer has five or six wives his creative anima has probably been running wild.

The woman, for her part, is given an animus, equally if not more important to the success of the love equation. At one time there was a kitchen scouring powder called Dutch Cleanser, the logo of which showed a Dutch maid brandishing an elevated rolling pin as if to menacingly chase all dirty comers away. The logo depicts the animus, the aggressive, hardheaded, get-it-done male side of female endeavor. When Susan B. Anthony stumps for woman's rights, Carrie Nation breaks the mirrors in the saloon bars and tosses John Barleycorn out into the streets, the woman's caucus insults the president in executive session, they are all exercising their Jungian animus.

But animus can be directed toward love, indeed is the essential ingredient of that relationship. A woman can merely accept the energy and the flattery of the male anima which, because of perfume and pretty clothes, sees in her the someone like Marilyn Monroe; or she can use her strength of character to straighten the man out about just who in fact she really is. And this is the proper function of her animus in love and in the socialization process that she has largely fashioned. By self-examination and rigorous introspection she must tell the man just who she really is, what she knows herself to be, and where she's honestly coming from, and above all what she is feeling. The guidance she gives him is true in a social sense, but it is equally true in a sexual sense where, despite all the adolescent or preadolescent courses in sex orientation, the young man gets lost in the myriad genital folds and doesn't have the foggiest idea what pleases her really or what she wants. She must not just ride his immense energy and go with the flow and remain diffuse and unaware. She must be actively passive, but emphatically active in telling him and showing him where she is and what indeed pleases her, otherwise he will never know. How could he? The term for a Marilyn Monroe, a woman of spectacular surface, who chose to be man's image of her, rather than who she really was within herself, is, in Jungian phraseology, an "anima woman." This is to be avoided at all costs, for the cost is often extreme. In the case of the famous film star the cost was advanced depression and suicide. She never knew who she was. When Elizabeth Taylor says "I do" to her fifth or sixth husband it is possible, despite her creative genius, that her animus has not been actively or accurately developed. The animus and anima out of whack accounts for much of the social life of Hollywood, as gossipy Rona Barrett relates daily for our eager consumption on "Today." Because there but for the grace of God go all of us.

The anima and the animus, then, have this necessary place in love. They are part of our soul, our God-given emotional makeup and as such have their positive and negative components. The male can use his anima to become a successful whoremonger, the woman her animus to whore, but the never-ending need for even these misguided souls is love, and history bears out again and again that every genius Dante, composing in the depths of the inferno, has always needed a Beatrice to lead him upward and outward toward heaven, where can be found the true anima and animus beautifully at work blending love divine, all love excelling. When the Bible says Adam knew Eve, it's fair to say that Adam discovered himself in Eve only because Eve's knowledge had become available to her through him. It is a necessary tautology—otherwise there would be no wholeness on either side. And in answer to another question of Yeats in "Leda and the Swan," "Did she put on his knowledge with his power?" we can say most certainly she did. But this was no unilateral male chauvinist swan. Putting on his knowledge was not a put-down. Old Zeus in disguise certainly learned as much about himself from Leda's femaleness as she from him.

Diffuse awareness is a natural part of growth to womanhood and goes to the heart of the consciousness-raising crusade young women are now embarked upon. To repeat, diffuse awareness is most emphatically not to be construed as a defect, but must be understood, appreciated, and loved as a natural evolutionary process in growth. *In a sense, as we will see, it is a part of nature's protective coloration to encourage woman to go through what she must go through in order to fulfill her biological nature and perpetuate the race. For* woman to be grossly otherwise when young is not only contrary to her nature but may be counterproductive. For example, there is no ulcer harder to heal than an ulcer in a young woman. There is no worse way to be pregnant than to be uptight about every twinge, or to intellectualize the comparative pigment chemical changes in the skin. There is no more difficult delivery than that of a woman who pretends to understand, because she has half-studied, the steps in a breech delivery. Half-smartness, admittedly a way station, is always the curse of knowledge because it seldom produces the resignation or humility we find at both ends of the spectrum. D. H. Lawrence put it this way in "Phoenix":

> *Are you willing to be made nothing?*
> *Dipped into oblivion?*
> *If not, you will never really change.*

Once I met an old fisherwoman in Mexico and we got talking about porpoises. She said porpoises were all female, because the porpoise and the water are one and the same. If you said to a porpoise the water was bad you would insult the porpoise, because to a porpoise she is the water, is one and inseparable with the water, and it is only when you become a fisherperson that you become separate from the water. So most of the fishermen were men—even she considered herself be be—who spent all their lives seeking the peaceful integration of the porpoise who was born one with the water and therefore a true woman. Years later a brilliant woman friend of mine began having recurrent dreams of swimming and playing porpoises. She went to a psychiatrist who explained that it was her unconscious sexual self pleading for attention in a progressively asexual marriage. At home for a time the woman attempted to porpoise, but alas, it became apparent that this successful professional woman was too intellectual, too far removed from the water, to be the full woman the fisherwoman was talking about, and so another marriage failed. Psychiatry only talks.

Such unconscious knowledge is young woman's greatest strength in performing biologically what she alone is privileged to accomplish. The I Ching says a woman always wins by waiting. As if there were any doubt about this three-thousand-year-old wisdom, the neat, comprehensive, anal-organized young mother soon learns that a patient diffusion of love and awareness, a judicious sloppiness, is the only successful way.

At Stanford, where a third of the undergraduate women now aspire to graduate school, at Columbia, where nearly half the medical students are women, they might carry with them this ancient truth. And to add to their enjoyment en route, here is this insight from May Sarton's brilliant novel, *Mrs. Stevens Hears the Mermaids Singing*. The heroine, an aged author, is being interviewed by a young woman who asks why Sappho, Jane Austen, and Colette were such successful writers. The old woman's reply is, "What occurs to me on the spur of the moment . . . is that the fundamental point is diffusion of sensuality. Colette could write better than anyone about physical things; they include the feel of a peach in one's hand. A man could only write this way about a woman's breast." Amen. Said by a woman.

Not long ago I traveled to my children's high school and gave a lecture to a group of seniors. When it was over a young man and woman approached me. The young man asked, "Is there any way you can measure the animus and the anima? Have any studies been done to really show it in black and white?" When I shook my head the young lady was quick to ask, "Why do we need all this? Can't two people simply love each other and get together that way?" Again I smiled and shook my head. They smiled at me, then at each other, and, turning, they walked arm and arm to the next class.

However maddening and confusing these differences for young men and women may seem, they are a necessary and intrinsically beautiful part of the race and bring the sexes together for mutual benefit and survival. Man must come to know that the specificity he can render his love through his masculine sexual self is hers just as much as his. And she must come to realize that her all-encompassing diffusion of warmth and love is not just a protection for herself, but one that can be fulfilled completely only in the arms of a man. None of this comes easily to our waking hours and certainly never all at once, but it does come because it must come in our life's journey, if we are to become whole. We need each other terribly.

FOUR

THE
RIGHT
CHEMISTRY

"Nature never breaks her own law."
—Leonardo Da Vinci

THE HYPOTHALAMUS is said to be the seat of our emotions, and its midbrain neighbor, the pituitary, the master gland that governs all our endocrine responses. The male or female imprimatur, which has been stamped on our hypothalamus at birth, does not begin its endocrine directives to the pituitary to any significant degree prior to puberty. Up until that time the pituitary is primarily concerned with growth hormone and regulation of water balance in the body. With puberty, however, we become manifestly sexual beings by virtue of endocrinological changes. In the male the hypothalamic message to the pituitary gland is one of tonic gonad stimulating hormone—constant, acyclic and progressive in character. In the female the hypothalamic message is a cyclic and periodic one, and the pituitary responds appropriately to these directives for the remainder of our lives.

The enjoyment of sexual potency is one of the prized possessions of manhood. From infancy man has come to count on playful erections of his penis, and he hopes beyond all hope to remain lusty into old age. As long as testosterone flows from the living cells of his testicles this will be the case. Some men do, rarely, have a congenital lack of sexual vigor, but this is usually related to a temporary deficiency in the testes and may be easily reversed by the administration of appropriate androgen hormones. True erectile impotence occurs in less than 1 percent of all males under twenty-five years of age, and the waning of potency and libido after that are so gradual as to be imperceptible as far as any organic basis is concerned. We will return to this later in discussing moods and rhythms, but the statistics are that at age sixty only 5 percent of males are impotent by virtue of testicular wear and tear, by seventy years less than 30 percent of males have insufficient hormones to be able to achieve an erection. Stated another way, 75 percent of the male population is virile for life to all intents and purposes. And this is because the male responds only to a necessary threshold blood level of circulating testosterone. Above that level he will be no more lusty, below it, as we shall see, he becomes impotent or feminized. Ninety percent of this required testosterone is secreted by the male testicles, the remainder by his adrenals. The adrenal flow tends to be intermittent, hence almost inconsequential, but the strong pulsating stimulus of the pituitary to the testicles is more or less constant and keeps him always potent and always producing sperms.

For practical purposes, then, the postpubertal male is always available for female stimulation, and when she does not arouse him she should think on psychic causes. One supposes, however, that the virgin they brought to cheer up the aging King David, who had been such a virile poet and warrior, was overcome with grief at her inability to arouse him. "To cheer the aging King David, there was brought before the king a virgin of unsurpassed allure—Abishag of the Shunammites. She cherished him, and lay in his bosom, that he may have warmth, but he got no heat on." Abishag should have been consoled that very old men do eventually peter out, however painfully frustrating that may be.

Ordinarily, man secretes in his adrenals female estrogen which is deactivated in his liver. Impaired liver function because of diseases such as inadequate nutrition or alcoholism may allow estrogen to run rampant in the male body and cause not only feminine changes, such as breast enlargement and skin and hair changes, but may decrease his responsiveness to women by suppressing ordinary testosterone effects. Many of our war prisoners retiring from the Pacific theater during the Second World War suffered from this kind of impotence because of inanition. Complete reversal was effected following nutritional and vitamin treatment. Alcoholism when combined with dietary deficiency may do irreparable damage to the male sexual function by enhancing estrogen takeover from the male's normal testosterone effect. Even in using sociable amounts of alcohol this may be apparent, as Shakespeare informs us in Macbeth II, 3:

Macduff: What three things does drink especially provoke?
Porter: Marry, sir, nose painting, sleep, and wine. Lechery, sir, it provokes, and unprovokes: it provokes the desire, but it takes away the performance. Therefore much drink may be said to be an equivocator with Lechery: it makes him, and it mars him; it sets him on, and it takes him off; it persuades him, and disheartens him; makes him stand to, and not stand to . . .

"Lovers nuts," a condition of painful testicular engorgement following stimulus, has nothing to do with hormonal flow. Rather it is painful congestion from repressed ejaculatory impulse. Neither are satyriasis, premature ejaculation, and homosexuality, three currently emphasized male sexual responses hormone-based. An inordinate lust, sexual gluttony of man for woman, is but a compulsive, goaty neurosis. Premature ejaculation is not as premature as it is immature, and, despite all the squeeze-me techniques, is best corrected by giving it another go. Coitus reservatus is most effective with rehearsal. Also, no remarkable endocrine alterations have ever been demonstrated in male homosexuals. Male homosexuals do not have female hormones. For modern man to justify his lustiness, his prematurity, his gayness on anything other than emotional grounds is contrary to the present knowledge about testosterone. Many years ago on a Saturday night, when I was on duty in the emergency room of the Cincinnati General Hospital, a man walked in with hands held behind his back and blood streaming uncontrolled down his pants. With a blank stare he brought his hands forward and presented me with a testicle cossetted in each hand. Fighting back my nausea, I rushed him quickly to the operating room to staunch the blood. As I passed one of the cubicles on the way, a psychiatrist leaned out to say to me, "If it will help you any, I believe that guy has a castration complex." It helped very little, since his personally severed testes could never be replaced. Six months later I got an invitation from him to attend his opening as a female impersonator. His estrogen had taken over. He had a high-pitched voice, fatty buttocks, smooth face, triangular pubic hair, and a lovely soft handful of breast. He informed me backstage *en cuirasse* that all he needed now was a vagina, and he was working on that.

Notwithstanding all the Donahue freak shows, where transvestites and transsexuals in a modern Barnum and Bailey parade and justify psychosexuality as normal variants, the full-blooded male is a constant repository of sperm for the female and is at all times under the tonic influence of masculine testosterone awaiting her beck and call. It's as simple as that. Christine Jorgensen, Myra Breckenridge, and Renee Richards have their own stories. For the rest of us men, testosterone constantly stimulates our sperm production and renders our sperm count always functional. That count is very good two days after coitus, better after three, and optimal at five for conception. But it's always good. It only takes one.

Because of the cyclic nature of the female hormone flow, a woman's endocrine changes are more diffuse and complicated than those of the male, who tends to have a specific titre of androgen hormones at all times from pituitary stimulus. By nature males are always fertile and available, but the female necessarily undergoes estrus periods of varying sexual availability and fertility. It is the pituitary action on the egg follicles of the ovary (the follicle-stimulating hormone) that causes them to secrete estrogen, bringing the ovum to a point of readiness that is concomitant with animal heat. At the time preparatory to ovulation, just when estrogen flow is maximal, a second hormone (the luteinizing hormone) is secreted by the pituitary, causing the rupturing through of the egg and the establishment of a hormone secreting bed in its wake called the corpus luteum. The corpus luteum of the ovary then secretes progesterone which inhibits the pituitary follicle-stimulating hormone from producing any more estrogen, and by direct action brings about secretory changes in the uterine lining to receive a fertilized egg. Thus a see-saw balance between pituitary and ovaries is set up in the normal female that involves four hormones, two from each structure, that arc in constant cyclical relationship. As progesterone falls off with the exhaustion of the corpus luteum, the uterine lining sloughs during the menses, and the follicle-stimulating hormone of the pituitary once again flows forth to build up the estrogen level and another cycle is begun.

Estrogen is best viewed as a preparatory hormone, not just locally in its proliferative building-up effect on the uterine lining, but in the general way in which it affects the female body during the first half of the lunar cycle. Estrogen increases body heat by increasing surface or capillary circulation. It adds tone and color to the body, often giving pink cheeks. The hot flashes of menopause are nothing more than the uncontrolled spasmodic outpourings of estrogen from the fading ovaries. When properly titrated, however, estrogen gives a sense of well-being and body tone. The dark clouds, so often described in the menopause or in the depths of the menses itself, disappear with estrogen administration or hormonal recrudescence. Cosmetics claiming an estrogen base have some validity. Especially do we know that estrogen maintains the healthy lining of the vagina and vulvar structures. Without estrogen these structures atrophy and may disintegrate beyond use. And estrogen used locally or given systemically has been shown to be equally effective. It is generally accepted that estrogen conditions the central nervous system for female feelings of lordosis, but it is progesterone that triggers the onset of receptivity.

The receptivity triggered by progesterone is short-lived, however, because it has been repeatedly shown that progesterone has an inhibitory effect on sexual desire. Women become progressively less interested in sex as progesterone titres increase during the second half of their cycle after ovulation. The initial effect of progesterone is to enhance estrogen behavior, then progressively to suppress it. Prior to menses, because of the drop-off in progesterone, women often note an increased sexual drive that continues, psychology notwithstanding, to rise throughout their menstrual period. Women who have taken contraceptive pills high in progesterone have noted an inhibition of sexual desire that was then reversed when the estrogen levels were brought into proper balance. With the increase of progesterone titres during pregnancy, women often note a falloff in sexual receptivity. Progesterone has had significant beneficial effects in the treatment of male satyriasis and female nymphomania by inhibiting sexual urge. It has been used to suppress inappropriate sex behavior in mental defectives. It has been used successfully as well to temper the ardor of uncontrolled homosexuals at their own request. It should be mentioned, however, that for the normal male it is circulating estrogen that has the dampening effect on his libido. Estrogen, which is ordinarily degraded in the liver, may accumulate in such conditions as hepatitis or cirrhosis or tumor when the liver is rendered nonfunctional. In such cases the estrogen level rises, feminization changes in the body become manifest, and man loses his libido.

In women something else exciting of a hormonal nature is going on besides these cyclical changes of estrogen and progesterone, for libido, frequency of intercourse, and ability to orgasm are demonstrably independent of the influence of estrogen alone. This clinical fact derives from the knowledge, demonstrated again and again, that when you remove the major source of estrogen production in women by removing her ovaries, such as in total hysterectomy, you do not alter her desire or ability to have sex, and frequently you even enhance it. Removing ovaries alone, thereby producing the functionally atrophic state of menopause, appears to have no appreciable effect on sexual desire and capacity for orgasm. We are left with the clinical conclusions, experimentally confirmed, that it is the endogenous androgens from the adrenal gland that cause most of the sexual drive in women. Since the degradation product of androgens is estrogens, it has been postulated, but not proven, that androgens in order to be sexually effective in the female must be first converted to estrogens. In support of this is the observation that certain close androgen relatives, such as androsterone, dihidrotestosterone, and chlortestosterone, that do not undergo conversion to estrogens fail to induce sexual receptivity.

Nevertheless, estrogens experimentally administered to animals or in clinical trials have little or no consistent effect on female libido, orgasm, or frequency of intercourse, whereas androgens definitely do. The focal point of androgen effectiveness seems to be clitoral where increased sensitivity is noted, leading to increased sexual drive.

Women who have an increased blood level of circulating endogenous androgen from adrenal secretion have increased clitoris awareness and urgency. When excess androgen is removed by appropriate therapy, the awareness and drive diminish.

Clinical confirmation of testosterone's (androgen's) libidinous action in the female derives from extensive experience in treating carcinoma of the breast. We know that female breast cancer is either estrogen-dependent or independent with reference to its growth mechanism. Thus a premenopausal woman still producing cyclic estrogen who contracts breast cancer will have an estrogen-dependent cancer. Similarly a sixty-five-year-old woman will have a low or absent estrogen blood level (and a relatively high adrenal androgen level) and her tumor will be estrogen-independent. In order to suppress the postmenopausal cancer growth, therefore, one must administer estrogen, but in order to suppress the estrogen-dependent tumor the treatment is obviously the estrogen antagonist, testosterone. It has been shown repeatedly that in women receiving androgen therapy there is increased clitoral sensitivity, increased sexual drive, and increased sexual activity. This has been shown to be true in the treatment of other endocrinopathy disease states, but the remarkable thing about the breast cancer experience is that these women have often had complete removal of their pelvic reproductive organs (ovaries, tubes, uterus) and elimination of the badge of feminity of one and sometimes both breasts, and still with the administration of male hormone their sex drive is enhanced, often above its normal state. There are those woman who even postmenopausally can be shown to have estrogen-dependent tumors by virtue of persistently high estrogen levels and low circulating testosterone levels. In these cases, once again, when testosterone is administered, clitoral sensations and increased sexual interest are described and often complained about. It is interesting that administration of testosterone to the androgen deficient male usually results in markedly increased sexual potency and drive up until normal blood levels are obtained. Beyond that, as if there were a saturation point, the male shows or feels no added increase in drive. In the female, however, at any age there is a geometric response to testosterone, so that the higher the level the higher the sexual tension and drive seem to be.

The other mode of androgen influence on the female sexual drive seems to occur centrally in the brain, probably the higher brain centers (the cortex) since the response depends upon prior psychosexual experience. Sexually inexperienced women may have increased clitoral awareness as a result of increased androgen levels but do not recognize its sexual connotations and, so to speak, do not know what to do with it. Frigid women, who long to achieve a sexual response, often have an increased sexual drive following administration of male hormones. However, these women, if not psychologically prepared for such experience, often note only a frustrating increased clitoral awareness without any change in their ability to perform or alter their fundamental aversion to sex. Masculinized women, such as female athletes and ballerinas, experience the same phenomena. In such women, by virtue of stressful outpouring of adrenal secretions over long and rigorous competitive situations, the androgen titres run high. These women are often amenorrheic (without menses) or have irregular periods indicating the lack of ordinary feminine cyclical changes. Nevertheless, they are exceedingly sexually active when conditioned by previous sexual experience, but in the absence of such knowledge, remain dedicated celibates with only increased clitoral awareness.

Before discussing the central nervous system's influence on the female sexual response, it is well to summarize the gonadal hormones' role. Women's sexual response is under two, main, peripheral hormonal influences: (1) the cyclical response of estrogen and progesterone; (2) the constant drive of androgen. Estrogen seems to be exclusively a preparatory hormone, not only locally in the uterus, but generally to make a woman feel good and appear attractive, two almost inseparable qualities to enable her to indulge her sex emotionally. Estrogen also brings her egg to ripeness and gives her pussycat urges to estruslike lying back and solicitation of the male. Progesterone, however, brings on the acute rupturing of the egg and establishes receptivity at the time of ovulation. It is the consummating hormone. But whereas initially it enhances estrogen action, it rapidly falls away from this function and becomes inhibitory of sex drive toward the second half of the menstrual cycle. Some have postulated that progesterone is nature's way of seeing that a fresh egg is fertilized, not one that has been hanging around and has partially disintegrated, which might lead to developmental anomalies. But overriding all this cyclical endocrinology is the high drive of androgen, an essentially male or masculinizing hormone secreted by the female adrenal gland. For the most part androgen levels are constant, but may be influenced irregularly by central nervous system changes. Their target organ is clitoral, a heightening of awareness in that area, an increase in libido, a need for sexual activity. Frequency of intercourse and success of orgasm are related to androgen activity. It is not too imaginative to say that the cyclical hormones are those of reproduction and those given woman to allow her to perpetuate the race, and that the acyclical male hormone is the one that shows her the way to enjoy it.

Although this sexual endocrine pattern is basic to all animals it is substantially modified in primates because of the development of the central nervous system and the neuroendocrine system of the brain. With increased cortical mass, mating becomes more discriminate and preference for specific partners is observed. Many subtle and poorly understood phenomena enter the picture. For example, pheromones are common in lower animals. These are substances formed by one organism that stimulate a response in another organism. Insects produce highly volitile sex-specific substances to attract the opposite member, and a pregnant mouse if she detects the odor of a new potential father, an alien male mouse, will, despite pregnancy, return to estrus behavior once again. This activity is carried out without sight of the male, merely his odor, and results in termination of her pregnancy to begin estrus again and another pregnancy. Odors alone may activate estrus in sheep. However, in humans the existence of pheromones has not been chemically demonstrated, only empirically experienced. Advertising by the cosmetic industry would have us believe that olfactory stimulus to sexual arousal is strong indeed, and man has been taken in by a whiff of perfume from time immemorial, as have women by the musk of men. In the human male with underdeveloped testes it is curious to note that anosmia, lack of smell or olfactory function, is a frequent finding. Pheromones, then, act as primitive sexual attractants, but are poorly described in humans and exemplify our psychosexual ignorance. Other areas of central nervous system influence are better understood.

Physicians who work with pituitary disease have long noted that the initial symptom of pituitary failure, such as occurs in destructive tumors (for example, chromophobe adenomas, craniopharyngeomas), is an invariable partial or total loss of libido. Inasmuch as the secretions of the testes and ovary depend upon the secretion of the pituitary gonad stimulation hormones this is not surprising. In the male this is simply gonadotrophic hormone, but in the female this is follicle-stimulating hormone and luteinizing hormone, as we have already seen. Secondly, the adrenal gland secretion is directly under the control of the master gland stimulus via the pituitary-adrenal axis, the so-called adrenocorticotrophic hormone. This pituitary hormone controls, among other things, the release of adrenal androgen, which we have already observed is crucial to the libidinous drive in both sexes. It is also possible that there are other pituitary hormones, as yet undescribed, that influence sex drive. Pituitary growth hormone has been tried, but produces no effect on libido.

Evidence that the pituitary-adrenal system is most important in female sex drive and that adrenal androgens are the principal erotogenic hormone once again stems from our extensive clinical experience with carcinoma of the breast. When breast cancer becomes extensive and spreads it is said to be metastatic and may need radical surgery to remove the adrenal glands or pituitary gland to eliminate adverse stimulatory tumor hormones. When the adrenal gland alone is removed, women note a dramatic falloff in libido. When the pituitary alone is removed the same phenomena occurs. And obviously when both are removed, the sex drive ceases. Once again, there is a clinical correlation of experimental data that androgens control sex drive in women, while that hormone, in turn, is under the regulatory control of the pituitary gland. It has been argued that such clinical analyses on advanced illness are invalid because of the debilitating influences on libido and sexual capacity wrought by the disease process itself. But postmastectomized women and women with metastatic disease do not necessarily report libidinous loss until almost terminal, and it is in this group that observations are most valid. In such cases, after pituitary removal, strength and well-being often improve—nevertheless, libido is suddenly lost. Also, in those rare cases of cancer of the male breast, pituitary removal (but not adrenal removal) has caused loss of libido and potency, indicating the pituitary gonadotrophin to his testicular androgen secretion has been removed. All of this confirms what has been demonstrated in laboratory primates: hypophysectomy (removal of the pituitary gland) eliminates sexual interest, sexual activity, and sexual drive. Loss of libido in any pituitary disorder, therefore, has grave diagnostic and therapeutic implications, in addition to confirming for us that this is the master gland of sexuality.

But as in the deviousness and intrigue of the ancient Greek myths nothing seems to happen within the body, especially the central nervous system, in a direct manner, but rather the pituitary comes under the influence of a myriad of confusing and conflicting stimuli. In general, the nervous systems within the brain itself are organized into (1) life support systems, (2) information processing systems, and (3) modulating systems, all of which have their particular influence on the pituitary. Category one relates primarily to regulating the body's internal environment. This would include such vital organs as the heart and lungs and the visceral nervous system, called the autonomic nervous system, which controls, among other things, the sex act. Category two includes all the higher brain centers of thought and the neural tracts related to the primary sense organs. Specific motor functions and learned responses would also belong here. In the third category we are dealing with the entrepreneurial modifiers, systems that function primarily to increase, decrease, or initiate cerebral activity and how it relates to lower brain centers. Thus, the modifying system sets a tone in the central nervous system. The hypothalamus lies right in the midst of this modulator system and is the prime influential organ relative to the pituitary. But it must be borne in mind that the overlapping activity of all these structures enables and allows neuroendocrine regulation immense flexibility.

There is no common blood supply or innervation between the brain and the anterior pituitary gland. Therefore, central nervous system regulation of the specialized cells within the pituitary that regulate follicle-stimulating and luteinizing hormones (the female gonadotrophins) is necessarily indirect and comes about through certain releasing factors (RF) that originate in the hypothalamus. Cells that synthesize RF are believed to be neurotransmitters, that is, they have the capacity to transmit nervous impulses, but at their nerve endings are capable of releasing or activating hormonal elements as well. Dopamine, serotonin, and norepinephrine may be released at such nerve endings and are good examples of neurotransmitters—hormones that arise as the result of nerve stimulus, which, in turn, act on other nerve receivers, in this case the pituitary neurohypophysis. There is good clinical evidence of dopamine's gonadotrophic or aphrodisiacal effect from the treatment of Parkinson's disease. These patients, who often have advanced debility, frequently note as a side effect of medication a tremendous increase in libido as the result of successful dopamine administration. It's possible that dopamine may be a major releasing factor in sex drive.

In the case of RF the cell nuclei are believed to reside in the lower part of the hypothalamus, but the nerve endings (axons, dendrites) terminate in a capillary blood pool that surrounds the pituitary. Thus, there is an intimate neurosecretory relationship between hypothalamus and pituitary, and the precise mapping of this relationship is constantly under study. Certain parts of the hypothalamus can be shown precisely to control certain parts of the pituitary as well as to relate to specific parts of the higher brain. It is too technical to delineate these pathways here, but certain generalizations are worthwhile. The midforebrain is highly developed in all primates as part of our information processing center. Fibers from this area can be shown to communicate with the hypothalamic nuclei that control gonadotrophin and adrenal-stimulating hormone release from the pituitary. The more rostral one goes, that is, closer to the forehead part of the brain, the more control over cyclical luteinizing and follicle-stimulating hormone is observed. This is important, because it is the forebrain that evolved last in woman and man and it contains all our higher human thought centers. It indicates, therefore, how intimately concerned our higher thought processes are likely to be, or at the very least can be, associated with our sexual stimuli. And it is the forebrain that contains man's developed emotional configuration and temperament, which, too, is intimately associated with our hypothalamic-pituitary sexual responsiveness. Prefrontal lobotomy, in which the nerve fibers of the higher forebrain are severed from the remaining brain, not only releases irremedial emotional tension but disrupts the normal flow of sex impulses. The same is true with medically lobotomizing drugs. Eliminate the forebrain in humans and you eliminate normal sex. While it is true that removing higher inhibitory impulses may enhance emotional sex in the sense that more primitive expression is allowed, the more frequent clinical observation from frontal lobe destruction is one of disruptive hormonal patterns and inappropriate sexuality. One of the first symptoms of a destructive frontal brain tumor in a famous man, who was consistently one of the ten best-dressed men in America, was his insistence on leaving his fly open at social gatherings.

Since the pathways are so clearly established, it seems almost academic to say now that woman's response to sex is intimately involved with a variety of external stimuli which are transmitted through her higher brain centers. Few would dispute this, though they would dispute the likely phenomenon of reflex ovulation, even when the reflex arc from beginning to end is established and so obviously apparent. Most insist that ovulation, such as we have been discussing, is strictly spontaneous and involved exclusively with cyclical alterations in hormones. And yet we know that certain animals (rabbit, cat, ferret, llama, mouse) undergo reflex ovulation regularly and will not ovulate until after coitus, and we know that anywhere from 30 to

50 percent of human conceptions occur outside of the so-called fertile midpoint of women with regular cycles. Stories are legion of the woman who gets pregnant out of phase when she has had an exciting evening out, or bought a new home, or adopted a baby, or taken a trip. Factors such as grouping have been known to influence ovulation, synchronization of menses has been described in college sororities. The incidence of conception following rape is strikingly high (35 percent), which goes along with some experimental data that shows adrenal outpouring in stress has both the ability to enhance and inhibit reflex ovulation, while adrenalectomized animals do not ovulate reflexively.

Perhaps the most convincing evidence of reflexive ovulation in women derives from the human condition of German females during two world wars. Germany was fighting wars of attrition on two fronts, east and west. At home, the women were undernourished and overstressed. Their periods were frequently irregular, their sexual drive and exposure to available males was minimal. The men, husbands mostly, would be given short twenty-four- or forty-eight-hour leaves at home in transit from east to western front or vice versa. And during that brief period of time an extraordinary number of wives became pregnant, during all phases of the menstrual cycle, enough to maintain the birthrate in Germany. Notwithstanding the fact that these women had been exposed to protracted stress and probably often anovulatory menstruation, this birthrate suggests very strongly that conception may occur throughout the cycle and may be reflexively induced. The rise in the birthrate several years ago in New York City, nine months after a protracted blackout would also seem to further the case for reflex and dampen the ardor of rhythm theory control. For we know that in times of public excitement ("Christmas conception week") private conception increases as well.

Now let us summarize the biochemical aspects of woman's sexual response so far as we are presently able to do so. Woman receives a sexually excitatory stimulus from the external environment through one of her five major senses—sight, hearing, taste, touch, smell.

These impulses are transmitted by peripheral nerves in the case of touch, but by direct brain-connected cranial nerves in the case of the other four, from the eyes, the ears, the nose, and the mouth, which act as an end receptor organs of sensuous stimuli. This information is gathered in the higher centers of her brain, the forebrain, where it is processed primarily with reference to previous learned experience and associations. Assuming this association is pleasurable, a message from the central nervous system will be directed toward the pituitary gland via the hypothalamic nuclei. Should the hypothalamic mediator be receptive, its nuclei will be activated to produce certain releasing factors for luteinizing and follicle-stimulating hormone. These impulses have come from specific forebrain centers, the luteinizing impulses further forward than the follicle-stimulating hormone. The same process, less well understood, is going on with reference to adrenal androgen release, and these impulses as well originate in the female forebrain and are subjected to releasing factor in the hypothalamus.

If the hypothalamus reacts favorably, its system of neurotransmitters is activated. These are tiny nerve filaments that have the capacity to secrete chemicals, such as dopamine, at their nerve endings which, in turn, influence the pituitary to action. Impulses are then sent to the adrenal glands and to the ovaries. In the case of the former the adrenocorticotrophic hormone does this work, in the case of the ovaries the gonadotrophic hormones, namely, the pituitary luteinizing hormone and the follicle-stimulating hormone. The adrenal gland then produces androgen, which we have already observed stimulates clitoral drive and enhances orgasm and desire in women. The ovaries, in turn, respond by cyclic alterations in estrogen or progesterone, and may even respond vigorously and reflexively in preparation for immediate and excitatory ovulation.

It remains to mention the obvious. The outpouring of male and female hormones within our bodies provides each sex with certain outwardly manifest, secondary sexual characteristics. "Tits and Ass," as one recent popular show tune has it. And hair and fat distribution, skin turgor, and a certain marvelous sexual air. These all have their place later on. We are not yet lusting. But the secondary sex characteristics, of which each and every one of us possesses our own wealth, now act on our environment to enhance the external stimuli and induce the sexually excitatory cycle to start again, and on nature's part to perpetuate the race.

FIVE

THE CASE
AGAINST
YOUR OWN SPACE

*Marriage is not commonly unhappy otherwise than as life is
unhappy; and most of those who complain of connubial mis-
eries have as much satisfaction as their nature would have ad-
mitted or their conduct procured in any other condition.*

—Samuel Johnson
The Rambler, *no.* 45

Amour and Psyche, Cupid and his love object, are relatively recent concepts in the equation of love. Love as we know it today was not described until the courts of the Middle Ages, and we are the inheritors of courtly love. Not only does this mean that modern romantic love originated with the troubadors in these knightly courts, but it means literally that courtship was and is involved. Helen of Troy was lusted after, fought over, and placed admiringly on a pedestal of beauty from which she could be coveted and possessed. Penelope, in her devotion to the absent Ulysses, kept knitting a web, which, she vowed to suitors, once completed, would enable her to consider their entreaties. But what she knit by day she secretly unraveled at night, to remain faithful to her husband who had been lost for seven lonely years. Beauty and faithfulness in days of old, yes, but romantic love is a modern concept. The free unmitigated pursuit of the love object, unencumbered by dowry or purchase price, is a late conceptualization. We call it romance.

It is no longer enough to say that love is a glowing state where one willingly displaces the ego for another whose very life becomes just as important as one's own. Love is too important to be left to the poets, it seems, and so there has developed a whole science of love. These "scientists" have discovered an "equity theory" by which people tend to seek out and get romantically what they feel they deserve from people much like themselves. Up until twenty-five years ago over half the people in the United States married somebody who lived within six blocks of them. Most people still become romantically involved with people in the same area of endeavor. Airline hostesses and pilots have something going, doctors and nurses, actors and actresses, all manner of academicians, and factory and businessmen and women at all levels. One editor, who is a very modern woman, has a male secretary who, she insists, sits on her lap. They are engaged to be married.

88

Another group of scientists insists that love and fear are analogous emotions and the sense of "falling" in love must really be present. Thus, in one study, scientists staked out two bridges across the Capilano River in British Columbia, one a dangerous rickety structure, the other smooth and easy. The lovely woman researcher, who interviewed men as they came off the two structures, found the more daring men had taken the poorer structure and were the ones more apt, by a wide margin, to make loving advances toward her. Shades of the inaccessible princess in the tower.

Many studies have shown that the all-consuming passion for another may not be purely sexual, but simply an emotional union or attraction, perhaps what we call platonic love. As a parent, one sees this in the surprising liaisons made as early as nursery school. Children seem to seek out each other as individuals almost as a matter of chemistry. Invariably, to a parent, it seems it's the snotty-nosed one who lives ten miles across town that Junior is attracted to and whose parents won't drive on Saturday. Just to make that chemical cheese a little more binding, phenylethylamine, a pituitary secretion that is abundantly present in chocolate, has been implicated in giving the "high" of attraction in human love relationships. This chemical is a close relative of amphetamine. It has been observed that star-crossed lovers, coming down off their romantic-high, often have an inordinate craving for chocolate. Sweets to the sweet.

Notwithstanding all this chemistry, romantic feelings are on the ascendancy and tests show that 85 perecent of our young men and women today would not consider marriage without romantic love. Over half of these same students twenty years ago would have accepted a "compatible relationship" for the prospective marital bond. I have contemporaries whose marriages were essentially arranged for them a quarter of a century ago by their respective interested parents, and I am fifty-five years old. No such equitable arrangement is conceivable among my contemporaries for their own children who are strictly foraging for themselves. I might add, however, that that foraging is done mostly in the same "equitable" pool. It is a fact that most marital relationships, while complementary in the sexual sense that males and females complete each other in that essential area, are established between persons with roughly similar emotional and intellectual interests, or at least what they conceive to be those common starting points. It is as if, sensing the frightening, unknown responsibilities of marriage, this firm foundation is a welcome groundwork. When you come right down to it, to put it metaphorically, most young women still want a solid ring on their finger and most young men want to see that his woman has it. But, really, how firm is that foundation? The answer to that now becomes a matter of temperament and long-term development within the circumstances of life.

Despite all their good intentions, psychiatry and its handmaidens, the numerous feeling cults, have done more to disrupt marriage in the western world than all the external paraphernalia of the industrial age. Psychiatry emphasizes self, self-indulgence of feelings, whereas marriage depends almost exclusively on selfless and unselfish regard for the feelings of those outside ourself whom we love. Day after day, hour by hour, across this country the couches in dimlit offices are filled by troubled people who are being urged to indulge their own feelings, as often as not at the expense of many others around them, when the real way to a successful life is to put other people's feelings first as often as you can. If you want to feel better, go ask somebody worse off than you how they feel. The famous playwright, George Bernard Shaw, said man was not intended to be a sniveling, groveling primate complaining daily about every little ache and grievous pain, rather he was intended to discover others in his work and be thrown at last, a bleeding and worn-out bag of bones, on the ash heap of civilization. If one would be successful at marriage, one would be unselfish. Incidentally, Shaw died in 1950 at age ninety-four and never made peace with psychiatry.

My second wife and I decided that we would, despite all else that had occurred that day, always have tea together on the green Chinese rug before the fire each night before we went to bed. We promised to resolve all our differences and never go to bed with an argument unresolved or unconcluded as we cuddled and loved each other to sleep. She had a big mug with the letter "P" for Patti, and I had one with "J" for Jim, and when my teenage son and daughter joined us, there would be mugs with "C" for Christopher and "H" for Heather. It was to be a beautiful pause in the day's inevitable tribulations.

Shortly after our marriage the four of us got talking late one night, and my thoroughly modern, uninhibited children were vitally interested in the frequency of lovemaking when you got married. I told them there was a tradition that if you put a penny in a cup for every bout of lovemaking in your first year of marriage, and then took one penny out for every effort thereafter, it was said you would never get all the pennies out. They laughed, and the next day I found in the kitchen cupboard, right beside all the others, an "F" cup; it still remained full of pennies two years later.

Here are the facts: During the first year we put 196 pennies in the cup, which comes to an incidence of .52, or making love every other day or slightly better. During the second year of marriage we removed only 98 pennies from the cup. The primary difference between the first and second year of marriage was the addition of a child, Stephen. Sometimes now the cup goes unattended for days, and often tea time is missed. After three years, at last count, there were still 30 pennies stagnating in the cup.

From the experience of all that has been taught, written, or told, this is the rather ordinary course of events and certainly no apology need be offered. What is offered is the obvious, but all too often misrepresented, fact that marriage has to be based on some numinous feeling that transcends our own petty indulgences and needs. The miracle of marriage is that any two people could ever get together, could ever be in the same mood for the same thing at the same time, when you consider what takes place in each life to dislocate the participants in any given day. But it does happen, because there is a need for it to happen, and that need we always come back to is love.

Some say *Hamlet* can be summarized in eleven words spoken by the prince himself near the play's end: "To be, not to be. Let be. The readiness is all."

Hamlet of course is referring to death, but he could as well have been talking about marital love. The readiness is all. This readiness is a matter of emotional advancement and building and occurs at different times for different persons. Despite all the current literature that outlines so nicely our life's journey in easily understood stages for men and women, these stages are nevertheless uneven and may be associated with quantum jumps here and there and long periods of remission and exacerbation in our emotional progress along the way. And most of this journey must be made within marriage. William F. Buckley, quoting a famous philosopher, advised his twenty-one-year-old graduating son to decide by twenty-eight what he wanted to be by the time he was thirty-seven. Notwithstanding the importance of the general life journey we are pursuing here, it is equally important to appreciate and respect the individual differences inherent in the process at any given point.

Take, for example, the matter of personality development, perhaps the most important ingredient in a marital relationship. Our personality depends on four, main, functional components. They are: thinking, feeling, intuition, and sensation. There are few if any facets of personality that are brought to bear on our life adjustment process or responses to life's problems or needs that can't be subsumed under these four easily remembered types: feeling function, thinking function, sensation function, and intuitive function. All evidence indicates that each of us is born with different potential in each of these four areas, and each of us develops at different rates and in different functional areas at different times. It's also true that the thinking function and the feeling function have a certain natural antipathy, so if one is hypertrophied through use or endowment the other tends to be atrophied by disuse. In a similar way, intuition and sensation tend to oppose each other. In marriage two persons may be at totally different developmental stages in the personality spectrum, stages that have nothing to do with the pat chronology so often described. Some examples will make this clear.

Suppose a young legal secretary has been raised in an atmosphere of warm, outgoing feeling, in a household where there was a free expression of love and a naturalness about sexual discussion. There is a healthy nudity about the house and an emphasis on good food and clothing and exuberant love of children and all the fun of watching them smile and pass gas just as soon as you've finished putting on a fresh new diaper (should you change him again?). She has in this atmosphere, developed at a young age a naturally uninhibited sexuality that is not promiscuous, just exuberant. Such a young woman obviously has a strong feeling function and one very successful to her personality. But because of the feeling emphasis in her household there is rarely time for higher thought, indeed such ideas are conceived as luxuries and extraneous to the business and real joy of living. To her, the differences between Brahms and Beethoven, Tocqueville and Dostoyevsky are matters of no importance. She comes at life through a strong feeling function and a weak thinking function, primarily because the latter has not been used. As if to acknowledge this weakness in herself, she has gone to work in a legal office where everything is thinking. Mind you, she is a college graduate and by no means stupid.

Into this office one day comes a middle-aged surgeon, a Viking, with a malpractice problem. This man was raised in a stringent, parchment-scrubbed Lutheran home where sex was dirty and love was distant. He has read the hundred great books and completed years of medical training, along with chemistry and physics, and knows calculus by rote, and is a first-rate cardiac surgical technician. In short, his thinking function is immense and his feeling function, as the result of birth, early training, and achievement, is stunted. But judging from his smile and good humor this potential is by no means absent. The secretary and the surgeon immediately get on famously.

I think it's obvious that this young woman and middle-aged man, so apparently at odds in a social sense, could make excellent marital

93

companions. Their personality function types for feeling and thinking are, as has often been observed, exactly complementary. The important thing is that they know this and recognize it for what it is in
themselves and each other. She is probably wonderful for him in bed
and in society, and he is probably wonderful for her to show her what
books to read and how to analyze finances. They are both overcoming their weaknesses.

Similarly we can analyze the intuitive function and the sensation
function, although the equation becomes somewhat more confused.
It's apparent that the surgeon, used to working with his hands, has a
strongly developed sensation function, and the woman, used to
working with her feelings, is apt to have a strong intuitive function.
But sensation is only tactile and has to be integrated with feeling
function to be useful to the personality structure, otherwise the surgeon (or the ceramicist, painter, tool-and-die worker) is merely a
technician. Similarly intuition is dangerous if it is not confirmed by
thought process, intuition always needs confirmation. An example of
an exceptionally intuitive man was Adolf Hitler. At a stroke he hit on
the image of the American Indian swastika symbol which touched
and fired the unconscious hopes of all Germany for twenty-five years
and led them finally to disaster, but not, however, before great
strokes of intuitive genius that enabled Hitler to possess nearly all of
Europe. He eventually failed because he refused to confirm his intuitive feelings with thought process. He kept following bad hunches
and would not listen to reason. Sensation needs feeling and intuition
needs thought, and all of them need each other and in good measured balance for a full personality.

I think it's apparent that all the recently described pat stages of life
are suspect in any given individual case, and that our personality
functional development can explain all kinds of permutations and
combinations of marriage; the middle-aged female executive and the
ski instructor, the airline hostess and her pilot, the cleric and the
countess, princess and rock star, the childhood sweethearts, Yin and
Yang, you name it. We are at different personality levels at different

times and always seeking wholeness and help along the way. The important thing for the success of the marital bond is to recognize signposts and be willing to enter in. We must not look askance when Fred Astaire, age eighty-one, wants to marry a female jockey, age thirty-five; when Marlo Thomas considers marrying Phil Donahue (her first marriage) at age forty-two; when ex-Jesuit Governor Jerry Brown of California is turned on by singer Linda Ronstadt and takes her to deepest Africa; when Tom Hayden admires Jane Fonda. If you asked any of them, they would simply tell you it feels right to them just now. My wife is half my age, which is the last thing it ever occurs to either of us to talk about, though other people are very concerned.

It is a truism that the female of the species comes at personality with stronger intuitive and feeling functions. As we have seen, this can be negated by a Madame Curie or Joan of Arc, but the reason woman does grow into a stronger feeling mold is that her biological destiny is a nurturant one, most particularly raising the young. The inability to bear a child has to be one of man's poorly explored latent frustrations, and, I think, the source of many of his own emotional inadequacies. "Because men cannot conceive and bear naturally," writes Günter Grass, at present the leading German novelist, "because even their blind and frenzied acts of impregnation spring from a dubious momentary caprice, they have to do clever little tricks, climb icy north walls, break sound barriers, pile up pyramids, dig Panama Canals, dam up valleys, experiment obsessively until everything on earth is synthetic, have to keep asking about the ego, about being, about meaning, the why, whither, and wherefore in images, words and tones, have to run themselves ragged on the treadmill known as history to make it spit out certified male products such as dated victories and defeats, church schisms, partitions of Poland, records, and monuments. . . . Women have no need to worry about immortality because they embody life; men, on the other hand, can only survive outside themselves, by building a house, planting a tree, doing a deed, falling gloriously in battle, but after first begetting babies. Persons who can't give birth to children are at best presumptive fathers; nature has not done well by them."

The maternal instinct we hear so much about is a gross misnomer. When my wife asks our pediatrician what to do when eighteen-month-old Stephen won't ever go to sleep before midnight, he advises, "Always follow your maternal instinct in such problems." But, you see, there is no such thing as a maternal instinct. An instinct is an inborn pattern of biological action as predictable as the seasons. It is what guides the monarch butterfly from Ohio to Pebble Beach, California, each year, brings the buzzards back east to Lake Henley and the swallows out west to Capistrano on the same predictable date each spring, makes storks return to the same rooftop nest in Dusseldorf, and eels return to mate in the slimy Sargasso Sea. But a woman walking down the street does not feel maternal. Even a pregnant woman neither has or feels any special maternal instinctiveness. She has no innate sense of direction. One would think the farther up the evolutionary scale we go the more refined maternal instinctiveness would become, but the opposite is just the case. Birds and fish seem to care for their young automatically, but monkey and chimpanzee mothers that are isolated from the group, and hence socially deprived, are very poor mothers indeed. Baby monkeys and chimps do cling most reflexively, however, and it is this activity that gradually forces a learning process onto the mother that is immeasurably enhanced in the informative atmosphere of a group experience. The human baby roots and sucks and has a rather annoying cry when it's hungry that can be silenced by putting it to the mother's breast. It is at this point that learning to be a mother begins, and in humans there is precious little instinct to help you along. Motherhood is an acquired taste. Here is what one mother, Nina Schneider, has to say about it:

The maternal instinct, in fact, cannot be imagined. Colette says it is born complete, fully armed and bleeding. Sociologists, not only male chauvinists, agree the race's survival depends on woman's self-abnegating, tender dedication. Biologists have claimed it inheres in a pinch more or less of magnesium. Whatever its source, I was unprepared for maternity, for what I have come to think of as the tragedy of Motherhood.

I don't mean the drudgery, the 365 days a year—day-in, night-in—on duty. And frankly, divining my night's fate by observing excrement was always disgusting. My lips are sealed about sandbox society, crayoned walls, playing Monopoly and even waiting until they've been bathed, fed, bedded down before being free to go to the bathroom, close the door and decide among a bath, hysterics or reading a book. That's all part of wanting to do the best you can so they'll be well and happy.

What I was unprepared for, and never learned to bear, was the hate. I've read Freud, and Frazer, and Frankenstein, and it doesn't help. I thought *my* children would never feel the vast repulsion that compels each thing created to reject whatever created it. To me that was theory. I planned to be the perfect mother, unambiguously adoring and therefore adored. I would nurture their tiniest talent, cherish them as individuals, be a confidante and friend. How could they hate me when I planned for them to be safe and happy?

But if there is no maternal instinct as such, there most assuredly is maternal, hence female, intuition. Intuition, as we have seen, is a function of our natural personality endowment and is congenitally predisposed. It allows a woman to have a certain sixth sense about her child, a certain hunch about what he's up to, an ability to sniff out trouble. Intuition once again is a gift, as intelligence is a gift, but it must be exercised to be useful. Standing alone, a hunch is not enough. A hunch is not reliable unless it is confirmed true or found false by experience. Intuition, therefore, is not a conclusion, but a sense of awareness to possibilities that a good mother must have in abundance. And woman does have this because it has been inbred in her by the process of natural selection. Thus, those women in the prehistoric tribe who were most capable of handling their children were always the ones whose offspring survived and the ones most likely to pass on—by example and behavior—those successful maternal qualities to successive generations of mothers. In all of nature there is only one constant predictable bond. That is the bond between mother and infant, and it is the basis of all primate social groups. A period of childhood education is implied in it, from which all higher orders of civilization are eventually constructed. The mother who is ready, willing, and able to discharge this ordained role will pass on this wisdom to those who come after her. This means that those women not so interested in or endowed for motherhood have been and are still being selectively removed from the genetic heritage of the race. Because the rearing of the young is often a guessing game of immense proportions, it has meant that woman's intuitive insights for childrearing have survived and hypertrophied over the millennia. This natural selection of physical, emotional, and intellectual abilities to rear children accounts for much of woman's "maternal instinct" and her natural way with children. Intuition is necessarily a big part of it. But once more a repetitious word of caution to all women, to all mothers: intuition is only a hunch, it always needs to be confirmed. If you go to the races and act only on hunches, you will be wrong at least half the time. And with children that's not good enough.

Motherhood is everywhere for everyone to see. It is its own reason for being, carries its own self-justification, is undeniably one of the great and good things that happens or can happen in this world, and young women grow up seeing this clearly all around them. Like Golda Meir (in a *Ms.* magazine interview), I can't imagine why any healthy young person, especially a woman, would not want biological fulfillment in heterosex and having a child. Notwithstanding all the world's terrible physical and emotional problems, lack of that desire would still, it seems to me, simply be a *form fruste*, a maturation arrest. But let the obvious be said here: There are many ways to make a living, many ways to create, to have and enjoy children, many ways to a full life. Celibacy, for example, is a time-honored way to heaven. But to deny children is to deny a whole precious part of yourself and your inherent debt to the world, if you are able to pay it. There is much to get straight before one marries, but above all, childrearing is the area that must be crystal clear. Marriage developed as a means of caring for children, and if we are not going to have them to care for, do we, will we always care enough for each other?

One of the anthropological reasons for a prolonged childhood in humans is the evolutionary achievement of the higher brain. It was necessary that the human brain be delivered through the female pelvis in an optimal state for survival, that is, not too big and not too small. Were the brain too advanced in size or function at birth the mother's contracted pelvis could threaten its integrity. If the mother's pelvis, on the other hand, were grossly enlarged for such an accommodation, she herself would be immobilized. Obviously, also, the delivery of a small or underdeveloped human brain into the world would not be in the best interests of the race. So nature took a middle road for us, delivering a well-developed infant brain through a female pelvis not totally incapacitated for walking and running in the upright position, but definitely inhibited in relation to the adult male of the species who was not so burdened. In addition to the safe delivery of that baby's head into this world, it was also necessary to provide for that brain's complete protection for a prolonged time while it further developed. This, then, meant a lengthy childhood in humans as the unique and incomparable zenith of our evolution.

A plant-eating existence tends to make people very self-centered. Vegetarians are solitary animals. They go out and tear off a leaf and eat it till they are content and then lie down and sleep. In nature this always meant lack of cooperation and a solitary, selfish existence— qualities anathema to child rearing and the survival of the race. When children's needs became apparent and the strong muscle portein need of man in migratory societies self-evident, early hominids left off plant-eating exclusively and evolved a special societal mixture of hunting and gathering. It was this unique organizational adaptability that enabled mankind to roam and inhabit the entire world, and, in turn, involved the acquisition of certain distinguishing social traits: one of these was a unit, a central unit, where infants could be cared for and meat and vegetables could be delivered. Women, who had to nurse and nurture, became the natural regional gatherers, and men, more mobile and muscular, the roaming hunters. Above all, there developed a tremendous sense of cooperation and mutual trust and care for the greater good of all.

Thus the establishment of a base camp, the division of labor, and the mutual respect and cooperation that followed, all derived in early societies from the needs of children. Sexual activities became more preferential and full of meaning. Refinements and internecine choices were allowed and, in natural course, the family was born. It was a place where *Homo erectus* repaired each night, about one and a half million years ago, to care for his children who had become almost wholly dependent on him for the first six years of their lives. It was a place where mother and father could provide the prolonged education necessary, teach the skills necessary to participate in an increasingly complex society, either by gathering or hunting. And, *au fond*, things at home haven't changed that much. The similarities are much greater than the differences when it comes to raising kids.

So the children come, but usually not before what many people consider an illness, at least to the woman of the species. In California, illness disability compensation is provided for time off for the pregnant woman. Thus the body's messages in pregnancy come not as a natural function to many modern women but as an illness, and society by such laws as the above encourages this. Instead of being inured to the temporary discomforts of early pregnancy, she feels her body put upon abnormally and used in an objectionable way. She is not the vehicle of a new life, but a transgression of the old. Her husband gets the message, not that she is incapacitated, but that she is sick and maybe he caused it. His reaction to marriage, and now to her pregnancy, is one of frightening responsibility. Jane Austen opens *Pride and Prejudice* with one of the most famous lines in literature, "It is a truth universally acknowledged, that a single man in possession of a good fortune must be in want of a wife." And well he might. What the man does not expect is that all the money in the world will not allay his frightening emotional responsibility for what he now sees is a person he has caused to be ill and distant, as she undergoes morning sickness, dizzy spells, and breast changes so painful he is no longer encouraged to enjoy her breasts. His protective instinct toward her is immense, and yet he feels helpless to do anything.

But all of this will change, and all of this is in the nature of things, and those persons who have had some actual familiarity with bodily change and function are much more apt to appreciate them. Such a young man will understand why his beard is no longer being trimmed and adored with such adulation as formerly, why his clothes are not being carefully laid out for him for the next day as she always did before, why the tea does not get sipped on the Chinese rug by the fireside every night, and why the pennies have stagnated in the cup. Such a young woman will accept herself and, no matter how uncomfortable she may be, will reassure him of her excitement about another life and the normal changes in her body. They are no longer two people just grabbing for all the gusto they can get, but are sustaining one another by love.

And when the children do come, just as Daddy said, this will all get much worse. The only advice my father ever gave me directly about anything (his teaching was always Socratic example) was about marriage: "Son, remember once the children arrive you won't be getting as much attention." And so as meals become a circus, as toys fly underfoot, as intercourse gets interrupted by the pitter-patter of curious onlookers, the marital bond is further strained. She is still amazed at the activity of his member, this male quality of being able to make love even with a headache at the end of a lousy day, or with kids screaming in the background. He is astounded how much has to be just right with her in order for her to complete herself and wonders if she will ever be able to be that way again. The modern circumstances of life are felt to conspire against them. After all, it's not as if these were pioneer days when each night for protection against the Indians of the Plains you had to put the wagons in a circle, one big unit, one united family holding each other together against the common elemental enemies. Something else must now sustain.

And that something has to be of a quality beyond ourselves, for if we look at the facts, are reduced by the facts, believe that facts speak for themselves, the answer is already written to doom this marriage, this human relationship, right at this point. It was Emerson who wrote that the first condition of love "is that we must leave too close and lingering adherence to facts, and study the sentiment as it appears in hope," and so if we follow the impulse of our soul, the impulse that man and woman have always sought in the stars and responded to down through the generations, we will always find love in the ruins, and this does sustain. Robert Penn Warren put it this way in "Brother to Dragons":

The recognition of complicity is the beginning of innocence.
The recognition of necessity is the beginning of freedom.
The recognition of the direction of fulfillment is the death of the
    self.
And the death of the self is the beginning of selfhood.
All else is surrogate of hope and destitution of spirit.

It seems only yesterday that all America was being called upon to have pity on all those who were over thirty years of age. Throughout the decade of the sixties, the youth of America claimed to be greening her alabaster cities from sea to shining sea with all the youthful glory of being under thirty. And although senility begins at birth, there was and always has been some sort of crossing of the bar when we pass thirty years. "Where are the snows of yesteryear?" wrote Villon in "The Testament" in 1463, as he lamented his long lost youth at the ripe old age of thirty, the sweet days that would never return. And T. S. Eliot at this same age was describing life as "The Waste Land." Ernest Hemingway and his young friends who had had so much fun in the sunshine and at the fiestas in Spain now had to face something else. At age thirty, in the conclusion of *Death in the Afternoon*, he brings a tear to our eyes for all of our lost youth:

Pamplona is changed, of course. . . . I know things change now and I do not care . . . and if no deluge comes when we are gone it still will rain in the summer in the north, and hawks will rest in the Cathedral at Santiago, and in La Granja, where we practiced with the cape on the long graveled paths between the shadows, it makes no difference if the fountains play or not. We will never ride back from Toledo in the dark, washing the dust out with Fundador, nor will there be that week of what happened in the night in that July in Madrid. We've seen it all go and we'll watch it go again. The great thing is to last and get your work done and see and hear and learn and understand. . . . Let those who want to save the world if you can get to see it clear and as a whole.

There is no doubt that something peculiar to our aging must be faced at thirty in a way that we confront no other birthday. Averell Harriman, one of our most enduring elder statesmen, has said if a person does not make major decisions in his life before he is thirty, he is not likely to make them afterward. And this may be the crux of the thirty trauma. When we are young we accrue many of life's benefits merely by avoidance of problems or procrastinating assignments. In America, especially, we respect the freedom of youth who are given carte blanche for a certain number of years to kick up their heels in the name of experience. But at thirty we must come to acknowledge that the avoidance of pain is not the solution to beauty, and if we do not so acknowledge and accept this truth, that the heart has only so much joy as sorrow has made room for, we are going to be miserable people and remain forever childish. We will never become adults.

The marital bond, indeed any bond between men and women, is stressed at this point in a way that is irrevocably linked to the female reproductive capacity. Until thirty women can "date," can play "the dating game," as one television program coyly calls itself. It is a game that men, and especially women, get very good at, particularly with reference to any disclosures about their heart's desire for children. I believe a writer feels he wants to be a writer very young, I believe a surgeon feels he wants to be a surgeon very young, and I believe a mother feels she wants to be a mother very young. Yet the number of women in their mid and late twenties who still give an ambivalent answer to whether or not they ever want children is immense. It is as if, while they prance about enjoying themselves, they are looking for somebody to answer this question for them, certainly one of the most important questions of their lifetime. The game is filled with "if I meet the right man" and "maybe later" and "who needs it" and months and years of confusion for the man who is trying to discern her attitude. The fact is that she has had years to think about it and knows, or most certainly should know, what she thinks about it. Whatever her hidden feelings may be, they become public reality by the time she is thirty when she faces possible barrenness in a relationship to a man.

Benjamin Franklin once said a person who does not get up early must trot all day. It's that terrible feeling of always having to catch up, of being late to the airport. It is a sense that life is out of your control, that it is acting on you and not you on it. Worst of all it gives you, as you go through your life, a sense that you have missed something, probably the worst emotion to feel as we grow older. Errors of omission leave a lingering bitterness that smolder and complain, while errors of commission most often scar over in a kindly way. If a woman has not acted on her childbearing function by the time she is thirty she may face all her remaining days in thrall to these uncomfortable emotions.

Though the years thirteen to forty-eight allow woman thirty-five years of ovulatory menstruation, her peak reproductive years are roughly from age eighteen to thirty. Prior to age eighteen pregnancy raises havoc with the still-emerging pubertal body which continues to need female hormone to round out the breasts, enlarge the pelvis, and complete the circulatory and bone changes for a sturdy adult woman. After thirty the female hormone serves a progressively regulatory or maintenance function for the female body. At thirty, therefore, with the twelve optimal years for childbirth behind her, a woman who has postponed or avoided or denied motherhood now must face the inevitability of her biological clockwork. Too often this comes as a shock to women, the sudden realization that she must play catchup baseball if she is to play at all. She may suddenly pull out her diaphragm or go off the pill, expecting the annunciation to occur next month. But life is not that way, and more than likely it will be a year, often of frantic perfunctory cerebral lovemaking, before she is pregnant, if at all. You don't just get pregnant because you want to get pregnant. It takes time, of which a woman at thirty has precious little left, if she really wants a family. As often as not such a woman is well into her early thirties before the baby comes.

In postponing a family till thirty or beyond, woman forgos her greatest protective device for pregnancy and the act of labor. It is true that uterine dystocia (poor or sluggish contractions) increases markedly after thirty and all female muscle tone becomes considerably more flabby. It is true that woman's heart and lungs are not as strong at that age and her metabolism is measurably slower. How many Olympic athletes, after all, can you name who are over thirty? Very few, and pregnancy is indeed Olympian stuff. But none of this physiology is, I think, of the truly protective essence of youth. What a youthful woman does bring to pregnancy is what the young male warrior traditionally brings to war—an emotional, adventurous idealism and a sense of challenge, a diffusion of reality that drives her onward and upward in adversity and sustains her. With learning, with sophistication, this balm will not return, and even her second and third pregnancies will not be sustained by this natural protection coloration of young womanhood. In nature, naiveté often has its own beautiful reason for being, and one of these is that experience makes a woman more capable of bearing and delivering children. It is its own anesthetic. When Rosalynn Carter was asked how she felt about campaigning for the presidency with her husband the second time, she said it is much like a second pregnancy. During the first pregnancy you are sustained by the adventure, but the second time around it's clear that you know what you are in for. You are thinking, and that makes it harder. Conscious, emancipated woman does not make for especially good gestation.

One emphasizes the woman at this point because her age is inextricably interwoven with her reproductive capacity. Not only is she limited in the number of children she can bear, but after thirty it is a stark scientific fact that the quality of offspring a woman produces may be low. For example, mongolism is of sufficient risk in women past thirty-three to warrant routine needle aspiration of the pregnant uterus (amniocentesis) to determine the integrity of the fetus. The incidence of diseases, such as diabetes and hypertension, also markedly increases. In short, woman has a biological destiny that comes to a head at thirty and that can be either accepted or finally denied. It is a crossroads in her psychobiological life that does not allow further procrastination, perhaps a character weakness she has been able to hide and use to great advantage for many years. But during those years she has been able to choose, and she knows deep down there are very few women who want marriage who don't now have it, and very few women who want children who don't bear them. At thirty she is reminded once again, and most poignantly, that woman *is* destiny, man merely achieves destiny, that one *is* a woman, while one *learns* to be a man.

As a physician, one is struck again and again by how many women who are at present declaring their freedom at this age are simply doing so because they are not healthily inured to their own bodies. Although they express an envy of men—to be free to come and go, to travel, to work when and where they like, to screw around, to be the captain of their fate—the truth seems to be at a more fundamental level. Do they really mean, in Freudian terms, that they envy man his phallus? Wolfgang Lederer in *The Fear of Women* puts such a woman's problem this way:

. . . freedoms have, at various times and in various places, belonged to women who for their sake did not have to stop being women. Freedom, like power, is not in itself male or female. In fact, both man and woman are free or unfree according to the customs of their times, and according as they experience these customs as congenial or oppressive. The only freedoms men have ever enjoyed that woman did not are the freedoms from menstruation and child-bearing and rearing; and if some women, understandably enough, wish to escape from the onus of their sexual fate, that does not mean by a far cry that they therefore wish to be men. No, these women do not wish to be men, they wish not to be women.

Such a woman can be likened to the goddess, Artemis, the Greek goddess of the hunt, who probably, like the ballerinas mentioned previously, masculinized herself to the point of not menstruating. In any event, Artemis was able to do without childbirth and mother-hood, and became a functional virgin huntress, free as the wind, roaming the lovely forests of Arcady. Thus, she achieved the goal of many a thirtyish woman of today—she remained exquisitely femi-nine, while successfully eschewing the male member as well as her own God-given biological fate. And yet the glaring reality is that Ar-temis above all else is barren and probably has made the fatal mis-take of confusing pleasure with happiness.

The young man at thirty has been well characterized in this quote from H. L. Mencken: "No matter how happily a woman may be married, it always pleases her to discover that there is a nice man who wishes she were not." Although at first glance this would seem to be directed at women, it could just as well be directed at man's sense of responsibility toward the woman, or women, in his life and his sense of adult responsibility toward her. Though he is not so chained to his biological destiny as she is, he is nevertheless chained to that destiny through her, and it is at this point that he must come to grips with the mature experience of marriage and parenthood. He comes to realize starkly that "marriage is only possible in a continu-ing human relationship when it is directed in the first place towards the procreation of children, and finds in its ultimate fulfillment a spiritual union of which the bodily one is but a premonition." So states Malcolm Muggeridge in A Third Testament, adding this quote from John Donne:

> Love's mysteries in souls do grow
> and yet the body is his book.

107

The Saturday night body shops of America, the local swingers' spots, are filled with men who make a career of hit-and-run affairs and the utilization of women for temporary release from the burden of their masculinity. A man at thirty has come to realize the drudgery of being low man on the totem pole at his place of work, of the rites of passage of his internship, of the frustrations of achievement. It is a syndrome that many women, especially if they have never worked toward a goal for any sustained length of time, will not experience until their next stage of life in the midthirties, but which a man feels full tilt at thirty. As often as not he would like to escape, say, to the lakes of Minnesota and open a bait and tackle shop. He feels put upon at work by the endless scut he is given to deal with, and by the end of the day or week he wants, and feels he deserves, women for pleasure. He can no longer respond to the boyhood appeals of courage and honesty and devotion to a cause because the entire energy of his waking hours confirms that this kind of nebulous thinking does not coincide with the cold reality of his life experience.

Such a man is apt to be acquisitive about women and pleasure-bound and will do anything short of giving his true self away to achieve this very evanescent end. What he fears most is what he needs most in order to become a man—love and commitment, but this of course takes him away from the fun of his childhood. One writer has called him the "Dance-Away Lover," whose repeated disillusionments stem from an incomplete intimacy with his sex partner and the morning-after loneliness that comes from lack of commitment. The Dance-Away is preoccupied with the fear of being trapped, of the insatiable need of the cavernous vaginal vault, and his own inadequacy to fill it. A woman will suck him into a morass of obligations and responsibilities, and he will no longer be free to indulge what he enjoys best, his freedom. What is missing in him is a sense of self-sacrifice and devotion to something beyond himself, which, in turn, stems from his own lack of confidence in his ability to perform. He needs love and commitment, but he remains merely a pathetic hustler. Herbert Gold, the San Francisco writer, in the midst of a painful separation, has this to say of this man's true soul:

Therefore I must be wrong about what I long for. I can't, it's too dumb. Sometimes I've walked alone, glad to be free, the day ahead just unlimited, just a field for play and invention. Now I wake alone and wish to love someone, that one. I have the comfort of children, but that's not enough. I can find the comfort of erotic sport; it gives nice sleep, but does not help me to awaken. I wake alone. The lyrical illusion is like those few times in a poet's lifetime when inspiration comes. Old poets learn that these moments are not enough for a long life; there are few contented old poets. I don't want drink, anesthesia, money, power, fame. I want that lady. I want love to be something I do for the rest of my life. Sport-fucking is not much more exciting than the Superbowl. It's a spectator sport in which the athletes are also the audience. I pick my way through the battlefields of my past. Gymnastic stunts leavened by giggles and tears do not suffice. I am saddened for an hour before breakfast. Mere protein deprivation can't be the cause.

Getting to unknow you. . . . The painful disentangling of intimacy, midnight snuggles and touchings, confidential lunches and strolls, the long process which began in the magic of courtship and continued into friendship and the common endeavor of a family.

Something and someone are gone.

If the married man and woman at thirty maintain the single focus for the sexes we have described, another marriage is doomed to fail. In fact, if even one of the marital partners (a point too poorly emphasized) maintains this juvenile cast of personality the marriage is likely to fail. Because it takes two people to get married, but only one to get divorced, thus it is one of the greatest tragedies of divorce that almost always one person is injured more than another. It is seldom a draw, an easy neutral parting, as many of the manuals would have you believe. There is pain on both sides yes, but disproportionate pain on one side. If the couple at thirty, however briefly they may have been married, is not working for something together beyond themselves they will soon find no need for each other. Because a successful life requires that we give our life away in order to gain it, whether it be to a person or a cause, both of which are necessary ingredients to a successful marriage.

The couple at thirty has had sex a thousand times. In the words of Gold and Dylan Thomas, they are a couple that whispers its night thoughts, lying together, *"their arms round the grief of the ages."* ("Night crying" sounds romantic. The facts are: diaper rash, bronchitis, sour stomach, mere hunger, energetic difference of opinion with parents about what hour it is, infantile angst, and the frazzled sharing of an endless enterprise that no one had predicted in advance.) They are a family that has to reckon with money, in-laws, conflicting habits, unpredictable new desires, emotions beyond the lyrical moments of courtship, each person paced in time by a separate rhythm of a desire. No wonder she has had her dry spells, he has had his premature spells. The element is old or worn in terms of the original flower. She is concerned that she is losing her attractive youthfulness, may even have to cut her long hair, and she may be tempted to some reassuring flirtation at the next party. He thinks that lack of fantasy may be the problem and tends to let his eyes wander toward the panty rims at the water cooler at work or a decolletage at the club dance. This kind of stimulus, properly perceived, is in the normal course of things, but when carried to the point where a marriage relationship is conceived as a license to perpetual promiscuity can loosen or even destroy that bond. A man and woman must require of each other and of themselves something of a higher order.

There is no seven-year itch within us humans, there is only an itch as old as a she-ass in rut. There is nothing to prove that our body cells turn over every seven years, for all the organ systems of the body have a different rate of cell replacement. A blood cell will last one hundred and twenty days, a stomach lining cell, destroyed by an evening of harsh drinking, will be replaced within twenty-four hours, brain cells are never replaced, and nerves to the arm grow out a slow millimeter each month. So it is for the liver and kidneys and bones and intestines, each organ system with its own individual idiosyncracies. It is wrong, therefore, to claim a seven-year exemption, such as Adam or Eve's itch, to account for our morality in marriage. Our couple at thirty must be beholden to something beyond themselves or they won't make it. Again, that something has to be love.

There are three broad stages of love in a life which if not carefully understood and pursued to conclusion can make for a disrupted maturation at vital points along the way. These are necessary steps filled with ingredients that redound all our life, in sickness and in health, to sustain us and show us the way to become a fuller person. If they are denied or stripped we are denied. For if the mind is set to work to avoid these often painful stages it will always be successful—and may eventually go on to avoid altogether emotional commitment and feeling experience of any profound order. Such a successful escape from the feeling functions of life has, in its most extreme form, been given the name of schizophrenia.

The first stage of love is the gimme-gimme-gimme infantile love need of a baby. It is our chthonic desire to get love that derives from the infant's yearning for warmth, cleanliness, and relief from the painful spasms of hunger. As those needs come to be slaked by the careful mother, the infant learns to associate them with somebody who cares for him in his helplessness, and this yearning for her comfort he comes to associate with love and a love object. The mother who exudes this unconditionally, who gives her child, despite all the turmoil and irritation of the day, the full-bodied and reliable mother warmth that child craves, has provided him with a basis of feeling he will carry throughout life. If mother love is thwarted by circumstance or lack of enthusiasm we know that children can be maimed for life. It is our birthright to experience this mother love, and a child sets forth daily to get this love for himself. It doesn't matter so much if that love comes from a surrogate mother, but it can be given only in a limited sense by a father. Foremost, a father cannot suckle an offspring and clasp it to his warm bosom. He can change it, he can give it a bottle, he can oogle it and tease it to laughter, but he can't clasp it nurturantly to the unconditional reassurance of the mother's breast. In the history of the world, few babies have ever been successfully raised by the male of the species alone. It takes a mother's love. The injured child cries first for mama, the very word being derived from her mammary gland.

The first stage of love, then, occurs when we are very young and simply want love. We want love for ourselves, love's approbation, love's regard and attention. We need love in a visceral way and will do almost anything to get it. It is a selfish state, but one that gives us the first taste of the real warmth and meaning of existence. It is the nourishment and security of being cared for, which at the end of every day as long as we live we will seek in our body next to someone else, or in our dreams as we lie down to sleep and enter the cocoon of the unconscious to be refreshed again.

If a child is secure in the love freely given by adoring parents, most particularly by the mother, one day, as every parent knows, the most astonishing thing will happen. The year-old baby, whom you have just given a cookie to munch on and hope will now be quiet, suddenly gives it back to you by attempting to put it in your mouth. He does this with laughter and a smile and will not be quiet this time until you, too, take the saliva-contaminated host into your own mouth and enjoy it, as he watches you relish and chew and swallow. The child is apt now to want to share pretzels, crunched in half, mouth to mouth, and wants to eat and have you eat everything on the table together. Mother has to show by occasional tasting that she too can handle that Gerber's stuff, as if that were a taste of her own medicine. (It has a certain sobering effect.) But it is in this act of giving, and then sharing, of his own substance that the child enters the adult world of love. The sooner one sees this in a child—the child who, at the cocktail party, toddles menacingly but naturally about from couch to couch, mashing hors d'oeuvres into people's mouths—the sooner the entrance into the adult way of love will be accomplished. If this does not happen early in childhood, there is a dangerous maturation arrest. Unfortunately, too many adults stop at the self-indulgent stage of love, when they should go on until they have learned in the soul that the only way to really get the love they

need is to give love. This comes home most naturally and most poignantly in our own parenthood when we feel this abundance of love
returned by our children, when this fundamental principle of reci-
procity is fixed in maturity where it grows and grows. And just as it is
hard for a rich man, in Jesus' words, to enter the kingdom of heaven,
so it is hard for the childless to enter the kingdom of love. For children take you by the nose and lead you there, as if to say this is the
only way you can make it and for damn sure the only way you can
make it with me. They require of you patience and selflessness
and losing yourself in the wonder of the world. If this aspect of
life is foresworn or avoided, the adult again is turned in upon himself toward self-indulgence. What was then his original childish
demand for his own indulgence by his parents remains just that,
and he is arrested in his love journey. There are many ways to replace or substitute or experience the parental love bond, but all of
them are necessarily tentative or oblique. Parenthood is nature's
way of advancing to another very essential and more mature level
of love.

That child with the pretzel, who can't yet speak, is telling us that
the essential ingredient of giving love is in gesture, not lip service.
Perhaps the most cloying kind of love partner is one who is forever
saying "I love you" into your eyes and waiting for a reply. While
purporting to be the quintessential giving soul of love, such a partner is
often merely abusing those three sacred words for his own selfish and
insecure ends, hoping to force some confirmatory reply. "Words,
words, words," as Hamlet said. Love is much more often and more
sincerely expressed each day in a thousand small things that take
place between men and women. A toothpaste cap replaced where it
was not formerly, an article saved from the morning paper, clean
sheets and pajamas, remembering a joke heard at the office, stopping
at the store on the way home for mustard, or taking out the garbage
without prompting. Candies and flowers I do not decry, particularly
Blum's caramels and wild California irises, but they are always of an
order that is more concerted. The gift of the Magi are not necessarily

selfless giving, for such magnificent gifts redound to the elegance of the source. It is consideration in little things, once that becomes our second nature, that is of the true essence of love. It is giving without self-consequence.

There is yet a third stage of love. It is the all-important mature stage and what the poet William Blake was referring to when he wrote:

And we are put on earth a little space
That we may learn to bear the beams of Love.

For the last stage of love is to allow love. Not to shut it out. Does our married couple at thirty allow love? Do they make a point of actively opening their hearts, not just to each other, but to the world about them, even unto the fat lady on the bus? Is a time set aside each day to have tea before the fire on the Chinese rug? Or do we, in our busy industrial way, in our zeal just to get things done, tend to exclude the whole poetic side of ourselves, because, as W. H. Auden once said, "Poetry never makes anything happen"?

Allowing love is not just a Pollyanna concept, for it begins in the very rudiments of ordinary propriety and politeness and extends through to the magnificent letting go of the sex act itself. The one introduces the other and perhaps, therefore, respect for others is the most important concept for adults in the modern industrial world.

From societal politeness we begin our own individual politeness to a considerable extent. *In veritas uno, in veritas omnibus.* What strikes foreigners often is how polite we Americans are. They laugh at all of us for the greeting, "How are you today?" when they say quite rightfully you don't really mean you want to stop and hear out all of their problems. But such linguistic expressions are truly symptomatic of a cultural concern for another's well-being, however superficial most of us usually are in using it. It means that people can care and do care to open themselves out to one another in greeting.

When I was first divorced, I felt rejected and lonely and wondered how you ever again met people in this world. I almost unconsciously began to smile at people and say good morning pleasantly to grubby people I hadn't acknowledged in years. I smiled at the fat lady on the bus and the man whose dog dirtied my pavement and the guard with halitosis who stamps my parking ticket when I consult for Blue Cross. Before long this disease spread, an amazing contagion, and I had some of the cutest numbers in town announce my availability to the world, and was inundated to the extent that I was considering becoming a sexual Scrooge again. And all of this because I set forth each day to open myself up to as many souls as I could, simply by being pleasant and congenial and concerned. In short, I allowed love to enter my life. Since that experience I have never had much sympathy with the young stranger in town who complains about not meeting people. The world is crying out for the person who allows love. As for those people you can't get along with, they must be treated as such relationships can only be treated—with courtesy and with distance. But even then the possibility of love can always be there, if only it's allowed. The crime against nature is to shut it off or shut it out forever, as is done much too often. There is an ancient Chinese proverb that states, "Always leave a door open so even your enemies can leave."

So poetry does indeed make something called love happen. It is our primitive lub-dub beat of the heart, the cadence of our every waking step, as the breath is the inspiration of our spoken lines. And if the man and woman at thirty are not nurturing this primal call within themselves, are not listening to the heartbeat rhythm of a life or tasting the inspiration of the breath, they are not completing the journey of love. For now that they have gratefully received love, and now that they have graciously given love, they must at last learn to bear the beam of love. If they would have each other, and the world as well, they must turn their hearts out and allow love. And that as often as not means pain, but without which there is no joy.

SIX

JUST LIKE
CLOCKWORK

Honey watcha doin' watcha doin' tonight
Hope you're in the mood
Because I'm feelin' just right
        —*Joe Garland and Andy Razaf*
                "In the Mood"

COMPARATIVE ANTHROPOLOGY is the study of divergent cultures in search of elements that may be common to the mind of all mankind. One of its remarkable revelations is that the collective human unconscious contains certain common myths that through the ages are persistent and recurrent as themes, however isolated from cross-fertilization various cultures may be. For example, Ireland and Japan are a world apart. They are culturally and geographically distinct, and yet, independently, at precisely the same time in the ancient history of both, long before any contact was possible between them, one finds the appearance of the Celtic cross. This is good, presumptive evidence that the mandala of a cross surrounded by a circle, as represented and expressed historically in those two disparate cultures, is part of the unconscious imagery of mankind. In a similar way, storied myths, such as the Oedipus and Electra myths we have already discussed, emerged and were absorbed and perpetuated because they expressed emotionally much of the unconscious fount of the experience of the race, in this case of all children and parents throughout history. We have, then, certain genuine myths that speak to our soul and survive because they serve a summary purpose that is time-honored and significant to everyone.

The trouble with myths is that they oversimplify. Unfortunately, sexuality, because of its highly charged emotionalism, is especially susceptible to attempts at reductive mythologizing so that everybody can easily partake of its promised ecstatic largesse. But we are not involved today in true mythologizing, we are only working on tentative and topical prejudices that are best referred to as old wives tales. Here for example are some old wives tales of my sexual youth, followed in each case by new wives tales on the same topic today:

OLD: Female orgasm is rare and corrupt.
NEW: Female orgasm makes the world shine every day.

•

OLD: Masturbation makes you nervous and is harmful.
NEW: Masturbation is better than intercourse because you can please yourself your own way.

•

OLD: True love is necessary for good sex.
NEW: Love and sex are unrelated. The thrill and enjoyment are all there are.

•

OLD: A big cock is necessary to please women.
NEW: The size of a man's penis makes no difference to a woman.

•

OLD: Poor people have a better sex life.
NEW: Rich people have limitless sexual activity.

•

OLD: Clitoral orgasms are inferior to those in the vagina.
NEW: There is no difference between clitoral and vaginal orgasms.

•

OLD: Orgasms experienced together are best.
NEW: Orgasms experienced in sequence are the best.

•

OLD: Deep Freudian psychoanalysis is necessary to correct sex problems.
NEW: There are technical ways to cure most sex malfunctioning.

•

OLD: The homosexual is emotionally maladjusted and unhappy.
NEW: Heterosexuality and homosexuality give equal rewards.

•

OLD: Sexual fantasies are mental aberrations.
NEW: Fantasies about sex are all healthy.

•

OLD: All healthy young people are virgins.
NEW: Every adolescent today is an incorrigible sexpot.

•

OLD: A woman who is raped brings it on herself.
NEW: Women enjoy rape because they fantasize it all the time.

•

OLD: Women put up with sex, they don't really dig it.
NEW: Women are sexier than men.

This is the Ann Landers' advice-to-the-lovelorn kind of revision-ism at its peak, which, while apparently holding out to you the gospel truth, is obviously very topical and tentative and hence permanently unreliable. It is this very attitude that stimulates the discipline of science, where clear rules are established to eliminate petty prejudices that might interfere with reported results. Such a discipline allows the cold hard light that scientific fact can throw on the confusing possibilities of current feelings.

Nowhere in recent years has science opened a more exciting vista than in the chemistry of rhythm and moods of the human being. We have come to realize that men and women share most of the same chemical basis for life and living, with one important exception: the female menstrual cycle. It's important, at this point, to establish what all we human beings share in common and then realize the interfaces and differences in the rhythms and moods of men and women because of the menstrual chemistry. It reminds us all over again that we are in this life together: first and foremost as human beings, and second as sexual beings.

Eons ago when life awakened and slithered its way out of the primal mud toward the warmth of the sun, our cellular forebearers in a mysterious way incorporated an affinity for light and darkness which is contained in microcosm within all of us today. Men and women have an amazingly consistent and immune-to-change daily biological clock that is always at work, measurable and predictable. Unlike the reproductive clock, unique to women alone, this shared circadian clock is independent of most kinds of external stimuli and amazingly free of even internal control. It has, nevertheless, immense bearing on the ebb and flow of our life, the going forth in the morning, the returning home at night, and largely controls the mood of our day.

The limits of the circadian cycle are strict. It is a twenty-four-hour cycle, occasionally reduced to twenty hours or expanded to twenty-eight, but generally encompassing the time it takes the earth to rotate once about its axis. In most latitudes this would allow for a period of lightness and a period of darkness. It can be shown that in humans, during this twenty-four hour period, the hormone cortisone pours forth from the adrenal gland at the end of a sleep period, usually in the early morning, giving maximal energy for the day, and then gradually diminishes with the day, to reach a nadir about midnight, only to be recharged again for the next day by sleep. This pattern is constant and invariable and common to woman and man.

Numerous experiments have demonstrated the integrity of our quotidian clock. It is independent of loud noise, strong odors, touch, severe stress, anoxia, anesthesia, alcohol intoxication, handling, electric shock, emotional trauma, and body illness, to mention but a few. It is independent of the ovulatory cycle in women and the testosterone levels in men. If you remove the gonads (testes or ovary) from man or woman, the daily cycle goes on unabated. For years it was believed that the master gland, the pituitary, was activated periodically to stimulate the adrenal with adreno-cortical hormone, thereby releasing a measured amount of cortisone into our blood stream. But it has been observed in patients following pituitary removal that the cortisone rhythm proceeds unaffected. This confirms experimental work on all manner of animals, including roaches, fish, mice, hamsters, and primates, where hypophysectomy (removal of the pituitary) leaves the biological clock unchanged. Furthermore, infusion of large amounts of adrenal-stimulating pituitary hormone seems to have no effect on the basic maintenance cortisone ebb and flow. The conclusion seems inevitable that our quotidian clockwork of cortisone is independent of every internal gland except the gland of origin, the adrenal. Even here there are exceptions, for some adrenalectomized animals (for example, rats) seem to exhibit no clock change and many adrenalectomized patients react similarly, although so much supportive therapy is given human adrenalectomies as to render any conclusions in human beings highly suspect. For this reason, some experimenters have chosen to localize the clock to the mysterious hypothalamus, which they have selectively ablated by electrocoagulation and in experiments with rats have thereby been able to shut off the clock. The facts remain that cortisone is the measurable hormone in our daily clock; a cortisone rhythm definitely exists; this hormone is only secreted by the adrenal gland; and the hypothalamus is not known to secrete any primary hormone whatsoever.

For the moment, then, we must assume that the equilibrilizing influence of our daily cortisone flow is adrenal in origin. Not only does cortisone flow display a conspicuous twenty-four hour rise and fall, but within that rhythm other minirhythms have now been described. These are called wobbling frequencies since they have a periodicity of eighty-five to ninety minutes, during which time one can demonstrate a rather consistent high and low titre of cortisone within the larger daily cortisone flux. Once again these minifluctuations are seen to be consistent and independent of pituitary control, occurring independently of the same external stimuli and with predictable periodicity.

Though there is still considerable doubt about what does not affect our daily hormonal clockwork, we know positively that the clock is (1) independent of everything but light; and (2) the manifestations of it result from the effects of cortisone on our body. It is postulated that the eye and the clock must have followed much the same evolutionary development and led to the recognition of light and dark periods within which animals selectively chose to function. The cortisone cycle of nocturnal animals, such as rats and ferrets, is exactly reversed from that of humans. Thus, their maximum flow of cortisone will occur at midnight when all through the house no other creature is stirring. The "dark" active rat and the "light" active monkey can be plotted diametrically out of phase, and both these phases can be reversed, but only with laborious training and conditioning because the mechanism is inherent and innate. For example, if this same group of monkeys and rats is blinded, the same cycle continues for a long time before becoming fragmented by truncated or prolonged cortisone-inspired activity. Persons I have known, suddenly blinded from trauma, exhibit this same peculiar persistence of rhythmic flow related to day and night, and remain curious about lightness and darkness to confirm their state of sleep or wakefulness. Although this persists for a long time, it eventually becomes distorted and internally irrelevant. Interestingly enough, animals or humans blinded at birth have a normal clock. So it is certainly a gene-controlled clock.

When you experience jet lag you are merely in trouble with your cortisone clockwork. Your rhythm wants to persist on Pacific daylight savings time and not adjust to Eastern standard time. It resists such adjustment, and you feel blah from lack of the mellifluous effects of cortisone. This hormone has a widespread spectrum of effects on the body, almost all of them beneficial and of a positive tonic nature. By acting on sensitive body receptor cells it is known to influence all our body systems like no other known hormone. It has an anti-inflammatory action, it increases our immune response, it increases our red cells and our white cells (lymphocytes) and our hemoglobin. It increases skeletal muscle, which withers away without it. It acts on our capillaries to increase circulation and thereby increases heart action and tone. By acting on the kidneys it maintains proper salt balance in the body, which, in turn, influences all other body chemistries such as potassium, calcium, and chlorides, which, in turn, regulate heart rate and hence blood circulation. Cortisone redistributes body fat and stores sugar in the liver to be called forth as reserves in hunger states or states of low blood sugar. Above all, by combining all these modalities, it maintains the functional integrity of our brain. The brain needs a constant energy supply to survive and function. Its cells are so sensitive it will die in a few minutes without this energy supply and become irretrievable to any circulation even to the most vigorous cardiac massage. By providing glucose stores in the liver and a constant blood flow tone to the brain cortisone maintains the integrity of our central nervous system. It is no wonder that one of the magnificent "side effects" of cortisone, ubiquitous in action as it is, is a great feeling of health and well-being. Cortisone does this to people—it makes them feel good. Cortisone is a high, a welcome shot of adrenalin. And men and women alike get it once a day in a huge adrenal outpouring crescendo, and a maintenance dose every hour and a half all day long to keep them going. In contrasting the hormonal differences between men and women we would do well to remember that we possess in common this basic similarity.

Though our daily chemical cortisone rhythm is reasonably well documented, relating these changes to mood and behavior is considerably more speculative. For example, we know there are "morning people" and "night people," the so-called "larks" and "owls" of this world. Studies have been done to show the more extroverted of us tend to be night people and larks to be introverted day people. The temperature of larks rises more rapidly in the morning, indicating a more vigorous early metabolism, and then falls off more rapidly in the evening. In adolescent girls, extroversion rates are higher than for boys in the morning, and boys rate higher in morning fatigue. It could be possible that there are more larks among adolescent girls, but the measurements of anxiety, stress, inability to cope, and depression for all groups at this age tend to show an increase in the late afternoon.

Late afternoon corresponds to the time of falling off of cortisone titres. However, when these same adolescents become college students, positive moods seem to increase and negative moods decrease at midday and afternoon compared to morning. Sleep habits seem to have the greatest effect on these moods. In adolescence the "sleeping in" habit is notorious, but by college years it has become somewhat more rigorously disciplined and regular. Thus, the displacement of the cortisone clock to a more normal routine may make more normal mood changes apparent. We know that shortening or lengthening the sleep period (too much sleep or not enough sleep) within the diurnal rhythmic pattern has adverse effects on mood. And we know that displacing the sleeping time, even if it's the same number of hours, within the twenty-four hour cycle will adversely affect mood.

And yet it has not been shown that these changes can be related to the overall cortisone ebb and flow, even in its circadian cycle or its miniflux of every ninety minutes. What is known is that altering sleep habits, such as in going from daytime to nighttime work, necessitates a change in clockwork, so that when we are asleep we are building up our cortisone levels and when we are awake we are running on maximum cylinders. Surgeons recognize this fact by trying to avoid emergency work in the middle of the night when not only the operating crew is likely to be at a low ebb, but the patient's clockwork is slowed as well. International airlines require long intermediary stops to reset the crews' clocks, and the state department, as well as most international businesses, requires its members to arrive in foreign ports forty-eight hours prior to important negotiations for the same reason. In all this adult men and women seem to share a need in common, and it can be shown that both sexes function best in a twenty-four-hour routinized daily cycle within a free but synchronized environment. Although normal mood and activity rhythms are maintained in a rigorously controlled environment (say in the cockpit of a plane) the amplitude of those swings of mood and activity rhythms is definitely diminished, hence less efficient.

There is no difference in the sleep-wakefulness cycle of men and women, both of whom exhibit consistent patterns as the result of innumerable documented studies in sleep laboratories. Two types of sleep are observed: rapid eye motion sleep (REM) and nonrapid eye motion sleep (N–REM), both with individual characteristics. REM sleep is associated with dreaming, nervous system activation, erections, and profound muscular relaxation. The N–REM phase is characterized by gross body movements, muscular activity, low nervous impulse, no erections, and verbal, repetitive thoughtlike expression. The electroencephalogram, which measures our brain waves, shows low voltage fast waves for REM and slower waves with greater amplitude for N–REM.

The most exciting aspect of our sleep patterns is that the REM and N–REM have a periodicity of approximately ninety minutes, precisely the same range now documented for the minifluctuations of cortisone in our daily circadian rhythm. Could these two be related? It is such serendipity that science is based on. For example, we know our circadian rhythm is present in all animals and in humans at birth. And now we find that REM and N–REM sleep patterns are demonstrable in infants, where no eye or body movement and spontaneous sucking respirations become measurable as REM at intervals of ninety minutes. Furthermore, evidence is now accumulating that wakefulness has its similar counterpart in daytime rest-activity cycles. These again are ninety-minute cycles of central nervous system activity, general muscular activity, and measurable oral activity analogous to the infant, which in men and women take on the form of smoking, eating, and drinking. A similar pattern, surprisingly, can be found in schizophrenic patients, indicating the constancy of the phenomenon as independent of integrated central nervous system control and possibly, as in the case of our cortisone cycle, under the rather constant control of adrenal output. Because the neurotransmitters of our hypothalamus, norepinephrine and serotonin, have recently been shown to have rhythmic variations consistent with REM sleep, that mysterious organ once again has been implicated in our sleep wakefulness REM patterns. But the most significant finding is this: activity, food intake, muscle studies, and brain studies all show a consistent sleep and wakefulness rhythmicity occurring in ninety-minute cycles of between ten and sixteen per twenty-four-hour period. And this is precisely the same pattern exhibited by our minifunction in cortisone in a twenty-four-hour circadian cycle. The association, which is similar for women and men, at this point seems more than just coincidental.

Although women and men alike share the rhythm and moods we have been discussing so far, it is woman alone who possesses a menstrual cycle. In contrast to the internal clocks that regulate sleep and wakefulness and body energy levels, the ovulatory cycle is often irregular, inaccurate, and unpredictable. Unlike the cortisone clock it is easily affected by external stimuli and is frequently beholden to the influence of the activity of the higher brain centers. It is woman's animal remnant of the estrus cycle, which can be demonstrably related to a feedback relationship between hypothalamus and ovaries, and disturbance in any of these areas can disrupt the normal cyclical flow. Odors, noises, shocks, handling, stress, toxins, altered environment are but a few influences known to alter estrus in the animal laboratory. It is an empirical fact of life that the cyclical-acyclical sex differential in men and women has an important bearing on emotional function and behavior.

Between the ages of roughly fifteen and fifty, a period of thirty-five years, woman spends 25 percent of her time in a premenstrual or menstrual condition. This is an immense amount of time, nearly ten years total, right in the midst of her most vigorous and energetic phase of life. Yet into this period of premenstrual and menstrual time are crowded an amazing number of psychoemotional and behavioral correlates: 50 percent of all female prisoners were in this phase when committing a crime, 50 percent of female suicides occur during this time, 45 percent of acute female admissions to mental institutions and 45 percent of punishments meted out to schoolgirls take place in this phase. A majority of automobile accidents involving women (60 percent) occur when they are menstrual or premenstrual, and a poorer showing by 15 percent on examinations is recorded in menstruating coed students. As can readily be seen, the conclusion is not too far out that in females a tendency to self-destruction seems to be related to the lunar cycle. This is the one physiological element that weighs more heavily on women than on men. Unfortunately, the mechanism of this is obscure.

Can it be purely emotional? Some have insisted those women do better who have been more lovingly and honestly prepared by their mothers for their first menstrual experience. Fear and depression tend to be more often absent in such women at menstrual time over the ensuing years, for these women have been helped and encouraged to value their womanhood, to understand and look beyond the "dirtiness" of the period process. It is possible that most women who suffer premenstrual or menstrual emotional lability had significant trauma in or around the time of their first menstrual period. It is hard indeed to account for this in any physiological way because so many, indeed most, women manage menses without emotional disarray. Yet we know there is a severe dropping off of progesterone hormone at this time, just as there is following delivery of a child, which is often accompanied by postpartum depression.

On the other hand, could menstrual and premenstrual depression be the result of lowered estrogen levels at the end of the cycle? There is certain circulating enzyme, a protein derivative, called monoamine oxidase whose activity can be correlated with mood and ovarian hormone production. The main action of monoamine oxidase is on the hypothalamus where it is known to inhibit the action of two neurotransmitters, our old friends norepinephrine and serotonin. The antidote to monoamine oxidase appears to be estrogen, so that high levels of estrogen suppress the enzyme and low levels enhance it. Thus, at the end of the cycle, when estrogen levels are low, monoamine is apt to be high, and inhibits the neurotransmitters serotonin and norepinephrine from being released to transmit their messages to the pituitary gland. Depression may result at just this point, because the message needed by the pituitary, as we have seen, is to produce ovarian-stimulating gonadotrophic hormones, which, in turn, lead to the production by the ovaries of estrogen. This, then, would suppress monoamine oxidase and commence another successful cycle, what nature at this point intends woman to do. So the relatively high incidence of suicides, depression, and accidents in premenstrual and menstrual women may be the result of low brain levels of releasing factors in the hypothalamus, norepinephrine and serotonin, secondary to high plasma monoamine oxidase activity, induced by low estrogen at menses. Thus elevated levels of monoamine in depressed women should be reversible by estrogen administration. And this is precisely the case—with dramatic improvement in mood when estrogen is clinically administered.

In large population studies the impulse to male and female self-destructiveness tends to occur in inexplicable "clusters," while maintaining a regular overall pattern. That general pattern consistently includes a random chance distribution for males, but always a menstrual orientation for females. Nevertheless, some scientists have

persisted in claiming a cyclical influence of testosterone on male behavior analogous to estrogen in the female. Let's pause to enumerate
more completely the effects of both estrogen and testosterone on the
human body.

Testosterone causes differentiation of all the male secondary sex
characteristics, including hair distribution and genital differentiation. It promotes growth in height and massive muscular development. It thickens the skin, increases oily secretion, and enlarges the
larynx, giving a deep voice to the male. It enhances penile erection,
and is necessary for sperm manufacture and maturation. With testosterone, protein synthesis in the body is increased and a general
building up and strengthening of tissues occurs. Water is retained by
testosterone administration, and sodium, potassium, and chloride are
also retained. In general, nitrogen stores are increased in the body.
Of all the steroid hormones, testosterone has one of the largest anabolic (or building up) effects known. In men, as the result of pulsatile
gonadotrophins from the pituitary, testosterone is secreted in irregular bursts that fluctuate unpredictably throughout the day. In
humans, about 10 percent of the androgen production comes from
the adrenal gland. This is not enough to control spermatogenesis or
secondary sex characteristics in man, but it is sufficient to have a sexually stimulating influence in woman. Testosterone has no proven direct and consistent pharmacological influence on mood.

Estrogens are largely responsible for the pubertal changes in girls
and account for those attributes that are usually called feminine.
They cause growth, hence enlargement of the breasts. They cause ac-
cretion of fats and the characteristic molding of the female form.
Closing of the epiphyseal end growth of bones and typical female
hair distribution are two other prominent effects. Pigmentation of
the nipples and nipple enlargement about the areola are estrogen-in-
duced. Estrogen is so potent that topical application to the skin may
induce breast enlargement through absorption, and oral preparations
are readily dispersed throughout the body. This is unlike the effect of
testosterone which is best administered by injection. But, like the androgens, estrogen does have an anabolic effect on nitrogen and salt

and water retention, but its building effect on body protoplasm is nowhere near as great as that of testosterone. Estrogen, as we have seen earlier, has a crucial role in the menstrual cycle and a peculiar tonic effect on the female mood. It is the hormonal remnant of estrus, or heat, in lower animals, and a preparatory hormone both for tissue turgor circulation and a sense of well-being. The psychological and emotional effects of estrogen withdrawal or administration at menopause are well known. A sense of hovering, dark, brooding clouds overhead is a frequent complaint of women, depressed after cessation of ovarian function, and this dark mood is reversible by the administration of estrogen. In pubertal girls it is estrogen withdrawal that causes menses rather than progesterone cessation. Later on, however, progesterone withdrawal seems to be the important element. Beyond this, progesterone seems to have little body influence, except to cause an elevation of body temperature (a thermogenic action) at the time of ovulation. It is for this reason that women measure their temperature to ascertain a one degree temperature change when progesterone is suddenly released by the ovulation process. The bottom line, then, is that among the three major sex hormones—testosterone, estrogen, and progesterone—it is only estrogens that have a proven direct pharmaceutical action on mood and a sense of well-being.

While progesterone has no measurable direct bearing on mood in the way estrogen does, its effect on sexual activity is definite because of its influence on estrogen. At ovulation progesterone tends to potentiate the estrogen activity and facilitate estrous activity. Following ovulation, with increasing titres of progesterone, estrogen activity is gradually suppressed. Ordinary monkeys, when given an extra shot of progesterone at ovulation time, show an inordinate sexual response. These same monkeys when the ovaries are removed nevertheless show a universe sexual response to ordinary estrogen administration. But this sexual response is then completely suppressed by progesterone administration. In general, it seems that progesterone in increasing amounts suppresses sexual activity. Perhaps this progesterone effect is nature's way of producing and then protecting the fertilized egg, first, by stimulating sex to get the job done, and then by discouraging any violent dislocation of the early implanted egg. The same influence to protect a fetus may be at work throughout pregnancy. We know definitely that, as progesterone increases during pregnancy, woman's sexual desire is progressively inhibited, presumably by progesterone's depressive effect on the hypothalamic brain. Most women experience a decline in desire for sex during the progesterone or second phase of the menstrual cycle, which, in turn, affects men's moods, not just their own.

How then to manage the mood swings during the menstrual cycle? It is important, first and foremost, for the male of the species to recognize and acknowledge that changes of a chemical nature do occur in women which have a direct physiological bearing on her mood. These changes are most marked four or five days prior to menses, the so-called premenstrual syndrome, a state in which a woman spends over fifty days a year. During this time 30 to 50 percent of all young women will be bothered by backaches, headaches, tension, depression, and general irritability. It is important for men not to discount the problem. A man in relationship to a woman is in relation with her twenty-eight-day cycle, even as she herself is in relation to that cycle.

The second thing for a woman and a man to understand is the moody influence of estrogen and progesterone and just when that influence is prevalent and what that influence is. Some people have equated estrogen (E) with energy and progesterone (P) with peace. That is, women tend to be more outgoing and active in the first half of their cycle when estrogen is running the show. They are more receptive to all life's activities during these first fourteen days. During the second half of their cycle, when progesterone takes over, women feel less animated and progressively less interested, hence more passive and resigned for all endeavors. Research indicates that women are more orgasmic during the first part of their cycle, reaching a peak around midcycle at the time of ovulation. In addition, most women note an increased libido just before menses when progesterone drops off and pelvic congestion may heighten their excitement. A number of women find themselves feeling very lusty right in the middle of their menses, perhaps at that time, for psychological reasons, craving the reassurance of the male member. All of this has idiosyncratic sexual implications for the particular marriage bed.

Approximately 10 percent of women are incapacitated by menses. Most of them cope with the minor discomforts mentioned. But husbands frequently accuse their wives of manipulating cyclic changes as an excuse to vent anger or for the secondary gain of attention. Neither the accusation nor the manipulation is psychologically appropriate. The couple should know the emotional vulnerability for both inherent in the menstrual cycle. Marital tensions are apt to be exacerbated in the already tense premenstrual state. What is emotionally subclinical may erupt out of all proportion at this time to dislocate or destroy a relationship that is otherwise happily controlled. Some psychiatrists have even suggested that the man should be allowed to "have his days" of emotional tenderness, perhaps a time set aside when the woman is energized by estrogen. The important thing here is that man and woman are honest about the cyclic aspects of woman's nature and that the possibility of controlling the volatility of that ebb and flow is real and available to an informed, loving man and wife. Most of this control is best exercised psychologically, but hormonal regulation is possible in extreme and uncontrolled medical situations.

It should be mentioned that the adrenal has not been completely absolved of influencing the mood alterations of the menstrual cycle. There is evidence to implicate a blood pressure-controlling hormone called aldosterone which is secreted along with cortisone by the adrenal cortex. Aldosterone shows both a midcyle and premenstrual peak commensurate with mood alterations at those times. At those times as well there is a measurable increase in the urinary potassium: sodium ratio which is one of the known functions of aldosterone. Also, levels of aldosterone are measurably higher in women suffering from recurrent premenstrual tension and cramps. Angiotensin, a hormone known to increase tension in the blood vessels and hence elevate blood pressure, is activated by aldosterone and may therefore be the

cause of "tenseness" and headache formation. Precursors of aldosterone are known to raise seizure thresholds and have a brain sedative
effect, while angiotensin itself has been demonstrated to decrease exploratory activity and to counteract the effects of anesthetics. But no
direct psychic or sexual effects have been demonstrated in the
human being as the result of the administration of aldosterone or angiotensin. It is possible that these hormones may work in conjunc-
tion with estrogen and progesterone to influence mood in some as
yet unexplained manner, related perhaps to blood pressure and fluid
retention in the body.

This brings us to the possibility of a testosterone cycle in the
human male. It does appear that there are measurable fluctuations in
male testosterone over a two-month period that may be cyclical, although there are immense fluctuations from day to day that may be
the result of pulsatile variations from gonadotrophin stimulation via
the pituitary, or possibly environmental influences mediated via the
hypothalamus. It seems that the male cycle varies from eight to
thirty days, with an average cycle clustered around twenty days.
Variations in low-level testosterone output average anywhere from
15 percent to 40 percent of normal for more than half the male population during this period of time, and diurnal variations are consistently recorded in some men. What has not been observed, however,
is any clinical correlation between lowered male testosterone levels
and mood changes. No anxiety, sleep, anger, or aggressive patterns
have been related to male testosterone levels, and no cyclical alterations correlated with testosterone levels in the blood. There is no
conclusive correlation between hormone titres and day-to-day moods
in men, although a possibility exists that high testosterone levels may
depress certain of the male population. Certainly, man is not as beholden to his chemical hormonal cycles as woman, and the influence
of estrogen on the woman is more empirically demonstrable than testosterone on the male.

Nor does the absence of chemical dependence mean that man is
not a moody or mood-prone character when compared to woman.
Many men show clear seven-day cycles, measurable by psychological

testing, possibly related to the conventional seven-day work week. In this respect women do not seem to test out the same, having (contrary to most hearsay) more mood equanimity from week to week throughout the days. Men seem to have more variable mood cycles, occurring anywhere from six to ninety days, with cyclical clusters between seven and twenty-three days and again at thirty to forty-five days, and this is true for about 40 percent of males. Thus, in 60 percent of males no measurable cycle exists by current psychological testing, but the significant finding seems to be that in those males where moods, such as anxiety, irritability, hostility, depression, and aggression, do exist they are idiosyncratic to the person and tend to exhibit more variability and shorter swings than in the female. It is impossible to get away from the fact that woman's moods are more hormonally linked than are the male's and, while both of them are moody creatures, even cyclical creatures, the female moods across the board are more likely to be the product of nature. Certainly they are more predictably so, notwithstanding all the traditional social and cultural pressures on the different sexes.

But if what all of us recognize as male moodiness is not chemically linked as it is in the female, how then to account for it? We must return to the realm of psychiatry for a moment for an explanation. Earlier we described the male principle in the female as her animus, and showed how the little Dutch girl logo on the Dutch Cleanser can, an aggressive busy-body woman brandishing a rolling pin, expressed the female animus characteristics to a considerable extent. We alluded to the male's anima as being that female part of himself that projects his creative impulses upon the world in general and the female person in particular. But there is much more to the anima than just that, and it is these female attributes within him that account for man's moodiness.

The characteristics of the anima are all the feminine cravings for sweetness and repose, for soft things and self-indulgent body care. They include a beauty rest on Scheherazade pillows and a beakfast of waffles and jasmine tea in a Japanese kimono at ten A.M. They include a manicure and a rubdown at midday after a racketball game, the smell of the fresh daphne and nasturtiums on the corner stand during a stroll at lunch hour. They include compliments for your new coat and tie and sugar-roll strokes at the office by colleagues and secretaries alike. In short, the entire indulgent quality of femininity is included in the anima which is contained within the male.

It is a short jump to appreciate that when this anima is not allowed sufficient attention it begins to complain. And these complaints are represented as moodiness in the male. We will have more to say about this later, but herewith the point that the blurting out, the nervousness, the headache, the vague discontent, the biting sarcasm, the insomnia, the dark brooding clouds are the male analogue of the female moodiness of a woman's cyclical chemical changes. In the male we find no such chemical basis, but we do find a feminine part of himself in his anima that must be properly recognized and allowed expression or it will be represented in destructive moodiness. In middle-aged man most of the work of psychoanalysis is to get the man to acknowledge the existence of the anima within himself as the unexpressed source of much of his difficulty. Once man acknowledges this feminine self, becomes familiar with its characteristics and demands, his moods show much more equanimity and he is a much more efficient and easier person. This is in fact what Bob Cratchit did for Scrooge, the therapist working on the miserly patient who, through a series of dreams, finally realizes that he has been a mean old bastard who has made himself crochety and miserable by not acknowledging his anima.

Before leaving the chemistry of rhythms and moods some comment should be made on the pseudoscience of human biorhythms. The advocates of this theory, which has received an exceptional amount of attention recently, claim that every living person, man and woman alike, has an idiosyncratic and measurable cyclical pattern that controls his or her physical, emotional, and intellectual capabilities. Furthermore, one can extrapolate any person's cyclical phases by simply knowing their birth date, hence make predictions of mood and behavior with reference to certain dates. The physical cycle itself is said to last precisely twenty-three days, the emotional cycle twenty-eight days, and the intellectual cycle thirty-three days. All three of these cycles are said to begin at birth and to proceed repetitively throughout our entire lifetime. Although there are bad days postulated for the beginning, the middle, and the end of the cycle, in a general way the first half of the cycle is a positive good half and the second half bad and negative. Thus we are supposed to perform at our best during the initial phase, whereas the second phase is filled with poor performance levels and even danger to our person. To confuse matters further, there happens to be one more positive than negative day in the physical cycle, and one more negative than positive in the intellectual cycle, while the emotional cycle is always evenly balanced. When one is in the interphase between positive and negative, one is said to be in the critical phase, which in each of the three cycles lasts only forty-eight hours. But the one day offset in the physical and intellectual cycle, and the fact that there are two critical days for all three cycle modalities, makes for a low statistical probability that they will all converge on any given day. This gives the biorhythmists plenty of margin for error on predicting anything.

Nevertheless, when the three cycles do reach a peak on any given day, the person is said to experience great drive, vigor, efficiency, and creative ability. If the cycles are in the critical interphase or negative stretch on any given day, the person is in a tentative state and apt to be sluggish and irritable, even accident-prone. One would think that merely to state such a statistically suspect concept would be to invalidate it, and yet many people have compiled charts and gone to great lengths to avoid certain so-called unfavorable life periods and wait for the good days. People have been known not to drive on negative days, postpone wedding dates, advance dinner parties, avoid shopping sprees, defer payments, keep babies at home. I know surgical colleagues who will not operate out of phase and actors who plan ahead to bomb on bad nights. Clearly, the implications of religiously following such "predictable" life charts is immense. It is rumored

136

that Jimmy the Greek, America's foremost odds-maker, will not act without consulting biorhythm, and has claimed that Senator Edward Kennedy was in a "critical phase" on the night of Chappaquiddick.

Fortunately, the theory of biorhythm lends itself to brilliant retrospective analysis. For example, Reggie Jackson was in the doldrums of a negative physical, emotional, and intellectual phase in the 1977 World Series. Nevertheless, he set an all-time home run hitting record, batted a roundhouse .450 percent at the plate, and almost singlehandedly led his Yankee team to a rout over the Los Angeles Dodgers. And all this contrary to the dire pregame predictions of the biorhythm experts. The same is true if one looks back on a hundred no-hit baseball games and a like number of boxing championship matches. Most of the pitchers were said inaccurately to be "physically negative" and "intellectually critical," and the preponderance of boxing's champs can in no way be biorhythmically correlated.

What strikes one as true in this sort of pursuit is man's insatiable need for control and tangibility, his invariable need to diminish what will always be the essential risk of life. What we see in the great Sir Alexander Fleming is only the scientific man who reached for a test tube one bright day and accidentally discovered penicillin. We don't see the long-suffering, careful investigator who had failed a thousand times before in his antibiotic research, and who, with a highly developed index of suspicion, finally struck on a moment of light and had the prescience to take the risk of failure once again and pursue a hunch. Life always embodies those risks, however, whereas science is but a method of altering moods and describing rhythms.

The great discovery about our human nature is that our similarities are much greater than our differences irrespective of which sex we are. The needs to eat and sleep, to be warm and sheltered, to work and to play, to love and have sex, to have friends of all ages, and a sense of the spiritual purpose of life are common to all of us and the overriding influence on our daily lives. When we explore our chemical natures, we find man and woman are fundamentally similar. Our clockwork cortisone is the same, and keeps us filled with energizers in both large and small predictable doses every day. Our sleep patterns are the same, and any stressful disruption in these basic protective mechanisms evokes the same disruptive response in men and women. The blood chemistry of men and women is predictable and interchangeable, as are, for the most part, their organ needs and responses and their physiological functioning.

What distinguishes woman from man is her reproductive cycle, which carries with it the burden of hormone-induced mood changes. It behooves man in relation to woman to understand that the first half of her cycle is under the mellifluous influence of estrogen, and she is apt to be then at her energetic and receptive best. It behooves woman to anticipate this feeling and act for him with it. Then it behooves both of them together to appreciate the upward thrust of ovulation, the initial urgency caused by progesterone, followed gradually by the depressive and inhibitory influence of that hormone. Then the fall-off during menses, which may be depressing in its premenstrual tension or may be a time of safe excitement and relief for the woman.

Man himself must be recognized for the moody creature he is, his moods reflecting a psychological need to allow expression of the anima part of himself. It is important for the female to love and encourage this part of him and tolerate his moods, for it is not so tangibly excusable in him to be moody as it is for her since her moods are organically induced. His moods are apt to be as cyclical but not as predictable, as hers and much more drawn out and irregular.

The trick of living male and female together is largely a matter of rhythmicity and identification of these inherent needs. This requires time, time that unfortunately fewer and fewer people have patience to invest. Because of the incongruencies that develop during our understanding of each other's rhythms there is the need for some concept of a spiritual order to hold us together while we struggle toward one another and fit together our apparent biological differences. Once these differences are known theoretically and experienced in actuality we gradually come together as a full physiological whole. While that slow process evolves and we are learning honesty of mind, body, and soul, the idea that holds us and sustains us has to be beyond ourselves and what we humans have uniquely come to call love. It is a journey, physiologically based, that goes on all our lives and gathers more and more and deeper meaning, and can only be achieved by pursuing it step by step to the end.

SEVEN

BREAKING OUT WITHOUT BREAKING UP

... unless Woman repudiates her womanliness, her duty to her husband, to her children, to society, to law, and to everyone but herself, she cannot emancipate herself.

—*G. B. Shaw*
"The Quintessence of Ibsen"

MANY YEARS AGO, so many in fact that I recall being astounded to have a woman offer to buy me a drink, I had one of the most remarkable conversations of my life with a magnificently accomplished eighty-year-old woman anthropologist in a San Francisco bar. While sipping Irish coffee she explained to me how the work of her life had revolved around interpreting aboriginal pictures in the *National Geographic* magazine, one of which we had open before us and kept carefully leafing through to document the progress of her thoughts. She set about explaining to me a difference she had observed early on between all tribal men and women which had puzzled and fascinated her for years. It was almost as if by now it had become her secret. As it turned out, as do most secrets once revealed, it was simply a transparent truth.

She first turned to pictures of the young women and, carefully describing features, demonstrated how all the young women of a tribe appeared naturally open and friendly, naturally warm and receptive. In their faces was a lovely curiosity that came across as a welcoming love and tenderness. They seemed content with themselves, with life and existence. She saw them most characteristically as embodying the natural state of mankind (her very word), as part and parcel of nature and what was left of our innocent and loving self from the Garden of Eden. The emphasis she placed was on the young women's willingness and openness, their idealistic friendly warmth and receptivity, expressed so well in their smiles and wide sparkling eyes.

Turning the page she quickly showed that at the same period of life young men were naturally suspicious and withdrawn. They appeared angry, hostile, their faces were contorted and warlike. They seemed to be uneasy warriors ready to strike out at anything at any time. Unlike young women who opened their bodies to you in a gracious and hopeful promise, the men hid and cowered to their advantage against or over you. And the men needed weapons to enhance their importance, whereas the women needed only themselves or perhaps an urn or some other household item intended to comfort. The men were painted to ferocity, the women to beauty.

But then this remarkable woman went on turning pages to point out that these attitudes apparently had a complete reversal in old age. She carefully called attention to pictures of old men, grandfathers, whose faces seemed lined with wisdom. There was a resigned warmth in their eyes, a feeling of kindness and understanding, tolerance for the outsider as if wishing to reach out and understand him, a true message of love and humanity. Often these men could be seen as a mediator of disputes among the lesser members of the tribe, and only rarely were their faces artificially embossed with dye or paint to the extent that the young men seemed to need or want it, though a single distinguishing mark was common as if some kind of chevron had been awarded them by others. The kindness they exuded was by now a natural and integral part of themselves; in a sense it was external to themselves and all they surveyed, since almost like artists they had become the vehicle of hope and understanding in the closing years of their lives.

The old women, on the other hand, she suddenly saw as hostile, devious, suspicious, withdrawn, perhaps even witchlike, with deep bitter furrows of worry and cruelty on their faces. As often as not they seemed to hiss at you from their hiding place behind trees or household utensils, anything to make you go away and not bother them or to convey the clear message that you were not welcome. And the women no longer did anything to enhance their image in the way of special dress or cosmetics; they seemed to want to be ragabones cutting off even any symbolic hope of affection, all in their own self-interest.

This progressive reversal, the anthropologist said, she had observed again and again in aboriginal societies where there was no special reason for female discontent, and had come to conclude it was a natural process, if left unattended. Men and women seemed to have equal shares of nature's good and evil, but distributed at diametrically different times of life. The young woman became the old man, the young man became the old woman. Was life then unfair, I asked her? No, she said vehemently. The solution was to civilize young men and old women. The trick was in the growth. Our natures are different, we necessarily come at life from different directions, but the endpoint *had* to be the same. We were proceeding to the same grave after all. I left the old woman still sipping Irish coffee far into the night, and walked and listened all night till dawn to the foghorns coming from all directions across the darkened bay. This woman had so beautifully completed within herself what she had clearly seen early on as her necessary personal fulfillment, and there was I with so much unlearning yet to do.

The curve of life that has been ascending for man and woman in relatively divergent paths until the midthirties now takes a turn toward congruency. For the man this is a leveling process and one of consolidation, but for the woman the turn is apt to be sharp, angular, and often a terribly traumatic time because she must face a departure from what heretofore has been her very strength and hold on life. Something happens to a woman at thirty-five. From girlhood she has been ahead of her male contemporaries in what had been given her in her self, her natural self. She has been born more perfect, differentiated earlier, achieved growth early, has been clearer in her expected role in life (whether or not she chooses to accept it). As a sixteen-year-old tennis player (for example, Tracy Austin) she has been strong enough to compete in the Nationals among the best women around. At nineteen a boy is seldom ready for such competition. He has had a tougher achievement row to hoe and is more used to failure. She has grown up learning and assimilating all the surrounding household accoutrements and amenities, and they have become a natural part of her woman's armamentarium against life. He has grown up realizing these things will one day have to be provided largely by him so that he may be comfortable, and so his emphasis turns not to the assimilation of such but to the provision process as he prepares himself to achieve. Her brains are easily equal to his, if not superior because he is less easily distracted, and in many respects up to now she has worked under less pressure because woman's history has not required as much from her. But in a sense, because of all this naturalness, her striving has been necessarily less than his, and so his life's apprenticeship has been largely served while hers in great part has just begun.

It is at this point that woman faces the central paradox and seemingly insoluble problem of being a woman. At age thirty-five so much of what has been her natural strength now comes to a close and more is demanded of her that must be derived from outside that strong central core of womanliness within her that has brought her so successfully this far. By now she knows her reproductive phase is drawing rapidly to a close with each passing month. She is able to look at her children or her past sexual accomplishments with a relative air of finality and say to herself, for better or for worse, this is what I have done and there is nothing more I can do about it. This comes to her as a tremendous advantage if she has felt constrained in motherhood because, unlike the male whose reproductive capacity continues relatively unabated for years ahead, she has been given an ultimatum by nature which conveniently forecloses any further possibilities. On the other hand, if she has been too dependent on her motherly role, she will now face the end of reproduction with dark clouds of depression and will cling too closely to her children and to what's left of her maternity. She may even go to great lengths to have one more child, often at the expense of her own physical and emotional well-being and against all advice, just to prolong her state of legitimate motherhood. Listen to Emma Bovary:

She wanted a son. He should be dark and strong, and she would call him Georges. The thought of having a male child afforded her a kind of anticipatory revenge for all her past helplessness. A man, at any rate, is free. He can explore the passions and the continents, can surmount obstacles, reach out to the most distant joys. Whereas a woman is constantly thwarted. At once inert and pliant, she has to contend with both physical weakness and legal subordination. Her will is like the veil on her bonnet, fastened by a single string and quivering at every breeze that blows. Always there is a desire that impels and a convention that restrains.

Emma, of course, had a baby girl.

Words like "emancipate" and "liberate" captivate the mind and feelings of women, especially at this time. Men take such words for granted, not only as integral to a self-evident truth as expressed in documents such as our American Constitution, but as an acquired and functional component of themselves as men. This is not naturally so with women, many of whom feel unfairly locked in to themselves and thereby inhibited from achieving all the apparently glorious things their male counterparts are doing daily. A woman at thirty-five, having expended all that youthful energy on her marriage and children, is frequently heard to announce that now at last "she's sprung," as if released from an imprisonment that was not simply of nature's making, but rather strictly circumstantial and one in a world that she could now completely control.

Emma Bovary, married to a dedicated and loving, albeit somewhat square, doctor husband now feels this way about her world:

There was a higher life 'twixt heaven and earth, amid the storm-clouds, touched with the sublime. The rest of the world came nowhere, had no proper status, no real existence. In fact, the nearer home things came, the more she shrank from all thought of them. The whole of her immediate environment—dull countryside, imbecile petty bourgeois, life in its ordinariness—seemed a freak, a particular piece of bad luck that had seized on her; while beyond, as far as eye could see, ranged the vast lands of passion and felicity. In her longing, she confounded gilded sensuality with heart's delight, elegance of manner with delicacy of feeling.

As often as not a rude awakening awaits such a woman. What happens is this: As woman becomes more detached from the firm female substratum that is her very being and strength, as she makes her first feeble forays into the competitive world, she becomes aware that the strength she could rely on in being a woman is no longer applicable and in fact the farther along this road she proceeds the less womanly (as she has come to understand and use womanliness) she seems to become. Thus her strong feeling function, her strong intuitive functions can no longer be used with abandon, but must be carefully particularized and specified by rigid rules and figuring. This goes against her nature and it goes against her successful life adjustment that has taken place during these past twenty some years since the turmoil of puberty.

This change, unlike so much else in woman's life, is disruptive and often is not gradual and demands from her what she sees as action, action she perceives as of a masculine sort. And so it is at this juncture that one often perceives women fumbling crudely and immaturely with their first attempts at animus expression and assertion, to put it in Jungian terms. Examples abound. One woman, the wife of an established lawyer, walks into a store and, seeing an attractive workman, goes up to him and propositions him. This is considered an act of courage on her part: it takes guts to go out into the world, see something you want and go after it. That's what men do all the time. Why can't I? No thought is given at the moment to the fact that, after thirty-five thousand dollars in psychiatric fees, which her husband will pay because he believes in his family and that hers was a momentary lapse of consciousness, she has irreparably destroyed her children, husband, and family life in one tawdry sexual affair. There is the woman who decides, against all evidence, that fluoride poisons the water and has nothing to do with preventing tooth decay. She attends city council meetings and disrupts the deliberate process because it is extraneous and irrelevant to her desired ends. She must no longer be a quiet, loving, composed, tenderhearted wife and mother, but now must grow up and be firm and assertive, and so to hell with tedious procedure. If you told her the history of fair government was largely the history of proper procedure, she would not only not understand you, but be suspicious you were bullshitting her because women had always been second-class citizens and this was just a way of putting her back in the place she had come from. There is the scrub nurse instructing the surgeon how to tie a bleeder she couldn't begin to control or ligate herself; the typist giving you the finger at a hopelessly crowded intersection; the woman screaming at the butcher who unfortunately only has on hand the meat he has to sell that particular day; the expert in nutrition who suddenly emerges by night at the PTA as an expert in leash laws for dogs and harangues everybody ad nauseam. There is England's leading actress receiving an Academy Award in Hollywood and using the occasion for a vile, inappropriate diatribe against democracy as she extolls the panacea of communism. There is one of America's leading actresses holding forth vociferously from a new podium each week claiming all manner of expertise on Indian rights, woman's rights, conservation rights, baby seals' rights, lettuce pickers, energy, you name it, and, while making scads of American money, decrying the very system that allows her free expression. When such a person travels to North Vietnam to reassure communists of her strong friendship it is "to help end the war." When such a person is turned down by the California State Legislature to be on the State Arts Commission because during the Vietnam War she "gave aid and comfort to the enemy," she quickly claims mistreatment because officially no war had been declared. She, of course, was only trying to help. In her mind there is no contradiction in this thinking. And when those very same communists starve four million Cambodians to death, she is able to separate that from her previous Vietnam friendship, and when Afghanistan is brutally overrun and peasants herded together and mercilessly machinegunned to death in Kabul Square, she remains completely quiet. What these emerging women must painfully realize is that equality means responsibility, and responsibility means self-effacing consistency and painfully habitual honesty in admitting errors, rather than manipulating circumstances for recognition.

All these and many more are daily strivings of the developing female animus to express itself. It comes out in little things about the household when a woman suddenly blurts out grandiloquent conclusions to matters that require distinctive thought and deliberation, thought drudgery in a manner the male of the species has become accustomed to, not so much by choice as by necessity, for since boyhood he has learned that in order to play a game you have to have rules, that you could fight over the game, but not over the rules, once you had agreed to them. For if you continued to fight over the rules you would not get to play the game, which was most important. And so rules become second nature, although it is an acquired taste that takes time. It will take at least that time for her as well. Meanwhile,

Emma was growing capricious, hard to please. She ordered dishes for herself and then left them untouched, drank nothing but fresh milk one day and dozens of cups of tea the next. Often she refused to go out, then felt stifled indoors and threw the window open and put on a thin frock. After administering a thorough scolding to the maid, she gave her a present or packed her off to go and see the neighbors—just as she sometimes gave away all the silver in her purse to a beggar, though she had little loving kindness and was not readily susceptible to other people's emotions.

What made life even more difficult for Emma was that her loving husband "Charles had apparently no notion of what she suffered. His unquestioning belief that he made her happy seemed to her a stupid insult; his complacency on the point, was ingratitude."

This phenomenon, at thirty-five, can be put into more comprehensive psychological terms that revert back to the previously discussed, relatively unconscious state of the female while young. Recall that this state in the female was sex-linked in the sense that the male's specificity of psychosexual urge, coupled with his innate muscle mass, set him off earlier in the more active direction of painful learning. The female on the other hand derived her strength from being more diffusely aware. This not only allowed her a certain incomparable fluid beauty, but was nature's protective mechanism to help her perform her biological need to reproduce and nurture her young. While doing this, however, she necessarily remained in a relative state of unconsciousness, that is, relative only in general terms to the circulating males of the species, not in absolute terms in any specific comparative case. Dionysus, the Greek God of wine, to whom many fructifying and orgiastic festivals of worship were directed, was said to be earthbound and was often depicted in a sleepy state of unconscious beauty. Opposed to him is Apollo, the god of sunlight, music, and poetry. The second god represents harmony, order, balanced character, the first represents strength and fertility. It is the leaving of the strength of that lovely Dionysian unconsciousness, now no longer so necessary, that displaces woman's equanimity and dislocates her confidence and causes her animus to complain—at first absurdly and violently—at this stage in life.

We know that Emma Bovary, to assert herself and overcome the supposed ennui of her life, takes a lover who deserts her. But she hasn't learned, her romantic longings persist, and she takes a second lover. "From that moment her existence became nothing but a tissue of lies . . . it became a need, a craving, an indulgence: To the point that if she said she had gone along the right side of a street yesterday, it was to be inferred that she had in fact taken the left."

The moment of epiphany comes when Emma, heartsore and penniless, is rejected in person and in purse by her second lover.

She stood in a daze, conscious of herself only through the throbbing of her arteries, which she fancied she could hear going forth like a deafening music and filling the countryside around. The ground seemed to give beneath her like water, the furrows looked like vast brown waves breaking into foam. All the thoughts and memories in her mind came rushing out together like a thousand fireworks going off at once. Madness was laying hold on her. Terrified, she managed to pull herself together, though in some bewilderment; for the thing that had brought her to this frightful condition—her need of money—she could not recall. Only in her love did she suffer; through the thought of that she felt her soul escape from her as a wounded man in his last agony feels life flow out through his bleeding gashes.

The remainder of the story is well known: how Emma brings about her own death by arsenic, while her devoted and uncomprehending husband stands loyally and tearfully by her side. "On Emma's satin dress, white as a moonbeam, the watering shimmered. She disappeared beneath it. It seemed to him as if she were escaping from herself and melting confusedly into everything about her, into the night, the silence, the passing wind . . ."

In the depths of the Civil War, with so much unspeakable tragedy all about him, Abraham Lincoln lost his beloved son Todd to disease. That death, said Lincoln, was the most painful experience of his life. The death of a child, as the death of anyone we love, is the death of part of ourselves, the loss of part of our soul. When John Donne admonishes us not to bother to find out whose funeral the bell is ringing for, he means that every man's death diminishes us and leaves a scar on our soul. But modern psychiatrists now tell us divorce may be the worst insult our souls can sustain, because unlike all the others it is a living death, a true death in life that goes on and on and on with all parties still surviving. After all, when there is true organic death, there is some sort of inaccessible finality. Unlike divorce, death is largely something we grow up anticipating ultimately.

Many brilliant modern women writers have described the animus "breakout" phenomenon. As often as not, this experience, which has involved a divorce and the destruction of the soul, has left lasting but not unhealable scars on all parties concerned. Emma Bovary's breakout and death is merely the nineteenth-century analogue of this trauma to the soul, how the animus can ultimately injure woman and man and family and friends if not properly understood and controlled. If woman, at this juncture in life, elects to employ the emerging animus to further the darkness of her life—woe betide!

One thirty-five-year-old woman author, after detailing this terrible traumatic time of life when she thought, that like Emma, she was going to commit suicide, finally saw the light and soberly concluded, "Well, I wasn't, I survived. I grew up a little, and all that seems a hundred years ago now." Rather than heaving a sigh of relief, we are tempted to say I told you so, it was nothing but the old animus coming through! And for you to be where you are, a wide swath had to be cut. Pity be to those in the wake of it, pity be to those in the throes, but there is nothing really new or revelatory in the process we have described here: it is but another brilliant and classic description of the rites of passage and birth pangs of the animus.

And what is the function of such disruptive change in woman right in the middle of her life? The answer is statistical: 8 percent of young brides regard themselves as boss in the family, 30 percent of married women in their forties say they are the boss. But 50 percent of wives in their fifties make this claim, and the percentage increases up to the end. As the more brittle powers of the male of the species wane, the more durable female assumes the ascendancy. It is nature's way. And it is for this reason that she must now tear herself away from the soothing waters of the unconscious and prepare to enter the harsh light of day. The sunlight at first is apt to be blinding, but soon she will be able to see her way and she will have it all.

To a man at thirty-five all this seems to be going on in the background. He is aware that his wife's astounding outbursts and simplistic analyses of many life situations frequently seem divorced from reality, but views this lovingly as the nature of the beast. He may have been called upon to bail her out of a few unbelievable situations that he couldn't imagine himself ever getting into, but he accepts these as expressions of the frustrations of her life and hopes that they will improve or go away. Often he is heard to intone at this age the old saw, "You can't live with 'em and you can't live without 'em." He comes to realize what Socrates meant when he said: "As to marriage or celibacy, let a man take which course he will, he will be sure to repent."

Like Emma's husband, Charles, little does a man know the inner turmoil within his wife as she struggles to assert herself as a mature adult woman at this time. Little does he appreciate the magnitude of the critical emotional transition that is now being required of her in order that her life may be fulfilled. When he takes it upon himself to solve her problems he seems to do nothing but prolong the absurdity of many of her efforts. Little does he realize that the simple ease with which he negotiates the insurance claim or the house loan represent to her horrendous problems in rudimentary learning, which she will never appreciate until she fumbles through them herself. Well into middle age, I complained to one of my old professors about the tedium of teaching young surgeons how to operate, and he said to me scoldingly, "You have forgotten how long it took *you* to learn."

Unlike the woman, the thirty-five-year-old man is like a three-year-old thoroughbred race horse. What was given to her at twenty-two for her job is now his at thirty-five for his. At no point in his life will his physical and mental abilities so combine to achieve maximum benefits as they do at this time. His muscle strength is still resilient, his eyesight keen, his sexual performance only slightly lessened by usage. His apprenticeship is past, or, stated another way, he has experienced enough failure and insult to have hardened to his chosen task and gone on with it. He has had his first taste of wisdom. Above all, he is still smitten with the desire for what one day he will come to recognize is only a young man's emotion—fame. Fame and recognition. This drives him upward and onward and consumes him and his masculine self. He is the boy wonder of the business world to whom all the most important tasks are delegated and the brevet colonel who jumps behind the enemy lines with the battle plans in his pocket. He considers that what he does is as much for those about him as for himself, and deludes himself that, as in some great convoy, others feelings correspond with his for the greater good of all. In this he is greatly mistaken, and in a few years is likely to get himself into trouble, as we shall soon see, for men and women are coming together, whether he knows it or not.

If for some tragic reason man and woman can't repair their differences at this crucial juncture and divorce ensues, man will be amazed at the desperate phone calls from her for help on the simplest matters, and woman will be astounded at how incapable she is of confronting life all alone. Man will be helpless in dealing with the simplest life-support systems from towels to toilet paper and woman astounded at what happens every day to the prime lending rate. So whether they like it or not, whether they want it or not, this man and this woman find themselves remaining in a relation to one another, and this always will be so as part of their very souls. Their lives were intended for, cry out to each other no matter what they do with them.

For woman to emerge into the full-blown light of day there are two facets of the mature nature of both sexes that are seldom, if ever, emphasized especially for her. I have reference to a self-identifying sense of comedy about herself and a sense of participating as a tragic figure in the drama of life. Both of these conceptual feelings are protective devices against the inevitable cruelties of this world, and they help us in the midst of the fray to remain above it and to endure. These two elements, comedy and tragedy, are strangely akin to each other in the sense in which I use them. Let me give an example.

One of the classic clown moments of all time was Emmett Kelly's Barnum and Bailey act in which he tried to sweep up the spotlight. The huge tent would be hushed in darkness and Kelly would appear suddenly in the center ring in a simple spotlight with a broom in his hand. He was always dressed in baggy black pants and a bum's cutaway coat and his face was made up to resemble the inscrutable mask of Greek tragedy. When Kelly begins to attempt to sweep up the spotlight all of us in the surrounding darkness laugh hilariously. Unsuccessful, he steps aside out of the light and approaches it from the dark, but the spot is always refocused on him. He looks around at us with his sad bewildered face and we begin to pity him. Before long we begin to tear and cry for him, he is so pathetic, frustrated, and confused. As the act continues, half the audience is in tears and half in uncontrolled laughter. By the time the clown calmly and resignedly shrugs his shoulders and the spotlight follows him out behind the curtain, none of us in the audience really knows whether to laugh or cry. We have seen a classic example of the blending of comedy and tragedy and the close kinship of one to the other.

One of the essential ingredients to health, I'm convinced, is laughter, although it is never included in the list of the basic human needs we all learned in school. Women, it has been said, next to orgasm love laughter, and one of the first things intuitively sought for in a man at that initial moment of meeting is a sense of laughter or good humor. For man, on the other hand, he seems to crave the company of his fellowmen from time to time to involve himself in a little billingsgate. This was true with Abraham Lincoln, as well as the late master parliamentarian, President Lyndon Johnson. Although pledged to humor, men and women are often at odds about jokes or even situations that entertain both of them. Young girls will giggle and twitter, while boys burst out in vulgar laughter, and some of this incongruency remains into our adulthood. One of the worst things then you can ever say about anybody is that he does not have a sense of humor. In fact, breathes there even the dullest clod who would admit to himself he was humorless. But the essence of humor is and seems always to have been the release of tension, usually suddenly and unexpectedly. For this reason it is imperative for woman to develop this element in herself, even as any soldier after combat will tell you that it was the laughs that kept him sane. Swearing and sergeants, my father claimed, won the First World War. But women have been derelict about self-directed humor. This has been reflected in our theater and in our literature. Günter Grass in *The Flounder* has this to say:

For literature is short on comic female protagonists. Don Quixote and Tristram Shandy, Falstaff and Oskar Matzerath—it's always a man who makes comic capital of our despair, while the ladies perish in unrelieved tragedy. Mary Stuart or Electra, Agnes Bernauer or Nora, all are in love with their tragedy. Or they pine and sigh over their sentimentalities. Or madness drives them to the moors. Or sin gnaws at them. Or a masculine power-hunger is their undoing—take Lady Macbeth. Utterly devoid of humor, they are handmaidens of suffering: saint, whore, witch, or all three at once. Or trouble turns them to stone, they are hardened and embittered, a wordless plaint. Sometimes their author allows them to go off their rockers like Ophelia and babble incoherent verses. Only the "grotesque old crone," far removed from all pleasures of the flesh, and the flighty chambermaid might be cited as examples of the female humor that is supposed to be "imperishable." But whether old and grotesque or young and flighty, only minor roles fall to woman's wit. And yet we need this cosmic female protagonist, we need her desperately! And the same goes for the movies. Why should it always be the men, the Charlie Chaplins or the Laurels and Hardys, who are privileged to supply the comic aspect of tragedy. I call upon you, dear ladies, to stage at long last the great feminine comedy. Let the woman comic triumph. Give the knight of the mournful countenance a woman's skirt and let her battle the windmills of male prejudice.

When we talk about humor and women we have to return for a moment to the fisherwoman and the porpoises in Mexico. Recall that she said if you insult the water you are also insulting the fish because to the porpoise the water and the fish are one and inseparable. So what we are dealing with here in humor may be something inherently different in the sexes, similar to that which we have already seen again and again. It is so poignantly exemplified in the matter of humor it is worth repeating. In order to understand and get along with woman, man must recognize that nature is part and parcel of herself and any insult to nature or nature's product tends to be a personal insult to her. A joke about the intimate functional organs of woman is not just an abstract element about the condition of mankind or womankind or their relationship one to another, it is a very personal affront to the woman hearing the joke, because she identifies herself closely with the natural feeling of her being that is questioned or is the butt of ridicule. This is not so with a man who tends to view a joke as a joke, no more and no less, with a detachment that allows his enjoyment however personal the joke may be. Furthermore, man has already had to differentiate himself from the female element in him that makes such assaults on a woman's being personal and he is now able to view them from a distance. If one would be a successful jokester with woman, he should use humor that is either directed toward his male self or has enough intrinsic detachment from her person not to threaten her nature. If you tell her, "All that clitoris not gold," you are taking a risk. Similarly, women do well to cultivate the essence of such humor because it will give them a sense of irony and distance and relief that has immense survival qualities for enduring in this world. Humor is God's manna to the overwrought.

The lacrymal glands, the tear glands, are located in the upper outer aspect of both eyes. They are no different in size or location or nerve supply in men and women. Why then is it that women cry more than men? In fact, contrary to much current observation, the emotions of crying may be just as frequent in men as in women. What is different is that men have a broader, anatomically more spacious, nasal cavity which can accommodate more of the tear duct flow as it egresses from the inner eye into the nose. In a woman, who has narrower nasal passages, this leads to an overflow and tears drop down her cheeks. Man, meanwhile, may only snuffle or blow his nose. But the upshot of this physiological difference is that man has a built-in disguise mechanism that can be misleading. Often he is crying and you don't see it. To say that men don't let go and cry like women may be a sociological canard. The fact is that neither sex has a monopoly on the tragic sense of life. Both sexes seem to sense this and feel equally that, in the words of the Irish poet W. B. Yeats, "There's a world of pity at the heart of love." As men and women grow older the melancholy inexorability of our lives becomes one of the profound forces that make men and women cling together in deeper appreciation and tolerance for our sexual infirmities. But if men and women are equally appreciative of this tragic sense, are they equally capable of being participants as tragic characters?

I have a friend who insists the one major difference between women and men, one almost never mentioned, is that women are not really capable of acting tragically. Tragedy always requires the garb of the male hero. Where, he says, in all history, is the female counterpart of Achilles sulking in his tent before the final battle of Troy? Where is the counterpart of blind Oedipus unwittingly doomed for mistakenly killing his father? Or of the pitiful Lear ranting and raving on the heath against remorseless old age? Are there women the likes of Willie Loman in Arthur Miller's *Death of a Salesman*, triumphant over death despite being a mere salesman? Is there the like of Ivan Ilyich, in Tolstoy's story about an ordinary government clerk who finally realizes he hasn't done anything in life, and in that very realization triumphs over death for all of us?

There are many rejoinders to my friend's argument, but I must say as he sputters off endless examples from literature and life, from sacrificial Christ to martyred Abraham Lincoln, I am at a considerable loss, or at least very hard pressed, to give many examples of women who fill the tragic mold. I must struggle. If tragedy is a "character weakness" (apparent to all but perhaps the possessor) that necessarily confronts circumstances that lead to inevitable doom, it's hard indeed to find many women who, for their own sake or for the sake of a cause, have died heroically and thereby become triumphant. I do not mean to say that they do not exist. There is Saint Joan burning at the stake, a tragic, triumphant idealistic hero of France if there ever was one. And there is lovely teenage Anne Frank writing in her diary as the Nazi henchmen screamed their sirens up and down the streets of Amsterdam looking for Jews to deport to their death. She could peep at the Christian church steeple from one small corner of a concealed window and praise the joy of love and living just two days before they carted her away. I think of the dignity of Florence Nightingale among the stinking war wounded of the Crimean War, killing herself with work, running the risk of contagious disease, as I have seen so many wonderful nurses do all my life.

There is heroism galore in all this, but the large, tragic characters of this world come more easily to mind as male. Even Hitler, the terrible son of a bitch we all wanted dead, nevertheless in the gotterdammerung of the bunker in Berlin at the end of the Second World War was a morbid, tragic creature. There was Nixon, the black wizard of Watergate who we all wanted out of the White House, nevertheless a tragic figure as he said his last farewells to his staff and resigned the presidency. There was Adlai Stevenson, defeated twice by Eisenhower, saying, "It hurts too much to smile and I'm too old to cry." The list is endless. But somehow Susan B. Anthony is not quite on it. She simply does not wear that garb in which, in the words of William Manchester, "the hero is a figure of massive integrity and powerful will, a paradox of outer poise and inner passion who recognizes the inevitability of evil, despair, suffering, and loss. Choosing a perilous course of action despite the counsel of the Greek chorus, he struggles nobly but vainly against fate, enduring cruelty and, ultimately, defeat, his downfall being revealed as the consequence of a fatal defect in his character which, deepened by tumultuous events, eventually shatters him."

I can't put my finger right on it, but my friend does have something here, even if it's only quantitative. I don't see Gloria Steinem or Bella Abzug capable of tragedy; in fact, they are closer to light comedy, and I'm hard put to find the quality I'm seeking among all the women I've ever known. They are often tragic insofar as they relate to their men. I think of the magnificent Lady Bird Johnson trying to keep the lid on her husband's coronaries so he wouldn't explode in office, as he did with reckless abandon several years later. I think of Eleanor Roosevelt throwing herself into the work of being a noble first lady while the president surreptitiously had his side affairs that pained her soul. I think of the nurse getting up each day at 4:30 A.M. to prop up an alcoholic husband to get him off to work by seven, only to have him return home again dead drunk by midnight and have to begin the process all over again. And there are all the nameless loving wives and lovers soothing their wounded husband's sores each night and miraculously holding homes together. Surely this is the stuff of heroism and tragedy. But not woman for herself. For that I must find exceptions, and I always return to Sylvia Plath.

Sylvia was a poet of the sixties and early seventies who hit the literary world, posthumously, like star rockets in flight. Unlike the Welsh wonder, Dylan Thomas, of a generation before who drank himself to death while yet proliferating poems, prose, and lectures, Sylvia's reputation, by her midthirties, rested on two thin books of poetry and a novel. Certainly by most literary standards she would have to be considered a lightweight. Her books are full of anger toward her parents ("Daddy, Daddy you bastard—I'm through!") and the self-indulgent paraphernalia of youth. Unlike Thomas she seldom described anything outside of herself, but like Thomas she carried on a romance with death and a suicidal impulse which was in her from an early age. Where Thomas undertook to destroy himself by drink, Sylvia, after several unsuccessful attempts, finally succeeded by putting her head in an oven. She left behind her two small children, a poet husband, and one of the coldest winters in the history of London, where she lived.

Almost immediately the sad story of Sylvia was revealed and fired the imagination of a generation of young women. Sylvia died for poetry! She described how she would put her little two- and three-year-old to bed and write through the night till dawn. If she collapsed from fatigue at midnight, she would set the alarm for three A.M. and begin again. Near the end, it was said, in her creative genius she often wrote two complete poems at a sitting. No doubt some of them are wonderful, beautiful, lasting poems. But she was not that good, especially with so meager a production, to warrant the outpouring of sentiment she received. What Sylvia managed to do, however, was to become one of those rare, female, tragic figures. She not only caught the spirit of her times when women were desperate to be liberated, but filled the female void of a sex generally lacking in examples of personal triumphant tragedy. For here were all the ingredients of true tragedy. Sylvia was a talented young woman, harnessed to a "creative" and "artistic" marriage. She had excelled in school, had left the comfort of a secure middle-class family to make it on her own. She was struggling with poems against all the odds of motherhood in a cold-water flat in London. As if circumstances weren't enough, there was that inborn suicidal weakness, a recurrent urge to do herself in. And in this she finally succeeded. Sylvia Plath was indeed a tragic female figure, caught in circumstances of mind and body that ran an inevitable course unto death. In dying, she indeed triumphed and lived on as a great heroic figure of her literary time—not so much in what she produced, but in satisfying a need as role model for many young struggling women. It is hard indeed to find many truly tragic figures among women, but Sylvia Plath is the exception that makes that rule. I am not saying that woman is incapable of tragedy; I am only saying in the broad sweep of history, with all the eons of opportunity, woman as such has not often chosen to be the personification of it. Through her man, yes, but for herself very seldom, and that in itself is its own form of tragedy.

So much is this sex differential the core—that men can stand outside themselves looking in and still be successful as men, that women can stand without themselves but run terrible risks as women—that comediennes and female tragediennes are very rare indeed compared to their male numbers, and that female accomplishment is considerably less over the years in artistic professions. In a larger sense the world of art is full of female artists of all sorts who have been unable to stand the separation of the artistic self from the personal feminine self that is required to effectively produce creatively. Often and finally women will opt for one or another life, always at a partial and painful loss to themselves and often with great destructive emotional turmoil. One thinks of Miss Emily Dickinson sitting all alone at her window in the yellow brick house in Amherst, afraid to go outside, and writing, even while the horrendous cataclysm of the Civil War raged on in the real world, "My life closed twice before its close / it still remains to see / if immortality unveil a third event to me." There was Emily, broken twice in love and thus choosing the seclusion of creativity, carefully and reticently folding her little paper poems and placing them in her drawer for posterity to discover love after her death. She could not both deal with the world and create. It was too hard, and hence she chose to pursue her art alone. There is unmarried Jane Austen circumscribing her life, and Mary Ann Evans Cross acting as George Eliot and Edith Wharton abandoning her sick husband for the creative solitude of France, and when Virginia Woolf's periodic schizoid nervous attacks were sensed by her long-suffering, sympathetic husband he carefully put her to bed for days at a time to preserve marital bliss in anticipatory prophylaxis against another prolonged depression. The late great poet Anne Sexton found the burden of her artistry too much in marriage, the terrible conflict of artistic creativity and womanly calling as lover, wife, mother, family member, all painfully so manifest in her writing, and finally she, too, took her own life.

Only rarely in the male artist is this guilt for neglecting family or being torn apart by virtue of conflict over it a consummate fact. The late Robert Frost was such an exception. He apparently lived his last years depressed and overcome with guilt at his neglect of his family in order to further his own art and well-being. More often the male artist, such as a Franz Kafka or a Thomas Mann, is apt to feel the conflict of simply being an outsider, on the one hand withdrawing from the world in order to create and on the other hand needing the world and the world's felt commitment as grist for his artistic mill. This ambivalence of not giving all his talents to doing something in a real way for humanity by actually experiencing it, rather than vicariously by creation, seems to be the more common conflict among the creative male. And so it is that great creative writers like Conrad or Tolstoy fathered many children while maintaining wholesome fatherhood and family life with no more than the usual problems. Women, on the other hand, have not been able to separate these impulses and frequently one has destroyed the other. It is hard to name a successful married-mother-happy-family-female poet, while the list of males is legion.

What all this means in practical terms has to do with what Lord Byron was referring to in *Don Juan* when he wrote "Man's love's to man a thing apart, 'tis woman's whole existence." The turmoil and conflict and guilt to women, and not only to those of artistic cast, are immense when they try to separate church and state, as it were, within their lives. The working woman spends her time torn between her desk and what she must plan for dinner and what the children will wear to the school play that night. When away from the home, she feels there is so much for her there to do that is of a natural and compelling order for her that she misses it as part of herself. It is not uncommon for me to do a surgical procedure where the nurse passing me instruments spends the entire three hours talking about housecleaning or what she plans to have for dinner.

At the same time if that woman is not out in the world, or hasn't one foot out there in the world, she feels she is missing something terribly important and the world is somehow passing her by. The confines of *kirche, küche und kinder* (church, kitchen and children) become so inundatingly monotonous and cloying she feels detached from all sense of reality and wants to scream "Let me out!" as, in fact, she often is heard to do. While there are no especially designated men's pages to newspapers, and men's magazines as such are rare, there are "women's pages" and "women's magazines" galore that daily describe this agonizing dilemma of women and hold forth with endless advice on how to combat the ennui at home and the anchorless feeling at work and how to resolve the difference. When the breakout time does clamor for recognition, when "Let me out!" echoes from wall to wall within the confines of a cloying, maddening home, woman should go bravely forth with two strong concepts as armamentarium against the strange new world: a concept of her own comic self and a concept of the tragic flaw in all of our lives. They are concepts she will find exemplified in every really good man and she will always find in them a momentary stay against the inevitable confusion she is about to confront head-on in the world.

It is well to pause and ask what all this means. A friend of mine once called to my attention that "even Jesus Christ had to withdraw to the hills to consider where he was from time to time." Because it would seem that we are doing nothing but raising and describing apparently insoluble problems. Though I have come to believe, however un-American it is to say so, that one of the greatest marks of maturity is the recognition in life that certain problems are just plain insoluble, I think we are dealing with something else in the male-female realm, which I feel is akin to ambivalence, rather than unsoluability. And he who best tolerates ambivalence has always best tolerated life. It is this element that maddens the precision-minded among us who seek to solve problems as if by formulae. When one in two California marriages goes down the drain, one in three end in divorce the country over, the popular wisdom is that there is something wrong with the system, the institution has got to go. The evidence today would seem to be all against marriage, all on the side of the Cassandras who say man and woman just can't make it together for a lifetime.

I come back often in my life to the words of General George C.

Marshall, one of my heroes from the Second World War. He was chief of staff of the army, and as such reluctantly relegated himself to a desk job in Washington while those men on the line fought for him the war he wanted to fight himself. But they indeed also serve who only stand and wait, and Marshall repeatedly admonished his subordinates, "Don't fight the problem, fight the solution to the problem." It is an admonition the surgeon has frequent recourse to. The element implicit in this sage advice, whether in love or war, is that a problem, if it indeed is one at all, must be isolated and its limits and characteristics clearly defined and established before it is solvable. To do this is to create the answer to most problems, because most problems necessarily hold the answer within them or they are not, in fact, problems at all. Listen to the patient, medical students are repeatedly told, listen carefully because she is telling you the diagnosis!

Years ago, after the indomitable New York Yankees lost some twenty straight ball games and wiped themselves out of the American League pennant after possessing a seemingly untouchable first-place lead, they asked the amazing Yogi Berra what the trouble was. He lowered his head, but then quickly replied, "It's simple. We made the wrong mistakes." Because, as any person truly alive knows, you don't feel badly very long about honest effort and honest failure. It's picking the wrong grief, which has you fighting the very existence of the problem, that really gets to you and upsets you. There is dignity and wisdom in an honest love affair that has turned bad. Better to have loved and lost than never to have loved at all, for this makes you sympathetically one with most of mankind. What isn't good is when that love was dishonest, insincere, demeaning, manipulative. Such people (and me too painfully one of them) find themselves consumed in the morass of fighting the problem of love, making the wrong mistakes, choosing the wrong weaponry, the wrong battlefield. How important it is for all of us to take that clear high road that Prince Hamlet describes so beautifully toward the end of Act IV, when he suddenly discovers, unfortunately much too late for his own salvation, that

164

Rightly to be great is not to stir without
great argument, but greatly to find quarrel
in a straw when honor's at the stake.

Such a clear high note was struck by General Douglas MacArthur at the end of the carnage of World War II. Standing on the deck of the U.S.S. *Missouri* at surrender ceremonies in Tokyo Bay, amid allies to a man who hated the assembled Japanese with a bitter venom, he nevertheless announced to the world in solemn, memorable tones, "Now we have had our last chance. If we do not now devise some greater and more equitable system, Armageddon will be at our door. The problem basically is theological and involves a spiritual recrudescence and improvement of human character that will synchronize with our almost matchless advances in science, art, literature and all material and cultural developments of the past two thousand years. *It must be of the spirit if we are to save the flesh . . .*"

These words are emblazoned above the magnificent Punch Bowl Cemetery in romantic Hawaii where lovers often go for the view. Ernest Hemingway, after that same war, making one of his rare public appearances, told a group of Idaho school children that the hell of life was that you could leave it at any time, but the idea was to go on and on and not quit until you had experienced fullness. The fullness he meant was based on certain classic, yes primal, impulses in men and women that allowed them to laugh and love together all along the way, and never could be destroyed by adversity. To understand our differences is to bring us together in pity and above all in love. For we need each other, and the race needs us.

EIGHT

ONLY CONNECT

Omnia Animalia Post Coitum Tristia Sunt

IT IS SAID that to have good sex is to die a little. It is perhaps preferable to say that good sex begins in delight, involves us and our body systems in every conceivable way, and ends in wisdom. Because we begin with the highest celebration, we are capable of seeing and wanting another human being and using language to explore his or her personality. We find this exploration sets off in us all kinds of hardly explainable feelings that our hypothalamus, in its primitively effective way, translates into body action. This involves our peripheral nervous system and our visceral nervous system and our endocrine system and our cardiorespiratory system. It involves our memories and our fantasies and the primal rhythm of our body and can leave us fulfilled as does no other part of nature. For years, biochemists and physiologists had pushed aside the sexual sphere of endeavor, saying it was so delightful there was no conceivable reason to investigate it—as if by knowing every line of a great poem you could somehow spoil the whole. But at last we have all come to realize it is indeed so delightful, so crucial, we simply cannot leave it alone. And when man and woman who truly love each other come together in sex there is no greater gift, no greater bliss on all the earth.

One of the most enduring phrases in the literature of this century is from E. M. Forster's novel *Howard's End.* "Only connect," wrote Forster, that's all we have to do among all of us and especially between the sexes. If we "only connect" everything will be all right. But if we are so divergent, man and woman, if the differences are so great and the true connections so difficult, how is it, then, we do happen to get together? What are the precise mechanisms of our connections, just how do we make this greatest of all leaps? We have already established the natural and inevitable attraction, emotional and physiological, of one of man's strongest basic biological drives, the sexual drive. It's now time for a piece of the action, as they say in dynamite Chicago.

The primary organs of sexual differentiation are genital. For each structure in the female there is a male analogue. The tip of the clitoris is called the glans and is analogous to the larger glans that covers the head of the male penis. The penile shaft and the clitoris and the prepuce (the foreskin) that covers each of them are similarly related. The erectile tissue of the clitoris and penis are the same, as are the large venous lakes (called *corpora cavernosa*) which fill with blood during erection. The labia minora is likened to the undersurface of the penis, which contains the urethra or urinary track of the male, the prostate gland equals the female urethral lubricating glands, the labia majora is the scrotum. One can similarly find analogous structures for hymen, upper vaginal vault, and lower vestibule in our primary genitalia.

At first glance it might seem that overt genital display would be the easiest and most direct approach to successful sexual communication. Until the advent of widespread pornography, the female genitalia was seldom exposed for purposes of sexual arousal. Even belly dancers or burlesque queens, who in low comedy might worshipfully don a male prosthesis, would rarely "take it all off" themselves. Yet, male phallic images and size enhancers have been noted since the dawn of civilization. The Egyptians used penis sheaths, Renaissance men used codpieces, and ancient Greeks carried mock phalluses in the festival procession to Bacchus. Among modern Africans the rhinoceros horn is still a symbol of male virility. With such persistent symbolic use it is surprising that male genital display has not been more often used for attraction, even in ancient civilizations, although it does occur in several species of primates. In human beings, however, it is invariably our secondary sexual characteristics, not our primary genitals, that are used to communicate sexual interest.

All communication has four distinct components: A situation or context, a sender or transmitter, a receiver or interpreter, and above all a message. This was true when Marconi tapped out his first telegraph message, and it is equally true with the sexual telepathy going on right now in Chicago at a swinging singles bar. But in the matter of sexual communication, we have first to acknowledge that all human communication may be idiosyncratic, may stem from individual creativity, and may not lend itself to any specificity. We must recognize that we are both creatures of instinct and creatures of culture and the two not only overlap but are in constant flux, just as women's skirts go up or down with the fashion of the season. We do, however, have certain built-in biological features, and certain acquired or situational features by which we communicate sex. Of these two the built-in features tend to remain steady and make for predictable distinctions, whereas the situational signals, by contrast, are more or less evanescent and fade rapidly.

It is not surprising that our permanent sexual messages to the opposite sex are related to our evolutionary past because of the secondary sexual characteristics we have acquired biologically over the millennia. Two main primitive features are still with us: first, men are larger than women, although the difference in body size seems to have progressively reduced in recent times; second, the female pelvis is broad, in response to the need to bear children. This keeps woman at a lower center of gravity and gives her a wobbling hip motion while walking that is characteristically sexual. When hip language is exaggerated, it may be used either to attract the male or to indicate the female is in a snit and wants to repel him. Rump presentation in primates may be an insult or an invitation. It is often used to indicate submission to a keeper or one higher up in the tribal pecking order, or it may indicate female submission prior to being mounted by a male. In human beings the buttocks play no such part in acts of submission. We bow or curtsey to the Queen of England, paying our obeisance with buttocks as far away as possible. In a dance such as the bump, partners collide buttocks in delight, whereas in vaudeville bumps and grinds, accompanied by rim shots on the snare drum, are equally a mark of female distinction and disdain for the all-male audience. In the French cancan the ladies lift their lacy skirts and thrust out their rumps insultingly. When I was a boy a famous jazz song went "Shove out Your Can, Here Comes the Garbage Man." Nevertheless, the great Dutch masters painting nudes accentuated the large curvaceous posteriors of their ladies as the height of sexuality, and we still see them peeking over one shoulder coyly and invitingly.

When man became an upright bipedal animal, prominent buttocks were further accentuated by the development of the gluteus maximus, or rump muscle, that was necessary for locomotion in that position. It is true that some Old World monkeys have calluses of enlargement over their hip areas, but no primates, who spend much of their time on all fours, have the true posterior muscular contour, the fat padding over muscle, that characterizes bipedal man. Female chimps and baboons undergo reddish discoloration and swelling when in heat, indicating buttocks' signaling of availability, but no such specificity exists in human females, and to liken this, as some have, to the erogenous significance of the human female rear is too far out for even the most imaginative evolutionist.

But bipedalism did have a certain influence on sexual signaling and activity. The female breast now was viewed head-on and became visible, and the human navel, far more conspicuous than its counterpart in most mammals, became a focus of sexuality. People began to face each other and had to confront facial looks and characteristics, instead of spending much of their time staring at the ground. Eventually this led to ventral intercourse. Although occasionally ventral copulation has been observed in the pygmy chimpanzee and the gorilla, this position is rare in primates other than man. Such a position accentuated the expressive face, the distension of the breasts, and the desirable erogenous feature of pubic and axillary hair, so rare in other primates. When the Christian missionaries first settled the islands of the South Pacific they found the backward natives still copulating piggyback, the male generally mounting the female as most animal primates do. Regarding this as disrespectful to the female, the missionaries taught the natives to have intercourse head-on in the ventral position. Henceforth, the ventral approach was called "the missionary position" and sex was enjoyed in the full abundance of viewing the sexual characteristics of the partner, as well as with the blessings of the church.

Two other anthropological legacies bear mention: The taboo on incest, and the accent on youth. Much old psychiatric literature claimed a unique feature of human sexuality was its imposition of cultural barriers against incest. This view was supported by anthropologists and sociologists and was acclaimed as a taboo that had enabled man successfully to shape human society. It also had gone a long way to channel and restrict sexual signaling within societies and, it was thought, ennobled man. Because of this it was shocking to have revealed recently by Japanese anthropologists that mother-son copulation was entirely absent in primates that had been carefully studied in the wild for over ten years. The reason seems to be that in all primates the close bonds created with offspring establish emotional barriers within a family that depotentiate the male desire. The inhibition seems to be directed exclusively at the male who is rendered incapable of the kind of dominance necessary to copulate successfully. He is rendered impotent.

Avoidance of mother and son copulation in primates is an example of negative sexual signaling to be sure, but one of extreme importance in human sexual relations. Whereas the end result seems to be the same as far as our choice of sexual partners in society outside our own family is concerned, it is important to realize that this choice is based in our biological heritage, not on man's higher nature. Incest is a biological taboo in lower primates as well as in ourselves.

Evidence for the accent on youth in sex stems primarily from studies in tooth reduction size in the earliest men and women. Progressively smaller-sized teeth, especially in the female, indicated a progressive juvenility. On occasion this proceeded almost to infantilism and is thought possibly to be related to the submissiveness that children show to both parents among primates. In this way infants elicit protection and love from their parents, as possibly did the young female from the protective male. Youth has continued to be the major realm of primary sexual communication for a variety of reasons, the most important being the energy required to reproduce and maintain the race, to sire and rear offspring. Labor is for youth.

The final built-in biological features that deserve special mention are the male voice and the female breasts. In the male, one of the main differentiating effects of the hormone testosterone is to enlarge the larynx, or voice box, and give man a greater range of vocal expression than the female. It allows him to whistle more easily at passersby, as well as strike deep resonant bass notes inaccessible to the female. It allows him a certain advantage in the use of the voice to charm and caress the listener or to mesmerize an audience. Indeed, one of the historical differences between men and women is the amazing paucity of women who have been successful, moving speakers. Acting and drama aside, the ability to move an audience with words, as in preaching or political oration may demand the full range of the male voice. Of course, it is equally true that the smaller female larynx has its own characteristic timbre and soothing quality that perhaps more intimately expresses love, as in a lullaby for a child or the reading of a nursery rhyme.

Studies show that women talk more than men, but men interrupt more often than women. Some have called this "conversational politics." The fact that men interrupt and thereby preempt the conversation when talking to women has been construed by some women as assertion of male power. On the other hand, women tend to use more adjectives in conversing and therefore draw out conversations with much circumlocution, which men often feel needs specifying. A woman uses three words to every one used by a male on the same assigned conversational subject. Hence, a male may feel the conversation is being monopolized as an assertion of female power, and that interruptions are necessary. My garrulous mother, for example, insisted she expected to be interrupted, otherwise she wouldn't know when she was finished. "How will I know what I think till I hear what I say?" was a watchword of her generation.

Woman's speech is characteristically different from men's, is more diffuse and expresses more of the feeling function. Modifiers such as "kind of," "I suppose," "really great," "practically endless" are common fare. Empty or mild adjectives, such as "lovely," "pretty," "divine," "scrumptious," are frequent. The intensive use of "so," as in "so awful crowded" or "so really cloudy," is common. Women will choose obscure, almost cute adjectives such as "puce" to describe

173

something, instead of coming down hard on a word everybody would clearly know. A questioning tone or phrase frequently occurs at the end of a sentence, giving a tentative coloration to what has preceded, such as in "don't you know?" or "wouldn't you agree?" And many women make a concerted effort at correctness in grammar that disallows the more pungent expressiveness of colloquialism. Then, too, baby talk or pseudo words are frequent. A party may be said to be "marvy" when really it was marvelous. At the opposite extreme life's unpleasantnesses are often euphemized or emotionally depotentiated by such talk. A woman will say she is in "a snit" when she is really pissed off. The baby will have "icky pants" instead of loose stool. The kitchen sink will be "grungy" and not greasy and smelly, and she is apt to "fuff" instead of fart—as men do.

The effect of this kind of talk is to coat the affairs of the moment with a kind of patina that often makes the substantive issue hard to get at. This has led psychologists to describe a definite male and female speech pattern that is often in conflict. Although the issue at hand may be the same, the verbal approach, the style, may completely confuse the opposite sex. To a woman, man's approach is often cold, calculating, and lacking in the necessary ingredient of feeling and care. To a man, woman's approach is indirect, obscure, and uninformative about the issue at hand. This leads men to converse differently with women from the way they do with their fellowmen. Conversations between men tend to follow rules that include turn-taking, respectful questions and answers, and a special concern with politeness, almost as if the participants were working in a vise. In male-female conversations, studies show a helter-skelter diffusion of such rules, with frequent interruptions on both sexes' part. Again, men try to direct the conversation by hopelessly specifying it, as far as women are concerned, and women try to usurp it by filibustering, as far as men are concerned.

The tentative language so often used by women has, in the past, in some lawyers' minds, rendered them poor factual witnesses before a jury. But those same witnesses have been used to great advantage when emotional impact is needed. Until recently the "authoritative male" voice was thought to be needed to bring us the daily news. We now know that women read the news as well as men, but interestingly enough, most of them have adopted the male approach in doing so. The same is true of women who have entered speaking professions, such as politics, the law, or the clergy. They have generally attempted to discard "women's language" for more masculine talk. Perhaps Margaret Thatcher, Britain's new prime minister, said it best when she declared about her profession, "Men talk, but women get the work done."

If it is true that women "work harder" to keep a conversation going, and men "succeed more" with the topics introduced, there is one work area in which women excel that delights beyond description: The area of inventing new words with specific meanings that are usually highly expressive and personal to each household. For example, the tiny lint balls you find in the recesses of little boys' pockets my wife calls "nerbies." When we are lying in bed together and she is stroking my aging skin, she frequently comes across skin tags, zits, or excrescences, or pimples or keratoses, and proceeds to lovingly debride them with her manicured fingernails. This she calls "brickling," from the verb to brickle, as in "you need to be brickled." Similarly "wabble" means just visiting and messing around in loving care. It could mean girl-talk or excessive demands by the cat for stroking. When I return home and ask her how the baby has been and she says "wabble" I know the demands on her loving care have been great. These delightful little expressions, incomparable in their usefulness, are a part of every daily office and every evening household, and usually are the inventions of thoughtful women. When my wife is suffused with cuddly loving warmth for a puppy dog or the baby or me, she says she has "sugars"—something every woman knows and will easily recognize.

Thoughtful men, on the other hand, often make the terrible mistake of giving formal names that dignify the most odious pursuits. Garbage men are now called scavengers and street cleaners custodians. Nazi Germany euphemized the Holocaust by calling it "the Final Solution," and every echelon of personnel from top to bottom in that terrible business was dignified by some gradiloquent title that made each one feel important despite the odious facts of what they were engaged in. Such is the nature of man that his ego can be so flattered by the use of titular words. Women have not been historically prone to such perfidy. A Miss Malaprop may call herself Ms. so no one can tell whether or not she's married, but she is not apt to invent words à la Joseph Goebbels to dignify (or obscure) the unspeakable death of five million Jews. That is corporate man at his worst. It is a sad commentary on women, however, that the Goebbelses of this world have always easily found women to do their typing and women to mother their children. For every Clyde there's a Bonnie.

Breasts seem to have been the focus of male attention in inverse ratio to their exposure. Thus, in aboriginal cultures, where naked breast display is common, little erogenous attention is directed toward them. But in civilized cultures where the breasts are hidden beneath clothing all manner of signals are given off and received. There are "breast men" and "leg men" according to preference, and women have gone to agonizing lengths to augment or flatten the breast structure in accordance with the whim of the times. In the twenties the vogue was for flat breasts, harnessed down if necessary. Corsets, bodices, breast bands, or brassieres have all had their way to titillate the male. In the sixties, women dared to become braless, to the delight of male onlookers, and in the seventies, huge injections by cosmetic surgeons of silicone substance could provide any contour to suit any fancy. Women signal with their breasts by posing or adopting a sexy decolletage in dress or gauzy see-through. Similarly the covered or smothered-by-clothing breast signals that a woman is probably not interested at the moment. In using the breast to communicate sexual interest, the female is taking advantage of the inherent child in the male who wants to suck on mother. Large breasts attract males because they remind him of mama (again from mammary) and the infantile pleasure of the suckling, nurturant mother. Small breasts attract many males because they are associated with youthfulness, perhaps innocence or young love. There is room

176

enough for all, for all sizes and shapes. No one is without hope. The smallest breasts may be those that become the most immense during lactation, and all breasts, male and female alike, have a sensitive reflex arc involving the pleasure center of the hypothalamus, which provides sexual enjoyment. Men have been known to come to orgasm merely by looking at a woman's breast (on screen or off) and women have been known to achieve orgasm by simple nipple manipulation (on screen or off). No wonder breasts are a fetish of our culture and one of the prime communicators of sexual interest. No wonder touching a breast is "getting to first base." No wonder all manner of succulent fruit has been used in referring to the breast; pears, plums, lemons, apples, peaches, persimmons, watermelons. Women's breasts have been called knockers and knobs and boobs and paps and dugs. When I was young they were affectionately referred to as "headlights." They are indeed often the guiding light to sex.

Odors and body heat occupy an interphase between purely built-in body language and the voluntary acquired characteristics of sexual communication. To be "hot" is to be sexually aroused. Awareness of body warmth enters into all kinds of human relations from shaking hands to snuggling up in a sleeping bag. The warmth of fresh new clothes just removed from the dryer has a sensuous feel against the skin. Women wear "hot pants" and can be "as cold as a witch's teat in January." When a dude is "cool" he is sexually under control, and when "hot to trot" is ready, willing and able. Most mammals have an acute ability to detect thermal changes, and because in many primates there are large areas, especially about the genitals, of exposed hairless skin, their thermal acuity is heightened in those regions. Some remnant of this is likely present in humans as they gravitate toward each other in meetings, or crowd next to each other in the "body shop" bars on Friday night after work. Some people seem to exude more body warmth than others, probably through heightened metabolism. Latins lose more body heat than Anglo-Saxons as the result of climatic adjustment over the years to warmer weather. Indeed, body heat was so indelicate to Victorian England that men who got up to give a lady a seat were encouraged to delay seating her for a time until the cushion could dissipate his heat.

Unlike our animal forebears the sense of smell is no longer necessary for protection and survival and accordingly has diminished its acuity in human beings. Yet each of us has a latent sense of smell that can be educated to great refinement, as in those who judge the elegance of a wine by sniffing the bouquet or those who savor tea or the quality of flowers merely by the scent. Each of us has a characteristic odor which we exude from glands at various erotic parts of the body where their concentration is numerically greatest. Kissing is largely a matter of savoring the taste and odors of cirumoral glands that we all possess in varying amounts (giving different odiferous tastes). The same is true of our axilla and genitalia which give forth characteristic odors attractive to the opposite sex. A healthy man likes the natural odors of women and a healthy woman loves the natural odors of men. Nevertheless, it is fascinating how the commercial concoctions to hide our body odors proliferate, and how very few of them attempt to simulate the natural alkaline smell of woman and the muskiness of man. Flowery and fruity flavors are frequent carriers of sexual impulses to the nose, and are frequently used topically or to "freshen" or "sweeten" the breath in the form of lozenges. Oils, lotions, soaps, powders, perfumes, sprays, ointments are the stock-in-trade of advertisements to improve your sexual image and your sex life. "Promise her anything, but give her . . ." that will make her smell like a delectable princess. All of this proves our immense susceptibility to sensuous olfactory stimuli and our essential lack of education and experience with this least used sense. I know men who swear they have been "fooled by her perfume" and women who will not believe so-and-so is a rogue "because he always smells so good." There is some evidence that today we are having a resurgence of once more enjoying natural things like the smell of the sea, a newly bound book, a clear morning after rain, and a child quietly asleep in his room. Lovers who come together and stay together always love each other's smell. In a sense it is the most basic and enduring of all our sensual senses, and one who loves strong odors is apt to be somebody who loves sex.

The biological and chemical aspects of situational sexual communication have endless fascination for us all. It would be interesting if we could delineate the chemistry of sex, say, as we first engage in an attractive flirtation at a bar after work or on the way home in a bus. But with the strong overlay of the higher brain centers and all the past personalized associations each of us has of breasts, body heat, odors, and human voice, the matter of sexual excitement takes on a highly individualized and idiosyncratic form that belies generalizations for any situational sex. We know that each of us comes to a social or sexual encounter with a certain preset working stage of cyclical hormonal availability.

As we have seen, this involves androgens in both the male and female, whereas in the female this involves her titre of estrogen and progesterone. It's important to realize that these hormones are cyclically foreordained and are not especially altered during a sexual encounter. Thus, somebody who turns you on is not at that moment altering or even working on your major sex hormone flow. The juices that flow are not sex hormones. The feeling we sense comes from other, more immediately acting hormones and physiological response systems. We know, for example, that in lower animals there are odiferous pheromones that attract the opposite sex, but no such data has been accumulated on human beings. So it is that we men cover ourselves with after-shave musk from the ox, a known pheromone in the rutting season of that lusty animal. Women use perfume to the same end. In the matter of body heat, we all have vibes that sense an optimal environment for erotic activity—the Scandinavian sauna is too hot for sex, the Japanese jacuzzi is even contraceptive because the testicles work best when they hang out in a cool place. The birthrate is highest in temperate climates where body heat is not overwhelmed by the extreme heat or cold elements of nature. Similarly, the image of the breast is a learned one as far as its erogenous evocation is concerned, and the human voice also elicits its psychomotor influence on the partner through first being represented in the higher brain. What I'm getting at is all these focuses of erogenous attention come through to the partner via nervous impulses that are immediately and uniquely transmitted and processed through our higher cerebral circuits in association with previously stored experiences. Thus, the breast comes through as a certain sight, a touch, a taste. Heat comes through via our spinothalamic tracts, which convey pain and temperature together to our higher centers. The voice is integrated via our auditory nerves to the speech centers of the higher brain where dwell the rhythmic circuits of language that go back to our earliest childhood learning experiences with primal sounds of love and anger, and are integrated there in our own peculiar, individual way.

Each of these sexually stimulatory factors takes on its own integral responsiveness in any one case and provides the endless fascination of sex. What the higher brain then does and can do with the hypothalamus we have already observed in scientific detail. It can, of course, do absolutely nothing. But by nerve control it can cause the heart to beat faster, and can bring on faster respiration by sending impulses to the primitive respiratory center in the brain stem thus mediating the contractions of our diaphragm. It can cause gastric churning, and activate our sympathetic nerves to cause the hair on our arms to stand up in excitement and our face to blush attractively. Our hypothalamus can activate our pituitary and thus get our adrenals churning out mellifluous cortisone and action-ready adrenalin, which makes the heart race, which, in turn, fills out blood vessels and suffuses our whole body with ready warmth and activity. All of these and much more, which we call a "turn on," derive from myriad suggestive external stimuli that evoke primal sexual associations.

Erection of the clitoris and the male penis follow. It should be borne clearly in mind that this is a voluntary act only insofar as the person who is sexually inclined has by the thought process of cerebration allowed exposure to the various auditory, olfactory, gustatory, tactile, visual, or imaginative stimuli available. For erection is fundamentally a physiological reflex response to a variety of neural stimuli. The erotic stimuli received in our higher brain are then transmitted via our primitive connecting system to and through the hypothalamus where they are gathered, integrated, transformed, and passed on as impulses to the spinal cord. In our lower spinal cord, as if it were its own autonomous primal sexual brain center, reside certain erection centers. If all goes well with this spinal receptor, automatic impulses go forth via our lower or pelvic nerves. Further tactile impulses of the penis or clitoris create neural impulses that go directly to the spinal erection center, which then directs reflex return action of the proper nerve fibers to the excited member. In this way, once cerebration has activated the process via the hypothalamus to the erection center, that same center in our spine sets up a reflex arc, and ignoring the ordinary impulses from the brain, sexual excitement proceeds on its own. What the parasympathetic autonomic impulses emanating from the spine do is to cause an opening of the valvelike structures in the erectile tissue of the member, thereby leading to and sustaining man's and woman's erection for sex. But that gets ahead of our story.

There remains to mention two negative aspects about erection that are painfully known to most of us. First, voluntary squeezing and control of the penile and clitoral musculature may increase rigidity, but this is a momentary phenomenon only. The mechanism of action is temporarily to obstruct the outflow of blood by containing it in the member. But it won't work long. Secondly, although the erection center in the spine is "its own man" it can be overcome by strong cerebral impulses from above. Thus fear and guilt and hostility activate strong neuroinhibitory impulses and dramatically suppress the successful autonomy of the spinal erection center. The neuroanatomy and physiology of these inhibitory pathways are not known. Theoretically, if they were, we could take an appropriate pill, disinhibit those pathways, and maintain a perpetual hard-on, although judging from a male disease process (Peyrone's disease) where that is the case, it would be a miserable, even painful, state of existence. Part of the joy of sex is its intermittency when our spinal center takes over for a time on its own and gives us surcease from the overworked brain.

We cannot leave built-in sexual communication without touching on the phenomenon of "sex appeal," so important to each new generation as to be almost a human need. One must wax poetic in alluding to this nebulous, yet very real, commodity which fills the masturbatory fantasies of each youthful male and female alike. In the twenties Clara Bow, the "It" girl was the sex symbol, Carole Lombard was the femme fatale of the thirties, and sparkling pin-up Betty Grable of the forties, sexpot Marilyn Monroe of the fifties, svelte Raquel Welch of the sixties, and hirsute Farrah Fawcett of the current decade. Slick-haired Valentino, he-man Clark Gable, tough-guy Bogart, lonely Montgomery Clift, smooth Paul Newman, handsome and virile Robert Redford were male sex symbol counterparts. All these people possess a certain characteristic message for the opposite sex. They carry erotic meanings that can be easily recognized from a distance and used by Hollywood and the media to convey to a great many receivers the sexual impulses of the time. For the most part such people are not aware of their unique possession until informed of it from without. And for the most part, they will strut and fret their brief moment on the stage and be gone, to be seen no more. Their talent, as the writer Hemingway once said of his contemporary, F. Scott Fitzgerald, settles on them as naturally as the dust on a butterfly's wing. Sex appeal is an intrinsic gift that catches the biological and cultural fancy of the moment, exuding a positive message of desire. It is recognized by common consent by those who encounter it, and it is highly marketable. William Faulkner's Eula was born such a person. The men in her small Mississippi town could never remember a time when she had been a child. Watching Eula walk down the street it was as if she had been born a whole juicy woman fit for sex from the very outset: "Her entire appearance suggested some symbology out of the old Dionysic times—honey in sunlight and bursting grapes, the writhen bleeding of the crushed fecundated vine beneath the hard rapacious trampling goat-hoof. She seemed to be not a living integer of her contemporary scene, but rather to exist in a teeming vacuum in which her days followed one another as though behind sound-proof glass, where she seemed to listen in sullen bemusement, with a weary wisdom of all mammalian maturity, to the enlarging of her own organs." If one were to question teenage Eula she would certainly have had no idea what they were all talking about, so unlike that did she really feel. and when women excitedly tore the clothes off Elvis Presley he must have thought them absurd, so little did he feel that way about himself. Most sex appeal is nothing if it is not a dressed-up gift of the gods for a moment in time. One is tempted every time he sees a *Playboy* cover girl in gynecological relief to quote the laconic quatrain from Auden's magnificent eulogy "In Memory of W. B. Yeats."

> *Time that is intolerant*
> *Of the brave and innocent,*
> *And indifferent in a week*
> *To a beautiful physique.*

For sex appeal has little if anything to do with sexuality, but rather more with haute couture or possibly even the culture that one comes from.

When Nikita Khrushchev, the first Russian Communist leader to visit the United States, saw our women he declared they were not short and fat enough to be attractive, as Russian women were. That was twenty-five years ago, and now my friends at the Russian Consulate in San Francisco aspire to the pinched blue jean image of the Western World for male and female alike. The basis of sex appeal is an intrinsically attractive person whose image can be so fashioned to catch the topical sexual spirit of the times. Zelda and Scott Fitzgerald did this for the twenties, sexually appealing people, an appealing couple, but to judge from all we know of them their sexuality was not exceptionally successful. What a shock for women to discover, years later after they had gone, that the manly idols of their youth such as Tyrone Power and Montgomery Clift really preferred boys.

The anima and the animus in us can be manipulated, if we are not careful, for somebody's commercial gain. The real appeal of sex rests on sturdier ground.

When sexual communication becomes situational it becomes flirtatious and tentative and lends itself to being surveyed more or less systematically. The dimensions of sexual communication in this secondary category include eyes, mouth, ears and nose, hands and face, posture and gesture.

The human eye is unique in respect to the amount of white it displays. Our pupils are relatively small compared to those of other mammals and primates and our white sclera relatively large, giving us more eye contrast, and making our eye movements more discernible and significant. In sleep, our eyes roll up, exposing more white. When we are excited our eyes widen, dilating the pupil to take everything in. Looking toward another as well as looking away conveys desire for attention from the opposite sex. Flirtatious eye movements such as winking or batting eyelashes play a salient part in human sexual communication, as does avoidance of gaze or glance in all higher primate communication. A wide-eyed female look may indicate energy or eagerness or "wide-eyed innocence." A sleepy, sultry male stare leads some women to feel they are being undressed or looked through. In Orientals the facial muscles are relatively immobile, giving a focus upon eyes whose eyelashes tend to be hidden by a thin fold of skin along the lids. Caucasians, whose eyes are of more variegated colors, more mobile, more labile, find the steady oriental Eastern eyes mysterious and fascinating. And, vice versa, the Asian often loves the animation of Caucasian eyes.

When we look at another human being our first contact is usually with the eyes. Further assessment, as in the case of sexual assessment includes exploration, again with the eyes, of secondary sexual characteristics, such as dress, adornment, endowment, demeanor, and availability, making initial eye contact that all-important open sesame. Eyeglasses, for example, have an attractive ornamental as well as introductory function. The enlarged rims of the sixties went along with "awakening woman," and the green-colored contact lenses with a fetching cat-eye glare. And though it was felt for a long time that women were only the object of visual stimuli, we now know they are very responsive in a psychosexual way to most visual stimuli. This is clear from such books as *Fear of Flying* by Erica Jong and female enjoyment of pornographic movies or magazines such as *Playgirl* where sexy men are paraded for their visual impact.

Modern cosmetics greatly emphasize the eyes, as if to acknowledge the ancient wisdom that gaze is the most important aspect of sexual body language. Scientific cosmetology reveals that there are "eye spots" or "eye ring" patterns, and demonstrates that human responsiveness and excitability is much greater to horizontally placed circles (eye patterns) than to any other patterns. Vertical traffic lights and diagonals do not arouse the same response in animals as horizontally placed lights. When horizontally placed "eyes" are ringed by concentric outer rings, response is enhanced. The women of ancient Egypt, Greece, and Rome all enhanced their eyes by circumferential painting. In the Middle Ages, women enlarged the pupils of their eyes with drops of the drug belladonna, which, in Italian, means "beautiful woman." Other investigators have proven that pupils dilate in response to erotic stimuli. Oriental gem merchants gauge customers' response to jade by observing eye dilation. Men's eyes apparently dilate when they are looking at attractive women, but not when looking at pictures of men or babies, and women's eyes measurably dilate when looking at pictures of attractive men *and* babies (!), but not women. Such a response can be exaggerated in both men and women when pupils in the pictures are retouched for eye emphasis.

Normally, two strangers will avoid or cut short any accidental eye contact. Ordinary eye contact in conversation lasts but one or two seconds. When this gaze is intensified or prolonged it shows inordinate interest, frequently of a sexual nature. So it is a glance held just so long, the "come hither" look in the bar, that look in a man's eyes passing in the street, a woman briefly seen at the airport or in the window of a subway—these are the moments of the poet, the eyes that promise romance. Each person will figure out his own eye signals even as each woman decides how she will make up her eyes. It is enough to know that there are all these marvelous idiosyncrasies, and the eyes really have it for introductory sex, even as newborns are first attracted to their parents' eyes. In deference to my aging mother I must also add one of her favorite admonitions, a caveat that I was raised on: "Always remember. Staring *can be* rude."

Next to the eyes the mouth is the most sensitive communicator of sexual interest. It is of course the organ of sucking and licking, and all primates can be observed to kiss affectionately and use their mouths to groom their mates and offspring. The mouth has a variety of sensory capabilities that includes taste, touch, heat sensation, and the moisture sensation of wet or dry that indicates thirst. The reason for veiling females in Islamic cultures is to conceal the sensuous mouth. Some folklore has it that you can judge the size and contour of a woman's vagina by looking at her mouth. A mouth can nibble affectionately at an ear, give love bites as dogs and cats do to their owners, or bite painfully. Mouth gestures may indicate all kinds of emotions: hate, fear, submission, sadness, humor, irony, tolerance, love, sex. The Spaniard exhaling hisses through his teeth at passing women, the striptease artist inhaling hisses through her teeth to take in the men, the obscene phone caller breathing heavily to convey his perverted excitement, all use the mouth for emotional expression. The mouth acts as a gripping or holding organ, sending signals by cigarette, pipe, even pens or pencils. In Arabia, a knife held in the mouth is the invitation to sensuous dance. In Japan, male kabuki dancers insert paper or handkerchiefs in their mouths to indicate female sexuality.

The tongue deserves special mention. The half-opened female mouth with the tongue slightly protruding is commonly used in advertisements to indicate sexuality, almost as if this were a vaginal invitation. Since the female in orgasm extends her head and opens her mouth, often giving forth a little cry, this may be an orgiastic gesture. A woman will baste her lipstick, moisten her lips with her tongue when expressing interest in a man. There is the analogue of the moistening vagina, the inviting vagina, when a woman is sexually available. Similarly, the male may dart out his tongue or twist it or curl it or lick the edge of a glass to indicate sexuality. He may encourage contests of curling the tongue in the middle or touching the nose with the tip or rolling a cigarette, all these with sexual overtones. It has been said that to mask the male or female face successfully the female should always cover her eyes, but the male should disguise his mouth. One sees this traditionally at costume balls, such as during Mardi Gras, where the women wear eye masks and men choose face or kerchief masks over the mouth. The male stagecoach or bank robber covers his lower face, because the mouth and tongue and the surrounding features, perhaps moustache or beard, have a characteristic give-away visual impact. The male seems to fixate on the female eyes, the female studies a man's mouth. We both pucker our lips to whistle and kiss. And when we kiss with our lips parted, touching each other's breath and tongue, we are said to be kissing with our soul. A soul kiss.

When I was growing up we children spent endless hours going to an ear, nose, and throat doctor. In my way of transliterating I called him my ear, nose and scrot doctor, as if to add some redeeming sexual attribute to those visits. However, the ears and the nose are not especially good sexual communicators. I can wiggle my ears for my children, but most people can't. In some African cultures enlarged earlobes are thought attractive. Accoutrements are hung on earlobes in the form of earrings to enhance this beauty, and perfume is placed routinely behind the ear. It is as if this structure needed emotional support. Like the ugly duckling our ears are often atrocious-looking structures. Bing Crosby and Clark Gable had lop ears and Jimmy Carter is caricatured with immense ugly ears. Nevertheless, despite having little surface sex appeal or signaling ability, ears are one of the most erogenous parts of the body. I love to watch the mother monkeys lovingly cleaning nits out of their babies' ears at the zoo, and adore having my wife debride my own. Most women love to be kissed on the ears, and sucking on an earlobe drives some of them crazy. In college we used to joke, "Take in it the ear for a beer," but I have never heard of anybody having an ear fetish. We might well have, though, because ears are not just receptacles for whispering sweet nothings. Though they are unable to send signals without help, they are one of the most erogenous zones of the body and should be exploited.

The nose can quiver, wrinkle, tilt upward, or flare outward at the nostrils. It can express love, as in a mother on the streetcorner smelling her baby's hair. By sticking our nose in the air we can express disgust, disdain, disapprobation. The nose can breathe heavily indicating excitement, or it can sniff as if chasing a scent of perfume. In folklore the bad guys are often blunt snubnosed bastards and the good guys have handsome cosmetic nose jobs. Exaggerated noses may be a phallic caricature, as in Cyrano de Bergerac. Just as a large mouth suggests a large female vagina, a large nose is sometimes claimed to indicate a big penis. Pinocchio's nose got bigger with each lie he told, while in contrast some American Indian societies cut off the tip of the nose for sexual transgressions such as adultery. Humor surrounding the nose has been endless, since high-living drink and spicy foods can aggravate a nose-enlarging condition called rhinophyma. Comedians W. C. Fields and Jimmy Durante ("the Snozzola") were said to be able to smoke a cigar in the shower, their noses were so big. Thus the nose can be both a sender and receiver of sensual stimuli. Above all it possesses the most daring of all senses, the sense of smell, the ability to detect beautiful and bad odors, from a distance or up close. It is our latent sensual sense that most needs educating and is to be recommended.

Hands may relax and open or tightly clasp and enclose, indicating tension and self-concern. They may have a fine pill-rolling tremor or sweaty palms, indicating anxiety. If soft and supple, they may be the hands of a clerk-typist or manicurist, if coarsened, those of ceramic artist or mechanic or housewife, if finely tuned, those of a musician or scrub nurse. In any event hands play a major roll in the paralanguage of sex and some say manual gesturing toward the genitalia was the original form of sexual propositioning. Primates commonly use the hands and fingers to explore each other's genitalia and fingers are commonly used to convey taste and odors to the nose. A woman's odor will often unexpectedly remain on the fingers of a man the day after sex, despite cleansing, and many men are seen sitting pensively, chin in hand, surreptitiously sniffing at their middle finger. Women will actually beckon with their hands by the wave of a carefully painted fingernail, or in contrast repel an advance by holding up the palm. My wife when she's had enough of a conversation not to her liking will simply give a little karate chop to "cut it off." All manner of people give the ultimate obscene finger gesture of disdain, called by the Nixon White House the "Italian salute," which simply means "up your ass"—with broken glass, my children always hasten to add. Bartenders and waitresses figure out elaborate hand and finger signals, much like a catcher and a pitcher where one finger may mean fast ball, two curve ball, three slider, four a pitch out. Men may cup their hands indicating the feel of a breast and women curve their fingers as if to encompass the male member. All things are possible, culturally different, but actual touch is always a moment of truth.

Whether it be playing footsie beneath the candlelit dinner table or gently brushing against the airline hostess in the ostensibly too-crowded aisle thirty thousand feet above America, the decisive moment in body language is always touch. This is what changes a social relationship to a sexual one and it is a transition that both men and women often find very difficult. Traditionally the man must "make a pass" at a woman in Western society, and equally traditionally she is heard to complain "he didn't even try anything." There are, of course, many socially acceptable noncommittal ways of touching that involve simple amenities, such as helping a woman with her coat, opening a door, helping someone across a street or up a stair, but with the liberation of women many of these subtleties have been discouraged or eliminated completely. Even dancing, once the best touch catalyst, has now been largely relegated to posturing movements at a distance from a partner and not pseudoembracing as once was the case. All this posturing and lack of direct verbal propositioning has the negative effect of producing much confusion and misinterpretation among the insensitive and unaware. Nevertheless, it seems essential, at least in our culture, to allow this vagueness so that the door to escape entangling alliances that soon appear doomed or unattractive can be accomplished with minimal psychic trauma. On Bali men can ask a girl to have sex merely by pronouncing the name of the sex organs, Lepcha women may do the same, and Siriono men may ask directly for sex if they whisper, but these forthright approaches are exceptions. Even in ancient societies, "love magic" or casting some kind of spell, which requires all kinds of indirection, is more the rule. All in all the heart seems to have its reasons which the mind does not always know, and trial and error, mostly by some sort of chemical indirection, prevails throughout most of the world. For this reason touch has become in most parts of the world a taboo. Handshaking and backslapping are frowned upon in the Orient, and social embracing in America is not common, though it is in Latin countries and Russia, where men readily kiss, as they do in France. Encounter groups in America have enjoyed great success, in part because they have eliminated the touch taboo and by thus "freeing people" purport in this way to educate actual feelings.

A dry sterile immobile face like Andrei Gromyko's may indicate that a person is a cold fish, is sexually unstirred and unstirrable. Exposed areas of our body are visible for analysis of sympathetic nervous system expression. A face may become flushed with excitement or blush with modesty. Fine beads of perspiration may appear across the forehead, at the roots of hairs, or across the upper lip. The moisture may give the face a fine sheen of excitement and add color to a woman at a cocktail party. The face juxtaposes and integrates all the characteristics we have discussed so far—eyes, ears, nose, throat, and the hair that surrounds and adorns the face. In Jefferson's and Washington's day facial hair was out and wigs were in. In Lincoln's day hair was out when he was young, and in when he became president. It was out for Grover Cleveland, in for Teddy Roosevelt's time, and out for Harry Truman. Ten years ago *Hair* was everything. Now my adolescent son "can't stand facial hair" or "long-haired creeps." That's what I said when I was his age. Now I have a beard. Some women report being kissed any place on their body by a bearded man is the most exciting thing they have experienced, others love a smooth-shaven, smooth-smelling, baby-faced man. *Chacun à son gout!* The face is the integer of our personality, whether it is the fixed jaw of a determined Popeye the sailorman, the lowered gaze of sanctity of the Madonna, Jimmy Carter getting his ears wet when he smiles, Liza Minnelli turning inside out on a high note, David Brinkley's overbite when he says good-night from NBC News, or the inscrutable Mona Lisa overseeing the second-floor crush in the Louvre. More than anything else our face is our personality and our personality is us. What we do with it bespeaks our vision of ourselves, both at the moment and what we would hope to achieve. Unfortunately, we human beings tend to have one facial feature better than all the rest and tend to highlight exclusively that feature to attract other people. All too often we wear a persona, a mask, that disappoints when inevitably it must be removed for love.

Body language, including posture and gesture, is important. Strangers will engage each other head-on for maximal benefit, while lovers will talk or walk beside each other, perhaps embracing or holding hands. The experience of sitting beside somebody on a bus, or perhaps even men standing at a urinal, takes on for strangers an unaccustomed intimacy. Crowded subways or airport waiting lines may force standees to a certain defensive posture or hoped-for distance. At nude beaches discreet distances are voluntarily observed. Inescapable gestures may accompany human encounters; a hand placed on an outthrust hip, a finger brushed casually toward the genitals, a woman thrusting her bust into prominence, a man cocking his head to one side, a woman in a laid-back pose, a man giving the benefit of his tight-pants membership for all to view. A woman will remove her coat as if unveiling, a man will thrust his vest out with pride. Some claim women in a courtship situation tighten their abdominal muscles, straighten their backs, lift up their heads, and shift to a more confident stride. Perhaps this imparts a visage of youthfulness and capability, perhaps the vigor available for sex. Men check their zippers and adjust their tie and pat their hair into place. Women use mirrors and have been known to brush their long blond hair in the line at the supermarket to indicate desire.

Body language has been divided into five main categories that include clothing, postures and gestures, angle and distance, eyes, and touch. Healthy women in all societies clothe themselves to best sexual advantage to display their bodies while carefully protecting their genitals. Even in primitive cultures where nudity among young females is condoned, they may be seen squatting legs akimbo, but with the heel of the foot carefully covering the vagina. Women sitting talking to men they like tend to adopt a more "open" posture, with arms parted and legs uncrossed, although such open postures seem to have no consistent relevance for men. Angle and distance are especially important. The male will often arrange himself to best partake of the visual stimuli he seems particularly prone to enjoy. A woman often feels, as in a picture to be taken, that she has a good side of her face or bust to display and will incline to show this profile to best advantage. In courtship, as in group therapy, people tend to come closer together and arrange themselves closer as intimacy progresses. Finally, people select each other and turn completely inward to enjoy each other as lovers, as if to shut all others out. Cultural differences in male "come-on" gestures are readily observed: Italians pull their ears, Arabs stroke their beards, Spaniards hiss through their teeth, and the Anglo-Saxon may simply pretend to ignore. Men and women both preen—he by adjusting his collar and slicking his hair, she by straightening her stockings and applying a new gloss of lipstick. Some say the American woman in waiting turns her palm outward and unconsciously strokes her wrist. Whatever the mode the psychodynamics are pretty certain. The attempt is always at nonverbal communication. And when this is the method used, a certain amount of feeling suppression takes place which allows for involuntary betrayal, via the motor body system, of desired feelings. Thus people betray their true feelings by gesture, hesitation, involuntary action, rather than by verbal expression or conscious action. Curiously enough the extremities, such as the feet and toes, rather than the central body parts, such as the navel or nipples, are the focus of this involuntary erogenous display. One of the leading feminists of our time is said to habitually rub her legs together behind the podium while publicly vilifying the male of the species.

Elizabeth I of England, under whose aegis the Spanish Armada was destroyed, was one of the most successful monarchs in the history of the world. To her, any lie was merely a tactic and had nothing whatsoever to do with scruple or morality of a higher order. Ends and means were never confused, since there were only ends. And she dressed the part in high-laced rigidity or gay deceivers as the occasion demanded. In a less devious way we all indulge in body alterations to communicate our sexual dispositions.

While there are negative sexual messages such as the habits of nuns, the cleric's collar, or Elizabeth's high starchiness, most adornment is intended to interest or arouse. Earrings and earlobe plugs are commonplace. Tooth sharpening, insertion of gold or diamond ornaments, or blackening, and even modern orthodontia are intended to attract. In Africa, the nostril is pierced and diamonds are inserted through the skin for cosmetic purposes. In Arabia, the navel is adorned with precious jewels. In Beverly Hills, nose-straightening is a common and lucrative plastic surgical procedure. African women often enlarge the lower lip with internal prosthetic devices, and precious metals are used to adorn them, once again by through-and-through piercing. Armbands and legbands are commonly used by Amazons, and ankle bracelets often have a vogue among American coeds. Waistband constrictors, all manner of breast molders and enhancers, and form-fitted clothing may suit the occasion for which women studiously dress to be appropriately attractive. For ceremonial occasions wigs, face paint, headgear, and foot and handwear may be quickly put on and removed, like the queen's tiara at a coronation.

Most sexual signaling with clothing is social and subject to change as fashions change. The miniskirts of the sixties allowed a marvelous glimpse of varicolored panties, which rapidly gave way to the tight jeans of the seventies. In all woman's fashions, however, the principle is the same—at least one erogenous focal point must be emphasized to excite the male. Thus the entire front may be covered, but the back must be generously exposed to add allurement. If the back and breast are covered, a skirt must be slit up the thigh. And if back and legs are clothed, some breast must be revealed, or at least tight buttocks. Usually it is one focal point, seldom two, that apparently distracts or confuses the unwitting male.

If a woman sits at a bar in Hawaii, a flower placed over the left ear signals she is taken. A flower over the right ear means she is available. One over each ear means she is both married and available, and if a woman grasps the flower in her teeth, she is saying to those across the room that she is undecided but worth a try. Most societies have certain conspicuous social signals such as wedding bands or rings, which in America are worn on the left hand, but in Europe are worn on the right. Fingers vary, but generally it is the fourth in Western society and a ring placed elsewhere is apt to confuse the viewer. In America many divorced people and some widows will shift their wedding ring to the right hand, whereas the opposite may be done in Europe.

Finally there is the matter of permanent body alterations; the whole gamut of cosmetic surgery from face lifts to breast implants to hair transplants is well known. Fingernails may be allowed to grow forever, to outdo the Guinness world record, hair and beard may be allowed to grow unabated, usually with various hair-dos interposed. Japanese women of fifty years ago bound their feet and toes so that they would remain petite, which was thought to be attractive and gave them a sexy, shuffling walk. Above all, body scarring and tattooing is permanent. Some lovers seal their bond in blood by slashing their forearms to commingle their blood and leave a scar. There is the Heidelberg scar from dueling, a sign of manhood among German youth. Branding and keloidal scarring occurs in some ancient societies to indicate tribal characteristics. I once had a man come to me for removal of a tattoo on his penis. It was a heart that adorned his glans penis on which was inscribed "Love Lifted Me." As he became erect the letters expanded, giving the inscription a pulsating neon effect. A woman once came to me with a tattoo that began at her navel and extended up over her chest and shoulder and down across her back to her buttocks. It was a chase scene, a dog chasing a rabbit, with the dog apparently gaining on the rabbit. The last tat-too, however, showed the exhausted dog sitting alone on her but-tocks gazing mournfully toward the rectum where the rabbit had ap-parently disappeared safely into the hole. I should add that both these people were circus performers, the man part of a high-wire act.

I have often used a tone of levity or mocking lightheartedness in referring to the communication of sexual interest. But as Robert Frost once said, "I am never more serious than when I am joking." Even if 90 percent of all communication is nonverbal the ultimate success of all communication depends on trust. This is no less true of communicating sexuality, which must be done with candor, honesty, and kindness. We've all heard it said that all's fair in love and war. But those who decry war are too often the very ones who most loudly exalt love in theory only. Our real sexual gambits are intended to lead to something more than the pent-up release of the moment. However therapeutic that may appear to be, the wisdom of the ages is that man and woman are reaching out to each other for something more. It does not detract from the playfulness and the fun to remind that the sexes can use each other's bodies honestly and respectfully, and notwithstanding all the modern license in sexual diversion, we each still crave someone beyond ourselves to live and die for. Those who claim they are free-swinging spirits are merely at a waystation where tentativeness is god. What they really seek is farther along the way, where the risk is surely greater, but the rewards become perma-nent. And this requires the use of man's greatest distinguishing at-tribute.

What we have said so far, regarding circumstantial sex, about the influence of higher brain centers and emotional needs on the func-tioning of the hypothalamus palls in comparison to the influence on it of language. Language is man's special attribute. It labels the things of this world that have come to involve our conscious life, and allows us reference to subconscious dreams and fantasy. It enables us to conceptualize ideas, unlike our primate forebears, so that we can select mates with reference to such considerations as race, looks, so-cial class, money, power, religion, ethics, and love. In humans, sex is almost never entered into without verbal exchange; only the most psychotic would rely on signals alone. Copulation based on seductive posturings or smell or facial expression seems to us barbaric or animalistic in the extreme. Human sexual behavior is immersed in words and our response to them. Male and female considerations in language have been so important as to give gender to all the nouns, the named objects, in such important cultures as the Latin, French, Spanish, or German. Words are emotional charges originating in the speech area of the cerebral brain, but transmitted by the feeling functions of our hypothalamus. The sex act begins with the hypothalamus at work with verbal foreplay—the use of language to touch the erogenous zone of our brain. Usually there is an initiating impulse involved, much like the poet experiences when he puts down that very first line of a poem from which all the rest flows. Years later lovers will remember the first words spoken. The experience begins in verbal delight and is rapidly surrounded by an aura of sexual tension. One of the characteristics is again the association with previously pleasurable experiences. These may include discussion of mutual areas of interest and appreciation, as well as emotional sharings of problems at work or the frustration of standing in line at the bank on Friday lunchbreak. A sense of feeling develops for the timbre of voice, inflection, nuance, humor, vulgarity, irony, laughter. Probes are made that can reveal sexual sophistication or inclination. Whispering can be exciting, but raucous laughter and loud noises are generally offputting to conversational progress. Young couples frequently make connections with language and imagery from their own childhood or with family usage of certain words. What older people need is a connection with the language of previous intimacies. Thus, they will share experiences that touched their souls—the death of a loved one, a view of the Parthenon with the sun coming up over the Aegean, the love of certain colors, or a movie mutually appreciated. The more mature the person, the more advanced this store of association, and so perhaps the more profound the potential of the relationship is. Whatever happens a selective process goes on and the dead wood of the relationship tends to get rapidly disposed of. Women are frequently heard to insist that their "heads be won before their hearts" and so the male finds himself in a persuasive role trying to find an area that pleases her set of mind. By tiny withdrawals she may reject, by open friendly warmth she may encourage. The result of this may be either a put off, or a greater closeness and psychic intimacy. Both partners then find themselves in an anticipatory atmosphere, which is translated into certain bodily manifestations: sweaty palms, a rapid heartbeat, rapid respiration, gastric hypersecretion, excessive salivation, garrulousness—vegetative functions all regulated by the hypothalamus in its neuroregulatory role. Women seem to be especially susceptible to verbal foreplay. Even a phone call may set their juices flowing. There is the classic example of the physically undistinguished male who mesmerizes the woman to sexual arousal. A male speaker can note the gyrations of the ladies' legs even if he is talking about Newton's Laws. One of my own female students at the end of a teaching hour once sidled up to me to whisper, "You know, you are a real mind fuck." It was the first time I'd heard the expression, though I *had* noted her legs. Thereafter I never doubted the power of the word.

The hearing organ of our inner ear is called our cochlea. It is a tiny spiral organ, two and one half turns around a central core, rather like a snail shell, and located near our balance mechanism in the spongy portion of our temporal skull bone around the ear. High-pitched noises excite the cochlea at one focal point only, but lower pitched noises, the language of love, causes the whole cochlea organ to shiver and shake and transmit impulses. As our verbal foreplay becomes more intimate, our voices lower and soon an illusion of physical attractiveness enters our nearby brain. We begin to make out and physically approach the love object. A second phase of verbal foreplay of a cajoling urgency is then entered. Each partner urges the other on to greater and greater expressiveness. As the sex act itself is entered, what was once relatively altruistic expressiveness is now apt to take on a more basic tone. A woman may now find herself totally inured to the appropriateness of the language of the moment. The foreplay has now become a foreplay to orgasm. But the verbal aspect regresses to whisperings and moanings, until at the end we find ourselves beyond words, left with only our primal grunts and groans, and the cochlea vibrating madly in our inner ear.

This, then, is the fantastic range and potentiality of our hypothalamic mediator at work. It has taken man's ability to speak and communicate in words and translated it into an erogenous activity, first at a distance on an ethereal plane, then allowing and encouraging our more primal expressions, which miraculously end in coupling. There is no better example of the psychomotor brain center at work. But the hypothalamus does not just receive sex messages from outside. It receives messages from within our body as well. These are being transmitted from our sexual organs via the nervous system all the time, especially during the act of sex itself.

Picture a cavity that is lined by a wall, say a balloon or a football. It's apparent as the empty cavitary space within is filled that it will gradually distend and the internal distension will impinge upon the inner lining. If there are nerves connected to that lining, they will register the tension change. In the case of the sex glands in men and women this is precisely what happens. Along the labial entrance to her vagina a woman has two sets of glands, Skene's glands and Bartholin's glands, as well as a generous supply of secretory vaginal glands. These glands, like tiny secretory balloons, are lined with cells that constantly fill their cavitary lumens with juice for lubricating the sex act when called upon. A woman finds herself in various phases of readiness depending upon the glands' fullness. When full the tension on the gland lining mounts, and nerve impulses are received in the hypothalamus, which may or may not be able to control the inevitability received. There may be a spillover because the glandular tension is so heightened. In such a case a woman driving home from an exciting lecture like mine may find herself gummy. Or she may later find she has dreamed the fantasy of being made love to on the Costa del Sol, and wake up swimming, all because of overdistension of her sex glands and a message to the hypothalamus.

In the same way the prostate of the male, and his testicles and seminal vesicles are all closed cystic structures, with limited distensibility and secretory linings, which are constantly pouring fluid into a central lumen. When that lumen is filled, the linings complain. A male feels a terrible fullness deep in his pelvis near the rectum where his prostate rests, and along the spermatic cords in his groin and in his testicles. Since there are more of these tension structures in him than in the female, a more bothersome surface area, he tends to carry a bigger load at a more constant level of sexual tension than the female. But at any given time her level of tension is apt to be just as high as his, even higher. His release is precisely the same, either through active response to the hypothalamic messages received or unconscious evacuation in dreams.

In all the systems of the body, one age-old law obtains: To every action there is an equal and opposite reaction. In our sex organs this is crucial. If we don't allow them periodic attention, not only will they complain, but they can go beyond complaint to a state of atrophy. This is sometimes called the atrophy of disuse, a process painfully achieved by celibates after years of denial. It is a state of suspended animation, a death in life.

What happens is this. If the higher brain centers by excessive exertion and negative impulse convey the message to the hypothalamus, sex is shut off and no effort or inclination is allowed in that direction. This leaves the secretory glands in a state of limbo within their little confines in the genitalia. Nevertheless they continue to secrete their juicy substances into the cavitary lumens, albeit at a slower, inhibited rate. Finally, when these little cysts have become maximally distended, the secreting cells lining the cyst cavity are collapsed back upon themselves much like little accordions forcibly compressed that can no longer play. This leaves our sex glands filled with stagnant juices and without further stimulus since the cells that ordinarily supply that function have been compressed out of use. This state is called the atrophy of disuse and is both physiologically and pathologically demonstrable. All secretory organs of the body that have lining cells and lumenal secretions share this characteristic. You can see it in a microscope.

In this way in time one can achieve a total atrophy of disuse, but

199

not without repeated complaints from our nature. Even when shut-off is achieved, there are always certain recalcitrant cells that manage to break through, leak, and cause the rebuilding of tension. Evacuation of the spontaneous and unconscious sort described above is the result. This will go on for years even in the most devout, but eventually the cells will dwindle in function and frequency and many will succumb to the atresia of time. In this state it is possible to achieve a virtual atrophy, atrophy of disuse, and triumph over our sexual self. Such is the nature of our unconscious urges.

For most of us abstinence does indeed make the heart grow fonder, sending desperate messages of tension to the hypothalamus which we all are compelled to act on. One truth about the human body is its fantastic resilience in the face of the appropriately designated use of an organ system. Our toughest muscle, the heart muscle, we now beat on, pound on, electrocute, and transplant, and it thrives on such abuse. If you take sex organs that have been dormant and grossly atrophic from years of neglect or disuse and suddenly reactivate them, they will be readily employed in a matter of hours, suddenly rejuvenated, doing God's work as intended once again. For most human beings disuse of their sex glands is a temporary state of affairs only, in fact and in fancy. And for this we can be grateful.

The relationship of the hypothalamus to our sympathetic and parasympathetic nervous systems now becomes the important psychosexual arena. It is easy for most of us to be in touch with the surface phenomena of our body, because sensory nerves transmit those messages to the brain in a manner which our higher centers can confirm by other means. Thus, if you are touched, you can look to see who touched you. But two other nervous systems are distinct from this surface system and are located deep within us. They are sympathetic and parasympathetic systems, together called the autonomic nervous system. They have their own autonomy and have a crucial sexual function. Each of these systems is detached from the main spinal cord and, except by indirect nerve trunks, work independently of our main brain routes. The sympathetic and parasympathetic nervous systems extend inside us from our neck to our pubis and contain multiple tiny brainlike ganglia dispersed throughout as regulatory bodies. The two systems work in a balanced perspective; frequently they are antagonistic in function. For example, the sympathetic nervous system will constrict blood vessels, close down sphincters, inhibit movement of the intestines, and cause sweating. If one would undertake to block, say, the sympathetic nervous system to the leg by injecting a local anesthetic such as novocaine along its spinal nerve chain, one would see (a) an increase in skin temperature (b) absence of sweating (c) redness of the skin from blood vessel dilation. In other words, these are manifestations of the now uninhibited parasympathetic system. If we could examine that system further, we would find it is our relaxing system, whereas the sympathetic counterpart is the stressful or tense system. Parasympathetic nerves cause the even flow of peristalsis, the regular beat of the heart, the looseness of our sphincters, and, above all, the flowing of our juices. One finds adrenalin at sympathetic synapses, or joining points, but acetylcholine, a relaxing agent, at parasympathetic junctures. It is the catalyst of the hypothalamus mediating brain waves at one end, these two vegetative nervous systems fighting it out down below, and all of them coming together that make for the successful sex act.

Parasympathetic effects are more localized in character, more conservative, having less to do with the expenditure of energy. It is not surprising that in the initial phases of the sex act we tend to be most in thrall of our sympathetic system. In the first phase of sex, the excitement phase, there is nipple erection in the woman and contraction of the tiny muscles that erect the skin hairs. This is a sympathetic function, just as the hair on a cat will elevate to a fierce stimulus. A slight splotchy rash, a reddening here and there, a regional type of blushing, as seen in embarrassment, is also observed and represents sympathetic activity. Similarly, a building of blood pressure, an increase in heart rate, an increase in respiration, a tensing of sphincters and voluntary muscles are all sympathetically induced. Adrenalin is released. But the flow of vaginal juices, the evacuation of Bartholin's and Skene's glands, the wetness of which a woman is most characteristically aware, result from parasympathetic overflow, as if a relaxing readiness were also slowly at work beneath the other more surface turmoil. It is tempting to say that the parasympathetic is our feminine and the sympathetic our masculine visceral nervous system at work. But both systems are in abundance in each sex.

Most prominent in the excitatory phase in both sexes is the vascular engorgement of the penis and the clitoral-labial area. Contrary to common belief, erection is not just the result of blood gushing in, but equally the result of failure of blood to be able to leave the organ. True enough, stimulus of the member does transmit pleasurable thoughts and feelings to the central nervous system which, mediated by the hypothalamus, sends an increased blood flow to the desired area. This causes increased flow of arterial or fresh blood and gives a sense of awakening to penis and clitoris. But it is the local tourniquet effect in these organs, mediated by tiny venous valves that trap the blood there and keep it from returning to the heart, that finally causes turgidity of the organ. Erection, therefore, is a phenomenon of the dynamics of penile or clitoral circulation. Two large cavernous bodies of elongated spongy tissue occupy the top of the organ (*corpora cavernosa*) and one the ventral or lower side (*corpora spongiosum*). These spongelike tissue areas contain many feeding arteries and exiting veins. When the penis is flaccid there are shunt valves that are closed so that the spongy lakes are not filled and the blood courses around these areas directly from artery to veins, going from the heart via arteries and returning immediately via veins. But neural impulses from the parasympathetic system in the sexually aroused open these valves between arteries and veins, and the spongy lakes are suddenly flooded with blood that pools there and becomes trapped as the organ distends. At first, arterial inflow exceeds venous outflow and normal tiny venous valves, as mentioned, further trap blood so that the organ has an accelerated phase of enlargement. Eventually, a hemodynamic state is established so that a sustained erection inflow and outflow equilibrate, the egress of blood beyond the valves being aided by the gentle milking action of intercourse.

One of the technical pearls of erection wisdom has escaped the sexologists, and that is the predominant venous role in the erection process. This requires the knowledgeability, the street smartness many on the heights of Parnassus can't be expected to have, that if a penis is grasped at its base and constricted partially, so as to compress the more superficial veins, but not completely so as not to clamp off the more deeply located arterial inflow, erection physiology is begun. It's important to emphasize that if you completely clamp off the penis (or any limb) you will get a *complete* tourniquet effect, as is the intention in amputation emergencies, for example. But in sex the intention is the more delicate venous occlusion only. As the member is stimulated, at its tip say, more deep arterial blood will be attracted to that point, but will not be able to return, because the valve of the lakes have opened and are pooling and the valves in the normal veins, like locks in a canal, have now been closed down by the excited pressure in the system. The shaft of the clitoris and penis behind these dams are filled with blood, huge lakes of blood accumulate, and continue to remain so long as stimulus is successful, aided by the peculiar elastic tissue distensibility these organs possess.

During the second, or plateau phase of the sex act, a surprising similarity persists in both male and female sympathetic response, although classically somewhat delayed in the female. But nipples remain erect, the scattered blushes continue, voluntary muscle tension persists, sphincters remain tight, heart and respiratory action rhythmically increase. In the male urethra one notes a mucinous discharge from the urethral glands, representing his parasympathetic discharge analogous to the woman's vaginal, labial, and paralabial moistening. But otherwise the parasympathetic nervous system still maintains relative inactivity.

It is not until the orgasmic phase of the sex act that the parasympathetic comes completely into play. And herewith the essence of what happens in the sublimity of the sex act, so poorly described by most sexologists. Because what orgasm is, is a sudden blissful shift from one governing vegetative nervous system to another, from sympathetic control to parasympathetic release, from intensive active state to relaxed rejuvenative repose. The splotchy flush now becomes a diffused erythema over the chest and neck indicating loss of sympathetic predominance. The muscles of the male penis contract involuntarily—a parasympathetic release spasm. The woman's pubic muscles contract, there are ripples of contractions along the body of her elevated uterus that spread into the lining of her vagina—an all-relieving parasympathetic discharge. Sphincters open, more release takes place, there is a lessening of the venous valves, a gradual detumescence of blood. And in the fourth or resolution phase of intercourse we become parasympathetically dominated animals. Our pubic congestion begins to resolve, the uterus comes down to its normal resting place, the previously opened cervical os closes, the penis softens, the clitoris goes back to its normal resting position in the anterior labial folds. Contractions taper off, we are consumed with rest and sleep. A bonus awaits the female of the species in the form of a soothing balm contained in the instilled semen in her vagina. We now know that certain "prostaglandins" (so named for their prostatic origin) exist in the ejaculate that cause a directed stimulation to uterine and vaginal smooth muscle. Thirteen such separate chemical compounds have been described. They are absorbed in the vagina, recirculated, and excreted in the female urine. Their effect is to cause gentle rhythmic uterine contractions and vaginal contractions that continue on and linger after the male has completed his orgasm. It gives the woman a lingering sense of sexuality and a gentle decrescendo sense of resolution and accounts in some measure for her need to be held and loved and cuddled long after he is done with it.

What begins with a circumstantial attraction between people that is based on our higher evolutionary nervous system ends in the act of sex where our vegetative or more primitive nervous self, the autonomic nervous system, is allowed full sway. At first, lust is a sympathetic response in which we are tense, excited, our heart races, our mouth may be dry from nervousness. Our parasympathetic system, while attempting to keep us calm, nevertheless breaks through and causes our palms to become sweaty, our stomach to rumble, our vaginal juices to become evident. In the male there is the prodramata of a mucinous discharge from his urethra and a throbbing can be felt in his penis. His parasympathetics have caused the discharge, his sympathetics the increased circulation; her parasympathetics have activated Skene's glands and Bartholin's glands and vaginal lining glands. The preparation for sexual reception in her has now begun. Her androgen drive of the moment may enhance her clitoral excitement, her ovulatory cycle may be in ripened phase, but the erection she now has is the result of parasympathetic opening of the shut valves in her venous clitoral lakes that pool from arteriole inflowing. The same is true of him, a little sooner, a little more intent, a good bit larger. But the erectile mechanism is the same.

During the second phase his sympathetic system expends extreme energy in heartbeat, lifting, moving, using all manner of male muscles. Sympathetic adrenalin is released, the blood vessels contract and blood pressure heightens. The head throbs. Her parasympathetic attempts to conserve. The vagina becomes relaxed, open, juices flow, the mouth begins to moisten. Her sympathetic system causes her tiny nipple muscles to contract. The nipples become erect, the hairs elevate. They are ready for manipulation, a heightened awareness now. As they enter the secondary or plateau phase of sex they are now man and woman in thrall of the predominate sympathetic system. The action becomes generalized. All sphincters remain tight. Gas can be released afterward. Heart and respiration pound away. All thought is gone and the brain has given way to the spine where the erection center works its own parasympathetic outflow from the sacrum continuing localized moistening and keeping the lake valves wide open. Miniorgasms occur, a sense of going from one state to another, but not quite yet. The sympathetics predominate, remain generalized—heart, lungs, exercise, thrust, move, moan—the parasympathetics moistening and hardening. The balance is sustained, he could go on and on, so could she. Now they are together, climaxing.

With orgasm comes the shift, the sudden fantastic release from tense sympathetic to warm paraympathetic discharge. The male penile muscles spurt their parasympathetic message. The female vagina ripples and elongates, the uterus elevates and gently contracts—all parasympathetic release. The vagus nerve of the parasympathetic system fires off impulses that slow the heart, sympathetic adrenalin is counteracted, respiration slows down. The last juice is milked from the member in parasympathetic spasm, the last juice flows from her glands as well. In one final spasmodic discharge the sympathetic chain causes a warm red blush to mottle the neck and chest of the female and that spreads over her entire face, now dry and warm. Parasympathetic sweat is converted to sympathetic hot and dry skin. The clasped couple is at peace. Organs settle back into place. The prostaglandins work their soothing balm, milking sperms up on their final way. Parasympathetics carry the lovers off toward sleep. Peristalsis resumes. Sphincters relax. She has to urinate. He passes gas. It's all over. It was good.

Among the basic biological drives of human beings—to eat, to sleep, to keep warm, to socialize—to have sex is at one extreme the simplest and at the other the most complex of our native urges. We can, like Old Testament Onan, simply indulge ourselves and masturbate in the shower to relieve the tension mounted by the tense glands in our loins. Inevitably, a sense of emptiness and waste accompanies this action and we look around to share our substance with another, not just in fantasy, but in fact. So we seek a connection with our opposite member. For this we can simply whore, turn a trick, for physiological release. A quick job in the backseat on the way home, no questions asked. But again we are left empty and lonely. Something is missing.

Inevitably as sentient human beings we are driven to seek something more and begin to socialize our sex. We become aware that what attracts us in the opposite sex in general are certain built-in features that come down through the ages. Men are larger and stronger, women are softer, more supple, smaller, with suggestive hips and breasts. We learn that there is an accent on youth and a taboo on incest, that because the male has a stronger voice box his speech is characteristically lower, quieter, more cajoling. We learn that women converse differently from men, using more adjectives, more soft words, more delightful original speech, fewer clichés, more long-drawn-out and playful conversations. Women will pose in characteristic come-on gestures with hip and breast to attract the male, who recognizes the gambit, and may exhibit a positive or negative attraction. Similarly, the female notices the shape of his body, the fit of his trousers, his shoulder strength, and may move toward or away from him with enticement.

Between purely built-in body language and acquired sexual communication there is an interphase where body heat and odors have their place. Although each of us uniquely have our peculiarly human odor, these odors may have an idiosyncratic appeal to members of the opposite sex, and as we become emotionally involved may become more pronounced. The sense of smell is comparatively dormant in humans, but may be activated under attractive circumstances. With the strong overlay of the higher brain centers and past personal associations of breast, body heat, odors, and human voice, the matter of chemical sexual excitement to these stimuli is too individualized to risk generalization for any two people. Sex appeal, however, has little to do with sexuality in our couple, rather it is a topical achievement stylish at any given cultural time and fashioned by external forces for the consumption of the moment.

Sexual communication, when situational, involves certain acquired or learned characteristics. These include use of the eyes, mouth, nose, ears, hands, and feet and the accompanying signals and gestures. Eyelashes bat and wink, mouths pucker and kiss, noses wrinkle, ears are adorned, hands beckon and put off. The sum of the organs of senses about the face gives it a certain expression that allows interpretation from a distance, whether right or wrong. Body language further involves clothing, angles, and distance, with negative and positive messages as intended: the nun's habit, the hustler's mini see-through skirt outside the church. Permanent body alterations intended to enhance may include tattoos, breast operations, male hair transplants, huge fingernails. Many, many things.

Pure psychic intimacy in humans increases only with language and the magic it can make in evoking pleasant past associations in a thoughtful partner. It can excite all the myriad hypothalamic media-tors to a point where brain and body alike are pulsating with excite-ment and anticipatory desire. It is the open sesame to sex and the excitatory first phase of sexual response. It causes our juices to flow and our members to become erect and ready for touch. Once begun, our special spinal erection center can proceed on its own to sustain its impulse and gradually cut itself off from any brainy interruptions. During sex, the cochlea organ of our inner ear vibrates in its entirety to low voice sounds as they enter the brain, giving us a whirling disco musical effect.

The sex act itself, once intromission has begun, is largely a payoff between our more primitive vegetative nervous systems, the para-sympathetic and the sympathetic systems. The latter is predomi-nantly the basic functional system of body stress, the former the sys-tem of body conservation. As they struggle one against the other within our primitive visceral selves, our higher brain centers are grad-ually released from the trials and tribulations of the day and all the preceding preliminary sexual confusion. In the end, the system of conservation always prevails so as to rejuvenate us again for our life and living.

NINE

CONFLUENCE
WITHOUT
CONFUSION

*And thou shouldst know that all have delight in proportion as
their vision penetrates into the Truth.*

—*Dante*
Canto XXVIII

IT IS SOMETIMES SAID that Freud is for the first half of life and Jung is for the second. Thus, Freud is for the erotic and Jung for the narcotic, or, as the joke has it on the West Coast where Jungian psychology has become so popular in recent years, Freud is looking down and Jung is looking up. One partakes of the genital, the other of the celestial. Although it is pertinent to point out that these two psychiatric schools need not necessarily be mutually exclusive for ordinary folks as we grow older.

So the trick is in the growth, the wonderful old lady anthropologist had said. Our natures are different, we necessarily come at life from different directions, but the endpoint has to be the same. And didn't she prove that within herself? A wholesome and beautiful woman facing the end of her life. The old women in the pictures had experienced no worse life than she, no worse life than any of the other members of the tribe in fact, but their clinging to a youthful state, an unconscious state, where so much had been naturally given them in their sex, had left them bitter and incomplete in old age. At some point they had needed consciousness, just as the old men, who in the precision of their hunting had known an overabundance of consciousness, must now be content to immerse themselves in the protective waters of the unconscious.

Jung's message of individuation is a process by which men and women, while developing their own uniqueness, become psychologically congruent in the second half of life. It is a journey, the Jungians emphasize, a journey that is constantly changing with the ebb and flow of life and one that requires constant tending, like a good warming fire in the cold wilderness of the world. But the position we find ourselves in at any particular time is a function of a natural process that will proceed apace in a beautiful and advantageous way if we will only understand and allow it. Jung made it clear, most emphatically, that this was not an invention or some psychiatric machination of his own fancy, but rather a process he had observed. And so in the way of psychiatrists he undertook to describe, even as he experienced it himself, what man and woman had often successfully achieved themselves by living a full life. The anthropologist had never studied Carl Jung, but she had most assuredly lived to fulfill her dream for woman.

So it comes about that at the age when they say life begins, we have, in the female, a person approaching forty from a relative state of sexually induced unconsciousness—a necessary ingredient to the job she has already been called upon to do, whether or not she has fulfilled her natural destiny. The male, on the other hand, approaches middle age from a state of excessive consciousness that usually hasn't allowed, in his achievement-oriented role as would-be protector and provider, the wonderful nurturant expression of his unconscious or female side. If these defects are not recognized and a restitution of the balance begun at this point, irreparable psychic damage is likely to ensue in time and another incomplete life will eventually result. But in early middle age this imbalance is a normal one. In middle age a woman's problem is her developing *Logos*, in middle age a man's his developing *Eros*. Both have their problems, separate but equal, as well as together.

I was born in 1926 and graduated from Princeton University with the class of 1948. When several years ago they polled all the alumni as to whether or not Princeton should become cocducational all the classes before mine voted against it, and all the classes after mine voted for it, but my class split fifty/fifty right down the middle (I voted for it). Middle-aged men apparently had some chthonic misgivings about having young ladies around while they were about the business of being educated, which seemed absurd to me. If these women met the qualifications, I thought, why not? Surely their minds were as good as men's, and from what I know, their bodies considerably more perfect. Why deny the world half the world's talent? When coeducation finally went through I thought it was marvelous. But then a strange thing happened. Heretofore I had always received pleasant formal letters each fall asking me to contribute to Annual Giving, and when I was derelict, which was frequently, I got a visit from an aged, regional classmate and a slap on the back, which I accepted or ignored as my pocket nerve of the moment allowed. There was no sweat. I gave ad lib, and when the spirit moved.

But then Princeton started having their coeds call me for money. I wondered why. I began to dream. If it were a young man I would simply tell him to go fuck himself, I'd pay when and where I damn well wanted to. Hell, I've got sixteen schools asking me for donations each fall! But this was something different. One night one of them came to my house, all parchment scrubbed and beautiful with her glossy hair strewn down all around her deep mother-of-pearl navel, wearing a gauzy, see-through, nippleoid blouse, and a skirt like a Tahitian loincloth. Her message was ostensibly monetary, but there she sat in a foam of purple gossamer clouds, pointing her perfect thighs at me from out a minimal skirt. I thought her interstices were checkered soft orange and black, the colors of my beloved Alma Mater, and I kept maneuvering my gaze around the palms and college memorabilia in my living room for one juicy glimpse of the little man up front in her canoe. And as she sat there coaxing me, all she said was money, money, money through perfect white teeth, the while taking my picture with her virginal moon. My middle manhood commenced to swell on me as I got up and, beautifully exposing myself, began to snake Priapus forward toward her. I apparently kicked my wife who let out a scream and we both woke up suddenly. I explained to her that I wished to hell Princeton would stop having their coeds call me for Annual Giving. I was a real sucker. My wife said it was time I started seeing women for what they really are. What a pity, I thought.

Seeing women for what they really are. Is this what a middle-aged man is supposed to do? Does a woman get all dressed up and decked out for him so he can see her for what she really is? Does she entice him with balm and perfume so as not really to entice him, but to allow him to see her undistracted for what she really is? Do all the models in all the magazines, all the fashions, the lingerie, the cosmetics, the whole process of being beautiful have nothing to do with pleasing a me? Do women indulge these things only to make themselves feel better, without a thought to him?

A million questions rise in a man when he sees a lovely woman and perceives the spell she casts over him in the ancient promise of offering him something he desperately wants. It is not possible for him to believe, in view of the feelings she arouses in him, even from a distance, strong as those feelings are, that she cannot see or perceive and hence intentionally desire to arouse him. To his mind what she does to herself in beauty she necessarily does for him, and if he is a robust and healthy male he will be responsive.

What a man feels terribly at forty with renewed vengeance is this feminine need in himself. He not only believes he has achieved what is or could be expected of him as a male in the competitive cauldron of an achievement-oriented world, he believes that in doing this he has often denied or sacrificed or disciplined out of himself much of the softness that he now craves so much as the truly beautiful aspect of existence that is his due. For him, woman represents this missing part, and he craves her, not with the ejaculatory exuberance of a teenager or eagerly as in his twenties, but with the lusty temperament of what he now perceives to be accomplished sexuality. He no doubt has had the experience of woman in all her darker malevolence, in all her fullness of pregnancy, in all her vagrant desires within and without a home. Yet he casts aside all this practicality to watch a woman prance down the street, her buttocks looking like two cubs wrestling under a blanket. He will sneak off alone to a pornographic movie, attributing all sorts of beauty to the tawdry ladies on the screen while surreptitiously covering Omar the tentmaker in his lap with his latest hat. And he sweats because he wonders if he missed something, because something seems to be missing, and he strains his imagination to become expert in details of pinks and blues and textures of soft and medium and hard.

Despite the experience of marriage or love affairs or children he is still the victim of Eros. The intense love affairs of our life, the real Eros that thunders and befalls us from time to time, have a life of perhaps a year or a year and a half. The heated part of that affair lasts several months at best, and this pattern has a relative consistency for all of us at whatever age. But the feeling of such a love affair is so immensely moving and beautiful that most of us carry its memory deep into old age, with beautiful, recurrent, conscious recall and subconscious fancy. The man at middle age, despite his experience as parent and lover, still longs to return to that youthful sensation and capture what he considers has been lost of his feminine self before it is too late. In doing this, he brings with him a sense of achieved independence and a sense that he has earned the right to display and seek his own fulfillment in this way.

Because of his vigor and his accomplishment he is obviously attractive to young, sometimes very young, women, who bring to him all the youthful softness and promise he feels he has lost in routinizing marriage and parenthood. She is flattered and impressed beyond measure by his attention, and the match seems a natural. But what may not be natural about his relationships now is the problem of his middle-aged Eros and whether or not he is seeing it for the manacle it really is or for the beautiful release in love that it can be, if the circumstances warrant it.

Not long ago I attended a dinner party for one of our country's leading philosophers who was celebrating his seventy-fifth birthday that week. He shocked many of the ladies by complaining that his anima still kept playing tricks on him and that this was one of the reasons he no longer accepted teaching positions in girls' schools. At age seventy, another leading anthropologist in academic circles finally, one weekend in California at Esalen, succumbed to the nude baths and let two young women give him a massage. It was an awakening of his Eros, he said in a lecture later, scarcely to be believed, and one that he had carefully sublimated since age forty when he had experienced wholly uncontrollable and, to him, unreasonable lust for young women.

Down through the ages, a man again and again has had to face the apparently unreasonable lust that overcomes him in middle age. He has thrown all responsibility to the winds—hearth and home, children, and career—for the impulse to complete himself with another who promises to teach him once again of himself. And that promise is always for more knowledge of his feminine self, which by forty has been too neglected and not allowed free enough rein in his personal expression. In doing this, in answering this crying need, man must be carefully aware of the Eros's unspecified darkness which, if pursued with abandon, will often lead him into depths of guilt and sadness beyond his wildest imaginings. His anima is to be respected for the creative and beautifully tempting flower that it is. But it is not to be uncontrolled and allowed unreasonable freedom lest it end up in total disaster. It is man's agonizing job at forty, the burden of his manhood, to recognize his erotic urges for the seminal impulses they are, what they really are, and place that energy alongside someone who will reciprocate it in love and elevate it, as a lily can be seen to grow from the mud. He cannot remain a man and abrogate his mature responsibilities to living, to maintain himself and his family against the trials of this world, and think that by giving in unrestrainedly to his complaining Eros he will complete himself. Yes, he is lacking in unconscious fulfillment, which his male person sorely craves and needs, but unconscious energy untempered by sober conscious thought and action is worthless and self-destructive.

While man's unconscious fulfillment or Eros needs attention, the woman at forty is struggling with her own damnable Logos, a word used here in the Greek sense of logic, meaning the conscious reason as a controlling principle in the world, as well as the wisdom manifest in our social institutions. It is not used exclusively in the sense of the opening phrase of the Book of John where it says "In the beginning was the word (in Greek, *Logos*)," by which is meant the spirit of God, although that is indeed part of what we are about.

The confusion in a woman's life as she struggles out of the strong urge and magnetism of the unconscious is immense and terrifying. What has been the comfort and beauty of nesting and protecting and caring for the young must now be left for the arithmetic of the real world, a world of masculine sharpies and hustling strangers who have little patience with somebody trying to move into their territory. Not in all literature is there a passage so telling of a woman's terror and feelings as she makes her initial foray into the real world of men, as in this by Lady Macbeth, as she contemplates killing her husband's rival:

> Come, you spirits
> That tend on mortal thoughts, unsex me here,
> And fill me from the crown to the toe top-full
> Of direst cruelty! Make thick my blood,
> Stop up the access and the passage to remorse
> That no compunctious visitings of nature
> Shake my fell purpose, nor keep peace between
> The effect and it! Come to my woman's breasts,
> And take my milk for gall, you murdering ministers,
> Wherever in your sightless substances
> You wait on nature's mischief! Come, thick Night,
> And pall thee in the dunnest smoke of hell,
> That my keen knife see not the wound it makes
> Nor Heaven peep through the blanket of the dark,
> To cry "Hold, Hold!"

Lady Macbeth as she faces the prospect of killing Duncan is terrified that her femininity will prevail and disallow what she sees as the masculine toughness necessary to complete her task in a man's world. Unsex me, she says, take away my tender womanliness and allow me the strength to do this man's job. But then her Logos gets all out of whack. She doesn't weigh and consider the possible methods, the possible contingencies, the consequences of this or that attack on the problem. No, the problem to her is the problem of feeling it right in her bones, the problem of getting in the proper "masculine mood," the mood she conceives men are in when they set about such an act of treason to depose a King. In her mind there is no logic to be considered as a primary approach to this problem.

Little does she recognize that even the worst demons in the life of man, such as a Hitler or a Stalin, have spent endless hours in preparation and conniving methodology before undertaking their dark deeds. With her the problem is her concept of man's logic in such matters of state, the problem of getting into the unfeeling frame of mind where her "keen knife see not the wound it makes." That is what a strong and courageous man does! In this respect, unfortunately, she is only leaving one darkness for another. What was the protective cocoon of her own dark unconscious female self, she now has replaced, not with the light of male logic, but with the dark side of man with which she is already so naturally familiar.

If a woman would achieve the maturity of her middle years she must serve her apprenticeship in logic. More than anything else she must value and make a point of specificity and reasoned thought and argument. She can no longer seek that specificity through the male as the primary arbiter of her own decisions. She can no longer cry out, "specify me" to her husband or lover. She must indeed specify herself so that she can learn gradually to light up her own life and dispense with the need for someone to light up her darkness for her. This means long laborious hours of concern for particulars that have a coldness and mathematical finality about them that seem harsh, cut and dried, callous, and wholly foreign to the development of her nature over the past twenty years. She must climb a hard ascent that man has largely already achieved and from where he stands looking back down on her, impatiently, yes, but with hope, certainly. Here's how one modern author, Nina Schneider, characterizes this woman's problem:

Failure of imagination is not listed among tragic flaws. Yet I nominate it for the number one spot. Wouldn't Lady Macbeth's enterprise have died aborning if her imagination had kept pace with her ambition? I imagined, if I imagined at all, that adding a lover to my orderly life would be an exotic embellishment on the order of adding a cage of tropical warblers to my houseplant window. I imagined "living in sin," free of routine responses, would be happiness. My smiles would be real. With my penchant for idealizing, and my denial of the specific, I was sure our love would inform every act and, as the verse had it—"life would be a glorious cycle of song."

It was the hunter Hemingway who once remarked, "It is no crime to kill, but it is a crime not to kill cleanly." The statement has largely been misunderstood as being cruel and unsympathetic. I have heard women vilify this outrageous "sexist remark" ad nauseam, with little understanding or thought for the reasoning behind it. I think for all of us to understand, particularly emerging middle-aged woman, the true tenderness of the surgeon and the essential toughness of the poet are two of the most important tasks in life. In the lay mind the surgeon is often a tough, cold, even cruel and mindless technical automaton. He derives from the butcher, albeit one step advanced. They feel the incontrovertible fact is "he couldn't be warm, sweet, kind, tender, and gentle and do what he has to do for a living." It is the liberal cast of mind again, speaking at a thousand cocktail parties, adding the caveat that "they all charge too much anyway." And as for the poet sitting in the corner with his shaky hands and exquisitely sensitive face, he is the real spokesman for all the love and kindness among us and wouldn't hurt a flea. Poetry never makes anything happen.

The truth is otherwise. A surgeon dealing with the human body is apt to be the most tender and meticulous person alive, the most respectful of a sleeping person's soul and wishes for posterity of any person on this earth. His feelings run deep into years of translating human thoughts and feelings into precise action for the betterment of one human being. And when he cuts he knows why it's best to cut cleanly and surely. His is the unbelievable, paradoxical tenderness of the surgeon. Emily Dickinson put it this way:

> *Surgeons must be very careful*
> *When they take the knife*
> *Underneath their fine incisions*
> *Lies the culprit—Life.*

And Emily Dickinson, tough and beautiful as she was, knew the logic in being cut and dried and tender all at once. And she above all others knew it was a crime not to kill cleanly and what the Logos meant for straightforward honest living with one another on this earth.

And there sits the sensitive poet quietly in the corner, dreaming up his latest love ballad to sing sweet songs for us and posterity. The truth of the matter is he is likely to be noticing that one woman needs to blow her nose, and a man is hustling the maid who grudgingly passes the hors d'oeuvres. If he is a successful poet he will tell you the trick of it is to get rid of all the damn adjectives and stick to nouns and verbs as Jesus did in the Aramaic language he spoke, which was so lean on modifiers. For it's words like "sweetness" and "beautiful" and "lovely" that confuse people, because we all have a different concept as to what it is they mean. The idea is to be tough and come down hard on nouns and verbs, making meanings utterly clear; to use definite adjectives like "careful" or "fine" as Emily Dickinson did when she had to; and to recall that Hemingway said any good writer has to have a good shit detector.

Against all logic many middle-distance marriages are destroyed by women who feel that man has been out there freely fulfilling himself in the exciting world while she, by virtue of her sex, has been consigned to the inhibiting confines of a home and children. In fact, most work is execrably dull, and 99 percent of the men of this world reluctantly drag themselves off to unexciting places to support the commonweal at home each day, so that the wife and children will be able to survive. The idea that a job "fulfills" a life and that the long-lost or inanimate wife who raises children will somehow "find herself" out there where the fun and action is, has to be one of the biggest hoaxes ever perpetrated by the liberal mind, and could only originate on the heights of Parnassus. Such professional folks have never taken a night call, and certainly have never met a payroll. In truth, most of us go out to the drudgery of routine again and again and deal with ennui and boredom. The world is full of men who would rather be off somewhere in the Little Big Horn Mountains of Wyoming, stalking deer, but find themselves for wife and family, whom they value equally with themselves, maintaining the job as safety director or night watchman at the corner bank. Most of us are grateful that even a blind sow turns up an acorn sometimes, and those rare sometime acorns are what all of us live for. When asked once whether or not he believed in drugs, the great and glamorous Frank Sinatra replied he was for anything that got you through the night. So much for the drudgery of his work. It is indeed a long time between drinks. In a Christmas column entitled "Visions of Sugarplums" for *Newsweek*, George Will put it this way:

Play, and toys, are increasingly important to adults. Most work, in law or medicine or teaching, as on an assembly line, is repetitive. But variety is inexhaustible in play. Almost all work has almost always been drudgery. What is new is that many people are surprised by the drudgery. They have believed that all of life, and *especially* work, can be fun, or, in the current argot, "self-fulfilling." Such a strange idea could only come from institutions of higher learning, and when it is refuted by reality, people assuage their disappointment by turning with awesome intensity to the search for fun in consumption. In affluent societies, most people have acquired the "necessities" (*very* broadly construed), so the consumption that refreshes, briefly, is the consumption of adult toys.

For a proper life perspective at forty it's most important for woman to have experienced this work-world drudgery at first-hand, and preferably at a young, premarital age. Many women who burst forth, wide-eyed and exuberant at forty, to attend endless seminars and consciousness-raising sessions are astounded that the stars don't shine forth each day to lighten up their lives. Somewhere along the line a woman has had to have experienced work for the hard discipline it is, the annoying people you have to put up with, the errors in auditing and the typos and the rejection slips and the people who are trying to beat the system by trading on your sympathy. If she does not have this to recall while she enters her term of motherhood, she will wholly misunderstand what her husband and the men about her are involved in doing for her every day. Her imagination as she prepares the meals and cares for the children is apt to grow out of all proportion to the reality of a world filled with sweat and agony more often than the fulfillment of "finding herself" that she feels her friendly psychiatrist has promised her. She had best have been there while young when the pus had to be drained in the middle of the night or when someone had to be pronounced dead. Because if she has not had the experience that life is earnest and life is real, her focus by age forty becomes aberrant and her aspiration level unhealthily out of proportion to what achievement really means. Fame, after all, is a young person's desire, and she had best have learned this early by working long fruitless hours. There is no more eloquent expression of this sentiment than in Rainer Maria Rilke's admonition to a young poet. Rilke, who has been called Germany's greatest poet since Goethe, addresses himself ostensibly to poets, but like all good poets he is speaking to all of our lives:

Alas, those verses one writes in youth aren't much. One should wait and gather sweetness and light all his life, a long one if possible, and then maybe at the end he might write ten good lines. For poetry isn't, as people imagine, merely feelings (these come soon enough); it is experiences. To write one line, a man ought to see many cities, people, and things; he must learn to know animals and the way of birds in the air, and how little flowers open in the morning. One must be able to think back the way to unknown places . . . and to partings long foreseen, to days of childhood . . . and to parents . . . to days on the sea . . . to nights of travel . . . and one must have memories of many nights of love, no two alike . . . and the screams of women in childbed . . . one must have sat by the dying, one must have sat by the dead in a room with open windows. . . . But it is not enough to have memories. One must be able to forget them and have vast patience until they come again . . . and when they become blood within us, and glances and gestures . . . then first it can happen that in a rare hour the first word of a verse may arise and come forth. . . .

Many years ago I built a house, a dream house by the waters of San Francisco Bay. We had searched for months for the right old house, which she wanted to do over, and had repeatedly failed. One day we looked at each other and agreed to build, and so after many more weeks of arduous looking, one day, starry-eyed, we hit on just the right spot. I would have a room right over the water, which a writer always needs, and my wife a studio down below beneath a lovely live oak where she could pot and paint forever to her heart's content. And so we cleared the land, and as the seasons changed I became more and more involved in the frightening finances of it and my wife went deeply into the design. She worked indefatigably with the architect over details, which I would oversee and participate in from time to time while worrying about the finances of which my wife took only a peripheral view. This arrangement I thought mostly a matter of energies.

An argument started, however, when the architect suggested that I might not be as involved with the creative aspect of the house as I should be. My wife picked up on this, saying what a rare and magnificent feeling it was to build your own house and that she felt I was not as thrilled with that creativity as she was. I agreed that was probably true because my feelings could not be separated from the money involved, that is, my life's energy would necessarily be required over many years, not just to build immediately, but to sustain the generous mortgage required. In my soul I knew and was willing to announce there was too much of the poet in me to be enthralled for any length of time by material things, and a house seemed to come under that general head. Saving a human life or helping someone in distress was soul-searchingly beautiful and rewarding for me. It was a recurrent and enduring experience. But four walls always had their limits for me, and even in the opulence of the Hearst Castle, which we visited at this time, the creative experience was admirable, but very evanescent and quick to be replaced for me by my own flickering inner light, which was poetry.

There was a permanence, however, experienced by my wife as the blueprints came off the drawing board one by one, and we would sit down over drinks and excitedly go from one room to another, taking measurements and adding a beam or a stucco covering here and there. I did my best to participate and share her enthusiasm. As money matters came periodically and frighteningly to a head, I went out of my way to involve and explain them to her. She would nod her head, I thought with understanding. As time went on I gradually became inured to the process, and seeing her love and enthusiasm with each new design, began to get excited and finally cast my money worries to a logical life-long perspective as I thought befit a man.

Then came the shocker. After all the months of planning, talking, clearing the land, getting the ordinance clearance, passing all kinds of inspections, meeting with homeowners associations, and struggling through the architectural plans and my own emotional misgivings—at last we were ready to build. At this point one night my wife looked straight at me and said, "I would be happy to quit now if you would." I was shocked beyond belief. And I learned about women from her. What I had been experiencing all these months was the terrible turmoil within myself of bringing logic to bear on the inchoate feelings of building and sustaining this lovely house for my wife and family. I had finally worked through those problems to the risk to me as a man that I was now logically prepared to take. I was set within my mind and body to do this, to take this horrendous leap for the greater good of my loved ones, knowing through them I would grow to own and love this magnificent place I had to work so hard each month to deserve. And I was ready.

But the woman in my wife had not been undergoing this same agonizing process. Despite my repeatedly bringing cold facts and data to her, she had avoided them and clung to the pure, unconscious, creative love experience in our projected new home, which she had enjoyed, as immensely happy in the process as I had ever seen her. But then suddenly when the logic of putting it all together, taking the first big steps to build, became a reality, she had frightening misgivings and was ready to cast all aside and quit. She had not worked through the process in a logical way to integrate thought and feeling. Despite the exposure to tough thinking, she had clung only to the joy of it, avoided the tough logistics of it. Years later when that marriage came apart she referred to that lovely place as a mausoleum, while I, who had invested so much of my life's thought and feeling, had grown to love it as my very own. And when I left, as it was then my traditional responsibility as a man to do for the greater good of the children, I was heartsore and broken as seldom in my whole life for any mere place, while she moved from it easily, with relief, as if she had never integrated the experience within herself.

It is important to act on life and not let life act on you, to control and be the master of your fate as far as is conceivably possible in this world of chance and ill fortune. And this means largely anticipating events and how you are likely to respond to them. Being prepared does not necessarily have to do with success in any endeavor. Ability does not guarantee prosperity. But being unprepared almost always ensures failure, because any success you then achieve must be the result of luck, which is rare and unpredictable at best. Branch Rickey, the famous baseball executive, once said, "If you have talent and work hard, luck is what's left over." And it should be.

Woman, who at forty has learned that so much has come to her in her life by simply waiting, must no longer make waiting a method of achievement. She must learn to act and act in a logical and enlightened manner and not be motivated by the fear of failure, which is, after all, only the other side of success. This means thinking in advance about contingencies, making lists, flow sheets of possibilities, recording levels of meaning, and putting forth game plans that include principles of fair play. In the matter of stress, she must face it headlong and combat it in the only successful way stress can ever be combated: (1) isolate the stress, name it, describe its particulars, understand it clearly; (2) pick an area of the problem that you can possibly do something about, concentrate on that, know it thoroughly; and (3) act on it. In this way she will learn to integrate thought and feeling habitually and will be astounded at her own ability to feel and control her life as time goes on. Above all, she should no longer run from tough decisions and allow others to make them for her. She can and should weigh and consider other opinions, but the soul-searching and agonizing final product must now be her own. She must no longer concern herself with another's approbation to the exclusion of her own, she must make distinctions, honor nuance and compromise, but always be motivated by the joy of winning and no longer by the fear of losing. This requires leaving the unconscious state for the higher road of logic, and it is her tough but rewarding job at this point.

Once, during the throes of my divorce, I sat in my psychiatrist's waiting room watching the Watergate hearings on television. At precisely five minutes past the hour the psychiatrist came out and sat down and without a word began looking at the TV proceedings with me. The two of us sat there silently, not saying a word, and spent the entire sixty-five dollar hour just watching TV in his waiting room. There on the screen was the usual parliamentarian atmosphere, the committees and subcommittees, the motions, the caucuses, the counseling, the votes on whether to take a vote on this or that issue, the interrogation of duly sworn witnesses, all a terrible bore, but obviously and unquestionably a necessary process. There was little progress and little more than the establishment of a few preliminary rules when I suddenly noticed the hour was up because another patient had rung the bell and come in. As I got up to go, the psychiatrist pointed to the TV screen and said, "Can you ever imagine women conducting themselves in that kind of manner?" It was the only thing he said to me that entire hour. But I noticed in parting the other patient who heard him speak looked at him angrily. She was a well-dressed woman about forty years old.

The clever point, apparently not lost on either of us patients that day, was the inherent respect man has for institutions and the burning necessity for them, whereas for woman, institutional respect is definitely an acquired taste. Part of the developing Logos is to realize that the history of successful human relationships in civilized societies has largely been the history of procedure. Formal and particularized institutions have painstakingly grown up to protect people and provide them certain freedoms in their person. There are reasons for them, based on precedent, which admittedly vary tremendously from culture to culture, but nevertheless stem from the Logos of holding the fabric of society to certain rules and regulations to promote what is considered the greater good. The law, therefore, is the Logos, and the law not surprisingly is preeminently a masculine profession, just as nursing and medicine tend to be a nurturant or feminine field. Psychiatrists have repeatedly told me that their hardest patients to deal with have been lawyers, be they male or female, because they are forever suspicious of the feeling function and the unconscious as a solution to any problem, which to them must always have a logical answer to be acceptable or it is not an answer at all. And it is just that apparent lack of feeling, this total disregard of her unconscious strength, that frightens women away from the Logos of institutionalization, lest once again she lose her strength as a loving person in the cold statistical impersonalization out there of rules and procedure.

Nevertheless, she must involve herself in the Logos for her own good, for understanding her business, her city, her world. She needs it and craves it desperately and will not be fulfilled without the painful risk involved in getting it. She must overcome her fear of it. In doing so she will soon awaken to realize that church and school and state exist for a reason that has to do with the greater good of all of us, and the regulations, often petty and overdone, are conceived as an aid to protect her self-interest, even as they have to be studied and logically revised along the way to be helpful. As Lincoln said, "As times are new, so must we think and act anew." Because, to repeat the point, the history of civilizations has largely been the history of procedure, painstakingly dull, odious, drab procedure. The famous Mayflower Compact is a perfect example of this process at work.

So for man and woman alike, it is our unconscious and our conscious fulfillments respectively that need attention and mutual appreciation at this time of life. It is not astonishing that a forty-year-old woman is likely to become excited by an evening of committee work, while her husband, having realized the futility in this activity, finds surprising satisfaction in the finite washing of that last dinner dish and putting the kids to bed. He never wants to go out; she always does. Instinctively, he's had enough of one, she enough of the other. Both are trying to fill their lives with what seems to them to be missing, and both should appreciate the process that is occurring in the other and enter in to understand and provide for that growth to take place. It is an occasion for allowing love by realizing the need the other is experiencing for the wholeness of life.

Pervading all this apparent incongruency and incompatibility is the never-to-be-forgotten realization that man and woman each possess something the other needs and wants badly. In the zeal just to get things done and achieve their personal journey, people at forty frequently shut out this primal need for one another and pursue their ends with theoretical knowledge that removes them from the feeling that they really need each other and still represent the essential complementary force in their mate's development. For woman, however much she may be struggling, the man in her life is still a shining light of Logos to which in the graver moments she must and will repeatedly return. To that same man times will come when the warm, nurturant mother-force of her natural, unconscious self will be necessary to soothe him against the terrible conscious friction of the world. And because we as natural men and women embody these qualities, it is our nature to crave them and need them again and again, even as we wake with the brightness of the sun each day and dive down into the swampy darkness each night. And so they are not to be denied, not to be excluded in our metamorphosis, but to be lovingly titrated one against another till we are each filled within our sex with the beautiful gender of our opposite.

It was Aristotle who said that temperance in all things is the one cardinal virtue requisite to a successful life. Thus, the man struggling to disallow much of his stringent and constricting Logos must not become an unconscious Bowery bum eating out of bean cans beneath the Brooklyn Bridge, claiming he is at last in touch with ultimate values. This kind of overkill will not enhance his masculinity one iota, merely divest him of the responsibility that is the burden of his manhood. It will not teach him to be more tender, more considerate, more feeling, more nurturant and loving, it will only carry him beyond the necessity of having to involve himself in the pain of developing and caring in a loving way. He cannot run nude across the Sierra foothills after each available sensuous experience and convincingly claim he is in touch with his unconscious. He dare not suddenly make a career of combing the Big Sur beaches in search of shells while surreptitiously hustling poon tang. He must realize the little things of preening and polishing that are the daily, almost delicate, feelings of the feminine side he has neglected. But in the process he must not become female or self-destructive, but rather enhanced in his ability to love.

And woman must not overextend her Logos lest she neglect what is her essential strength and firmament. She must not become too logical or she will lose the blush of love. One of the crimes of liberation has been too much emphasis on intellect, on intelligence, for this merely divorces woman from the side of her nature that loves. She becomes "too into her head" to function in the sexual, often motherly manner which is nature's duty for her. Women all over this country have equated the Logos with the intellect and have destroyed by the process of thought the process of feeling their sexuality. A man and a man's member become things to be thought about, analyzed, or deliberated over, as if there were some syllogism to erection or orgasm, rather than the natural flow of her marvelous sexual self. Women who are too intellectual not only destroy their feeling tone, but destroy their ability to love and create the needs for love they so desire and crave as part of their essential self. Physiologically, the male has a hard time sublimating the tension in his prostate or testicles, repeatedly brought about by the millions of sperm swarming inside the confines of his constricting sacs. It is hard for his mind to cut off huge midday erections, and midnight ejections by using logarithmic thought as a substitute. But thinking woman has a considerably easier time of drying up and shutting out all impulses to sexuality, if she chooses. And many women, so bright and accomplished in that same logarithmic fashion, simply shut down and exclude their wonderful nurturant self. It can be done with relative ease. Such women claim this is their option on the Logos. Nor does anybody doubt their ability or right to guard the Unknown Soldiers tomb at Arlington, fly commercial nonstops, try cases before the Supreme Court, become an atomic physicist, run a department store or a steamship line. All well and good. But not if the cerebration excludes their essential, unconscious sexuality and destroys this in the process. It is not intended that the developing Logos in woman place her precisely where man is, when by the time he has reached the age of forty he has so often risked impotence by the overuse of the powers of his thought. When woman becomes too objective too soon she destroys herself, her very strength, by masculinization through misdirected Logos and runs the risk of becoming asexual. In this way she might just as well not be woman. Unfortunately, with increasing frequency, it is anorgasmic woman, too intellectually involved, who is destroying many human relationships, especially marriage. In any given case it may be right for her, but it is wrong for her soul and her nature.

Need we even ask, then, if women should join men in military combat? The question is really moot as now posed in our society where feminist pundits are clamoring women can perform just as well as men, and machismo men are clamoring they can't. Hell, you can train chimpanzees to orbit the earth, and that adorable Russian bitch Laeka was the very first astronaut hero long before men and women went into space. Creativity is a congenital gift, but you can *train* human beings to do almost anything from plumbing to typing to surgery, and above all else, the military is a matter of training. The thirty-inch army regulation stride can be learned or modified for women. The upper-body strength superiority of men can be altered by lighter fighting weaponry in small arms. Women's relative extreme temperature intolerance can be altered by clothing, the hourglass configuration of the female body can be made to fit into all manner of new vehicles, and she can even study karate instead of boxing for the good of the breast. In a pushbutton war why require women to do thirty-five pushups, as men must, when eighteen is enough? What's the difference if the Pentagon measures female recruits at only 55 percent the muscle strength and 67 percent the endurance of men? The Army can train women to do almost anything, including using a special disposable cardboard tube that will enable her in the field to urinate standing like men without undressing or even revealing her wet urethra.

The question is not women's ability to kill or talent to participate in combat warfare, the question is whether the shit-piss-fuck ribald billingsgate and deadly offal of the trenches of the Somme, Mount Suribachi, Pork Chop Hill, or Da Nang are her milieu and best serve her human nature. For women have always been the keepers of our civilization, the chalice of love and the family, and in the dark ages, along with the Church, it was women alone who preserved our cultural accomplishments and handed them on to future generations while men conducted the odious necessity of war. It was women, not men, who stuck by Jesus in the end. Again, what is at issue is woman's soul. Writing in *Newsweek*, George Will puts it beautifully for us:

The question is not just, or even primarily, whether women are physically "tough" enough. The question, at bottom, is whether this society wants participation in war's brutality broadened to include women.

Society is a seamless web and cannot anticipate all the consequences of abandoning an ancient practice that is deeply felt and subtly related to some of our civilization's best expectations. The almost instinctive and universal exemption of women from combat draws a line against the encroachment of violence upon havens of gentleness. It confers upon women a privilege of decency. It has been inseparably involved in the organic growth of societies committed to such things as the sanctity of the family, and civilian supremacy. Before a nation breaks that cake of custom, it should have a better reason than the presumption that the settled practice of civilization is, suddenly, anachronistic.

As a boy attending a very strict and classically oriented prep school, I used to complain to my teachers that having to know every line in Caesar's *Commentaries* was absurd and only ruined the beautiful overview of the work of art by disrupting the flow. My criticism never varied, but the answer was always the same whether it was math, history, English, religion, or Latin. To know the particulars of *King Lear* was to progress to the general. Even death got more interesting and less frightening the more you knew about it. And that would be true of love one day too, so exacting and inevitable the particulars, in which male and female will come gradually together in that long journey.

TEN

THE LAW
OF BALANCE

What a man knows at fifty that he did not know at twenty is, for the most part, incommunicable ...

—*Adlai Stevenson*

WILLIAM CARLOS WILLIAMS, an American hero, the doctor-poet, was fond of saying women were his energy and men were his inspiration. This was a real switch in perspective for the years of the twenties and thirties of this century, for when I was young the image of a woman being man's inspiration was the popular myth. Movies were made of it, songs sung to it. There was always a man gazing at a woman, singing into her eyes while seeing only himself. But the poet was doubtless closer to the truth. Because if anything characterizes woman at fifty it is the tremendous surge of energy that seems to have been welling up inside her for years to be used at this precise moment of life. And yet what, in fact, is climacteric woman to do? The energy is there, welling up inside, urging her onward and outward. She must do something. And she usually does.

Recently I was watching a television commercial plugging the new West Coast spectator sport of volleyball. The commentator was a woman who observed that, while modern men and women now both make money, it is still generally women who direct how it is to be spent. Therefore, the volleyball pitch was directed at women, and to this end the vigorous mixture of the sexes on the teams was emphasized to the exclusion of male or female play alone. It was the commentator's point that there would be no problem in arousing the young of both sexes to attend the game, but the audience to attract was the middle-aged woman from whom all family blessings flowed, since she ruled the money-spending aspects of our society. When prognosticators predicted to Winston Churchill that women would rule the world by the year 2100, he replied, "Still?"

What gives a woman at fifty this immense energetic power is a sense of the liberation at last from the confines of her own body, at least her exclusively female functioning body, and from the strictures of childrearing. Taken together, these two have a liberating effect that produce an immense flow of available energy. Any male who has ever had a mother-in-law has probably felt the full force of this flow.

Most mothers-in-law are in their fifties and descend on a young marriage with an ebullience that shocks. They don't come visiting as live-in parasites, as dependent dollies, as clinging vines—most of them are there, by God, to help out. And help they do with a vengeance. Both of my mothers-in-law from two different marriages arrived dressed within an inch of their lives for their first visit shortly after my marriage (within three weeks). Within an hour of their arrival they had donned old clothes and were scrubbing the oven and reconstructing all the beds. They were there to organize the new house and give the benefit by fiat of their immense experience in domestic arrangements. If a little later you managed to go away for a weekend, they would announce upon your return that your eighteen-month-old son had been suddenly (and completely!) toilet trained, Deus ex machina! If you had an idea for a quiet evening out, you'd return with your wife to find her mother papering the downstairs bathroom. If it was merely conversation, you would get it full tilt and with expertise. If it was errands that had to be run, they would be run at a gallop. The traditional mother-in-law gag is invariably directed at somebody who has come to interfere, to fix things up, to polish the silver, rearrange the furniture, not some middle-aged bump on a log or clinging vine who is a burden because she's another mouth to feed. No, middle-aged mother-in-law is Little Miss Fixit grown up, bursting with helpful hints in the bedroom and out, ready to translate everything into action. My own astonishment at this exuberance must have been the same as that of most young (or middle-aged) married men. And my own adjustment was probably the same—courtesy, but a good distance, so that the juggernaut could pass by as peacefully as possible and one day perhaps leave life quiet again. The middle-aged man slumps pensively in his chair, chin in hand, toilworn and worried about himself, his family, the attrition of years. But not the woman. She senses her time has arrived, and she is full of life and ideals and means to be up and about and out there doing something about it. Mother-in-law bursts forths with energy because nature is now on her side. But she does have one more hurdle to overcome.

The female climacteric, the menopause, differs from that of the male in that it is much more chemically based. It is true that the dwindling of testosterone production in the male accounts for diminution in sexual drive, but this is at best a very gradual, often imperceptible loss. So much so, as we shall see, that middle-aged male impotence should be presumed to be psychogenic until proven otherwise. Few other areas in medicine will allow such an approach, where you can first safely presume a nonorganic cause for dysfunction over the organic possibilities. But menopausal woman contends with the very real effects of the dying ovaries. This is essentially the loss of the effect of estrogen on the female body. As we have seen, this effect is ubiquitous and accounts for all those attributes we have come to know as feminine. The tone of the skin, the color in the cheeks, the fullness of the breasts, the integrity of the bones, the retention of body fluids, the capillary circulation, the maturation of the genitalia, are but a few of the functions diminished as estrogen lessens. Above all estrogen gives woman a "sense of well-being" without which depression can engulf and immobilize her. And so the hurdle of menopause, woman's final release from her cyclical self, requires an organic understanding. Estrogen may be a necessary ingredient as replacement therapy.

Many women cease to menstruate abruptly and bring down a sudden climacteric upon themselves that is wholly unanticipated. Most women do have some merciful warning by irregularity of periods and most of them would do well to prepare themselves for the change. The hot flashes experienced are nothing more than the uneven spasmodic secretions of estrogen from the dying ovaries, manifested by sudden circulatory changes. Estrogen treatment directed at this and other symptoms is merely intended to smooth out the estrogen release, allow it to diminish gradually, so that the normal atresia of the ovaries can take place. In the voluminous medical advertising that crosses a doctor's desk is the recurrent image of a fifty-year-old woman kicking up her heels with her skirt high above her head. The caption, pushing some particular sort of estrogen therapy, always reads, "The life of the party right through the menopause." The well-taken point to be made with menopausal woman is, unlike the male, her symptoms are likely to be organically based, and she should not feel her spells of depression and weeping are necessarily caused by a deranged psyche for which her brain is responsible. Treatment with estrogen will help remove the dark clouds. Estrogen has a specific tonic effect on the female at the climacteric, for which there is no analogy in the male.

I am fortunate to work in one of the venerable old hospitals of San Francisco, which grew up originally as a women's and children's hospital, although it has long since expanded to include all manner of cases. With the original charter, over a hundred years ago, was established an exclusive Lady Board of Directors, which persists as a unique phenomenon in American hospital administration. Most of these two dozen ladies are approaching middle age. They have all been carefully screened, highly selected, are eminently qualified for their responsibilities. Certain characteristics emerge from studying them at work over the past twenty years that bear out Virginia Woolf's observation in *A Room of One's Own*:

The nerves that feed the brain would seem to differ in men and women, and if you are going to make them work their best and hardest, you must find out what treatment suits them.

One is struck by the time and energy these women give to the job. They will work night and day volunteering their lives for what they consider a worthwhile cause. They hold meetings morning, noon, and night to serve "the health needs of the community." They man an office that is available to any member of the hospital with any complaint at any time, and are in constant liaison, not only with the multiplicity of hospital services within, but the crucial night and day needs of the community without. Their intelligence and dedication is exemplary, the envy of many other institutions. The one quality that strikes you about these women is their endurance.

At a very young age the female learns to say no in such a way that her yeses will have more meaning. As keeper of the keg it places her in a natural judicial role that gives her great authority. It gives her an added emotional clout when finally she does agree to something with a man, who probably has already been exhausting himself in an effort to please her. Unfortunately, this youthful posturing can become habitual, a life-long game, and continue in many women as a character weakness well into middle age, by which time nay-saying should always be straight talk and not a confusing juvenile patina. Woman's job is to end this game at fifty and come clean. Woman's temptation, the sentiment within that she must be in constant struggle against, is expressed in *The Woman Who Lived in a Prologue* in this quote from Elio Vittorini:

But we're not satisfied with what we ourselves have learned about the world and about ourselves. We're always waiting for a stranger to come and tell us something more. And "something more" means "the rest of it," and that's what we need most; we miss it. So go ahead stranger! . . . tell her what she herself is, beyond what she already knows she is . . . her life, her years, her great expenditures of self, what of herself is honey and what is gall on her tongue, the hunger she has, and the hunger she sees.

Such knowledge, such approbation, comes strictly from without, is only tentative, is superficial, and is to be ultimately resisted when beneficent nature has now provided her with the true key to future excellence. She must not be content merely to accept this gift and become part of the vacuous ambience of life.

That confused, hence confusing, ambient woman was so much a part of my childhood in the Cumberland Valley of Pennsylvania! This lush valley is the northerly extension of Virginia's lovely Shenandoah where the early summer sun casts some of the most beautiful spectral colors in all America. But the smaller Cumberland even outdoes Virginia's splendor, translating the summer ground into a fertile crescent of some of the best soil in all the world. And this I can vouch for, because when I was growing up the Cumberland Valley was one beautiful rolling lawn after another, the result simply of mowing back the weeds. Everybody had a gorgeous lawn and on these lawns were given an endless stream of lemonade parties. It was common for them to occur at least thrice weekly all summer, with people scattered in groups of threes and fours over several lovely green acres. Into this milieu, in magnificent flowing magenta, or flowered silk print with radiant white-brimmed hat to match, was injected the ambient woman. My mother was such a person, dashing from here to there amid laughter, scuttling conversations, pausing only for effect, constantly on the move as if she were some essential angelic catalyst. She was, of course, what I later came to know as "a hostess." One of the many 1930s divine busybody hostesses as it happened. I recall once tiring at one of these noxious affairs, trying to keep up with mother for my own essential needs, and I suddenly grabbed a pink sash that was hanging decorously from her waist and loudly demanded, "Please tell me what the hell you are doing!" She looked down at me as if from heaven and replied, "Oh, I am merely circulating." It wasn't till years later, reading the urbane poet Wallace Stevens one afternoon, that I discovered my mother, the consummate, ambient middle-aged woman. Stevens grew up in nearby Pennsylvania and knew the same garden-party milieu and hostess genre very well. In "The Pleasures of Merely Circulating" he brings it all home beautifully, describing first the spacy hostess, then the men's nonsensical heavy-handed talk, then the women's worthless gossip, ending with wonderful instructive satire:

> The Garden flew round with the angel,
> The angel flew round with the clouds,
> And the clouds flew round and the clouds flew round
> And the clouds flew round with the clouds.

Is there any secret in skulls,
The cattle skulls in the woods?
Do the drummers in black hoods
Rumble anything out of their drums?

Mrs. Anderson's Swedish baby
Might well have been German or Spanish,
Yet that things go round and again go round
Has rather a classical sound.

There is, of course, a lesson here for all of us from Stevens, but there is a special admonition for the middle-aged female to make better use of her time. A word to the wise is sufficient. Much more is required.

What strength of character is called for in many situations for middle-aged woman is what is demanded of the surgeon when he finishes a hopeless cancer operation that is wholly unexpected in its results. The family which he has misled in preoperative conversation now sits outside in the waiting room, just beyond the operating room doors, waiting for the expected good news. Now he must leave the sterile security of his surgery and painfully go out and sit down and tell them eye to eye just what happened, where he was mistaken, what went wrong, and what can be done. That is the strength of character that is required. Nothing less will do. A woman editor, for example, can do a thousand things to show she is a mature middle-aged woman worthy of dealing with sensitive writers. She can suggest other editors, suggest agents, recommend some recompense, carefully return an entire manuscript with comments, make an explanatory phone call extending her sympathy and apologies with the clear message that she tried, so that you believe she did. It doesn't matter that none of this is customary in her field of endeavor. We are concerned here with the fact of middle-aged woman's personal fulfillment as a human being, and that requires much more than the rudiments of a cold industry in which there are no promises worth noting. It requires that her own promises ring true, that even in failure her honesty and dignity are what you are convinced of. By middle age every person knows that ability does not necessarily mean prosperity. We all know, along with Hamlet, how "Circumstances do seem to conspire against us." And so we accept this as part of the package. It is never the fact of the knife that is bad, it is when it is unmercifully used. An editor, a good critic, in the words of Alexander Pope in his great "Essay on Criticism," should "fan the poet's fire." This requires an honesty and kindness based on straight talk and truth that should not mislead. Above all, it means oxygen and clean air to allow that fire to burn. And this is a matter of character. She simply cannot opt for the dark side of a life when the light is what is needed. Commerce alone does not justify such machinations, or make her feel good.

Because of woman's generally healthier state from beginning to end, life insurance policies on her life run at a consistently lower premium. By age fifty, man's premium jumps perceptibly ahead of hers because of his susceptibility to stressful disease states to which she is relatively immune. As we have seen, these include such diseases as heart attacks, lung cancers, stomach ulcers, high blood pressure, brain tumors, strokes—nearly all diseases except immune disease, for example, arthritis. Woman at fifty, of course, is peculiarly susceptible to breast cancer, which will strike one in ten American women. Men have the counterpart in carcinoma of the prostate, which some statistics say is present in 30 percent of all male autopsies after the age of sixty. If a male lives long enough, survives the stressful diseases of middle life, the chance that he will develop prostatic carcinoma is exceedingly high.

What this serves to remind us is that the female in her fifties is an exceedingly healthy, vigorous, active, and capable human being. While her man may be riding the full flowing tide of his maturity, his potential is nowhere near as great at this point as hers. She is still a creature of the future if she wants to be, whereas he is only a creature of the present. Nature has now provided her with the key to future excellence. You can prove this to yourself some evening when you are out to dinner. On one side of you may be a young couple with an elderly couple on the other side. Across from you sits a mid-dle-aged group, men and women in their fifties. With the young couple, the man is apt to be doing most of the talking while the young woman listens or occasionally interrupts with opinions or questions. Generally, she is content to let him go on while she re-mains part of the ambience. The old couple on the other side sits there quietly not saying a word. They stare at each other or stare into the middle distance. The young couple can't imagine, and deplores, that the time will come when they are old and they may sit there without a thing to say to each other. How sad it must be to be old! The old couple, on the other hand, know that it is no fun to be young like those two struggling to communicate. When you really know and love someone there is nothing more that words can say. What was all the fuss about anyway? But what of the two middle-fif-ties couples across from you? You will note the men are quieter now and the women's voices are shriller and more pervasive. One is plan-ning a trip to the Greek Isles, laughing about wanting to see the Isle of Lesbos. The other has just ordered the waiter to take back her husband's entrée because that's not the way he likes his prime ribs. The man, a successful county judge, was reluctant to chastise the young waiter unnecessarily. One notices that the women are in charge, quick now on the ascendancy, and one sees that the men could be happy with pipe and slippers and sustaining what mostly is already done.

The central event in the life of every civilized person over fifty years of age still has to be the Second World War. A boy born in 1926 was fourteen in 1940 and had grown accustomed to what peo-ple called "a depression" all around him, as well as the dark clouds of brutality and lawlessness that had come over the world from beyond our shores. I stood on the darkened boardwalk of Atlantic City after dinner with my frightened parents and gazed seaward through binoc-ulars to see ships explode and sink right off our shore, destroyed by slimy Nazi submarines. And my friends were already spread all over the world—Africa, Alaska, Egypt, Norway, China, South America, New Zealand, Scotland, Panama, Hawaii, the Philippines—and some of them were soon dead or dying everywhere imaginable on the earth. The war not only divided this century in half chronologically, not only dispersed it geographically, not only split these hundred years atomically, but did something much more disruptive to our moral fiber. For all that young adolescent knew, standing there on that boardwalk, was that life was a miserable place and all you had that made it barely meaningful were certain nebulous but necessarily very real feelings and principles to sustain you. These principles came to things like thrift, honesty, steadfastness in adversity, helping others like yourself, and, above all, courage. It was important to have family in these times and the value of intelligence unassumingly conveyed. There was real righteousness in loving your country and being willing, as a matter of duty, to die for a cause as dear as liberty. Above all, the life of that young person was pervaded with a spiritual dimension, which he was yet too sophisticated to willingly call God, but which made his heart sing and called him armed with what was really right to challenge all the world's ills. And nowhere today, in anyone over fifty who confronted head-on the near-destruction of all that was just and beautiful in this world, is there one who can ever feel otherwise than that it was and is these verities that sustain us in the darkness of our life. At fifty the spirit takes on new and fuller meaning, the meaning of our soul.

The great discovery of our protracted middle age is that the law of the psyche is the law of balance. This is the secret, the essential lesson of psychiatry so poorly and often so grudgingly conveyed. One of my favorite framed magazine rejection slips reads, "Everyone here agrees this is a fantastic article. But I'm afraid it's too balanced for us." No wonder ulcer formation is so high in publishing; trying to strike that proper imbalance!

For imbalance is contrary to our nature—it's likely to drive you crazy. We don't need a Watergate or a Middle East crisis to tell us that if we let one part of our psyche get out of hand, its counterpart will always complain. If we don't get enough rest, we become cranky and irritable. If we get too much sleep, we become slothful. Too much desert, we see mirages. Too much noise and crowd and we close ourselves out. Most important, if we don't allow the female side of ourselves to emerge, the male side will complain. What's good for the goose is good for the gander. If you want to confuse the hell out of your psychiatrist (and who doesn't) go one week and be as profane as a guttersnipe and next week give him the Beatitudes by heart. One week give him lusty hard-core and the next week the Venus de Milo. One week your mind, the next week your body. Because, you see, all he's looking for is wholeness, a balance between these naturally competing systems that require tolerance and expression or they will complain. Once a patient came to me, looked me straight in the eye, and complained that sparks flew out of his ass when he had intercourse. I thought this was marvelous and saw no need to change things, but he returned in a week to say that his wife thought the sparks she kept seeing over his shoulder were abnormal and disconcerting to her own completion. I had them both come in and explained to them that I saw no special surgical problem and they should continue to enjoy each other. I said it sounded to me like a gift, that sparks should fly out any part of you while making love, let alone your ass. They felt I didn't believe them and vowed to return in a week with a specimen of one of them caught in a bottle. And sure enough, in one week they returned with one of those Skippy Peanut Butter bottles emptied to the last lick. It had been carefully relabeled "Spark for Doctor," with the date of the catch underneath. Smiling and laughing proudly like two screaming banshees they confidently presented me with a sealed bottle. I held it up to the window light and, of course, saw nothing. Afraid to open it, I suggested they see another doctor, a specialist down the hall who was a psychiatrist. Late that same day I got a call from him. All he said was, "These two people you sent me today are *unbalanced.*" He was serious.

When I proselytize for balance in our sexual selves at middle age I am not advancing the cause of bisexuality—quite the opposite. It is most emphatically, to reiterate, to teach us tolerance for our own inherent ambivalence and enhance the sexes coming together in the delightful, incomparable way they have always needed each other. In

Kentucky, a morgue attendant once put it for me in the most memorable way: "It don't matter where you get your appetite as long as you eat at home." Carl Jung would have agreed the man had a good handle on middle age.

When one hears that someone at fifty is at the height of his creative or professional powers, what is meant is that at no other time of his life will the flowering of mind and body be so congenially disposed. He will in after years become brighter and wiser in the ways of perfidy and taste for excellence, but he will soon disintegrate in his ability to do much about it. It is early fall or fall in all its ripeness at fifty when a man can think and feel as perhaps at no other time. He is filled with the confidence that only comes from being certain of what you do not know. It was Adlai Stevenson speaking to the seniors at Princeton University in March of 1954 who put it this way:

What a man knows at fifty that he did not know at twenty is, for the most part, incommunicable. . . . The knowledge he has acquired with age is not the knowledge of formulas, or forms of words, but of people, places, actions—a knowledge not gained by words but by touch, sight, sound, victories, failures, sleeplessness, devotion, love—the human experiences and emotions of this earth and of oneself and other men; and perhaps, too, a little faith, and a little reverence for things you cannot see.

Self-knowledge, which seems to jell at fifty, is best described as a knowledge of the art of the possible with the material, mind, and soul you've been given to work with. A patient once told me being fifty meant waking up one morning and finally realizing you weren't going to be president of the bank. This realization of self not only temporizes ambition with a merciful sort of resignation but gives tremendous impetus to what you are confident you *can* do, whether it be pumping gas or courting women or preaching the Sunday sermon at the First Presbyterian Church. In another way it is a stylistic comfort with what has become your particular mode with the world. This is primarily a knack of selecting detail.

What an executive sees in his underlings is a tremendous confusion of facts and figures as the answer to administrative problems. What the surgeon who is teaching the young to operate sees is a plethora of technical talent and energy and only a modicum of judgment for the real-life issue at hand. And the seasoned choreographer sees boundless energy wholly undirected, as the ancient politician knows what strings to pull and doesn't have to be out early in the cold of a Battle Creek, Michigan, morning in November to shake hands with the cereal makers of Captain Crunch. And Arthur Ashe at age thirty-six could still compete with the youngsters because he's a master strategist. All this comes to is a selective process that has gone on within the mind that has purged itself over time of the extraneous nonsense needed to perform a given task.

Man at fifty selects out what is important. He is able to go to the heart of the matter and pick out the important kernel needed for decision and he is able to act on it. Just as a writer must write for years simply to lavage himself of all the bad words, so he has purged himself of the excess baggage, factual and emotional, that will waste time, thought, and energy. If he is a tool-and-die worker, he works his lathe with minimal tension, if a lawyer, he knows when to object. In this he is aided by now being somewhat beyond the jungle of cutthroat competition that he has already struggled through; he now owns part of the ladder. For those on the way up behind him he has understanding and a certain nostalgia for the old competitive fervor that made him a man. And his knowledge of this background goes a long way toward giving him his insights into what constitutes real excellence, as well as all the darker tricks of the trade. There is no good without bad, they are mirror images, and the knowledge of one liberates us for the greatness in the other, and the mantle of this ambivalence sits on the man at fifty in a kindly and challenging way.

The challenge, however, often leads to great misgivings, and coupled with the male climacteric, can be a time of tremendous emotional upheaval and change rivaling the conversion of the libertine Saint Augustine to a man of God or of Saint Paul on the road to Damascus. Something very serious can begin to happen to a man at fifty if he continues to pursue an essentially unrelieved work life that is not to his unconscious liking as it is to his and his family's conscious need. Thus it is that a general reconsideration of life is so common at this age, presenting problems that the honest man must assimilate, because all too often he had not foreseen them in his busy life. My father was a crackerjack trial lawyer who at this age was making, and could have gone on to make, scads of money trying law cases. Instead, he became a poorly paid county common pleas judge and labored in that tough vineyard for twelve hard years till he died, always living and dying for justice. At his funeral the flags over the state capitol building flew at half mast, the first time it could be recalled that this was done for any ordinary judge in our state, and the small church crowded in 1,500 people with not a dry eye in the place when, at his request, so intentionally filled with great good humor and irony, they quietly read the lines from Tennyson:

> Sunset and evening star
> And one clear call for me
> And may there be no moaning of the bar
> When I put out to sea.

But the Bar did moan for the loss of this great man for many years, one man who wrote scores of brilliant and still-acclaimed opinions that have been regarded as exemplary down through the years. He was a man who in middle years had had an agonizing reappraisal of the material aspect of his life and had headed off in a new direction to make his mark in a new life given up wholly for others in later years.

Thus, a man will write the book, as I am doing, that he always wanted to write. A man will start a second family, as I am doing, that he could never imagine he wanted. For a young woman who wants wall-climbing multiple orgasms, fifty-year-old men go off and have their vasectomies reversed. They will go through psychoanalysis just for the hell of it, or decide to get a camper even though they hate mosquitoes, poison oak, and outdoor defecation. One of my friends, a pharmacist, became a clown in the circus for several years, then returned to a midwestern university where he took his doctorate in clowning and now has a respectable graduate school going in that discipline.

The male climacteric is a very gradual process, but none the less very real. When impotence comes down suddenly in middle age and persists, however, it is, I repeat, almost always a psychological problem, one related to self-worth and self-esteem. Abstemiousness in sex often comes easy to a man at fifty who is able by now to throw himself into work to avoid that side of himself hungering for love. If this occurs, it usually further potentiates his impotence by cutting him completely off from the emotional part of himself. It is for this reason that Freud made the point that the real test of any adjusted person is his ability to love, and his ability to work. These two, these two abilities alone, make for a wholesome life, a love life devoted not just to mutual sexual enjoyment, but related to the events of the day, and a work life devoted not just to personal indulgence, but to the furtherance of the needs of others.

Samuel Johnson at age fifty went into a deep three-year depression. The great literary man who had compiled the magnificent first English dictionary had said of it that it "was written with little assistance of the learned, and without any patronage of the great; not in the soft obscurities of retirement, or under the shelter of academic bowers, but amidst inconvenience and distraction, in sickness and in sorrow." These dark clouds of age forty-six could no longer be hidden four years later when he assessed his life achievement at fifty. Two-thirds of his life was behind him, he felt his contributions empty as the vanity of human wishes and for days he would weep and despair of living. He made lists as a shopping housewife might to get himself going—Tomorrow: rise early, send for history book, arrange mail, scheme your life. He spent late hours carousing in taverns, reluctant to return to his empty lodgings where there was no love. What he most enjoyed—books and conversation—seemed to content him least. Then two things happened to him that turned his life around, and drew him out of the slough of despond and enabled him to go on and provide our world with one of the greatest twenty-year periods in all literature. He met James Boswell, who would one day write Johnson's biographical masterpiece, and through him he experienced the love, concern, and admiration of a young colleague. About the same time he met Hester Thrale and experienced the care, attention, and tenderness of a young woman. Together these two brought Johnson back from the brink of madness—Boswell by flattering Johnson's ego by recording endless conversations and taking him off on a trip to Scotland and the Hebrides; Hester by taking him into her home and providing the intimacy of love and prodding him to work. The result was to get Johnson out of himself and the dark brooding clouds that had been mounting for years. It was soon thereafter he wrote his noble preface to Shakespeare, a landmark in the history of literary criticism. From there it was a matter of reaching toward immortality.

Johnson, eighteenth-century literary genius, exemplifies so clearly the male climacteric as to be almost classic: a man so full of love and feeling he had spent most of his life giving himself to his work. And yet again and again the loving side of his nature would break through and complain, only to be repressed by him in work. Finally, at age fifty, the dark side of his psyche began to complain, expressed itself, and overcame him with depression. He had not allowed the balance so necessary to an integrated emotional life. Despite his generosity, his forays into love were painful and unrequited failures, and this threw him more and more into his work. This, in turn, suppressed his terrible need for love and appreciation and led to more complaints from his unconscious. He became impotent in love and impotent in work until Boswell and Thrale rescued him. Parenthetically, it should be added, that these relationships were not primarily sexual, but one of relatedness and face-to-face intimacy. These are the ingredients of the antidote to the male climacteric—warm love and respect and care—and in Johnson's case they were curative.

I once had an aged grandmother-in-law (my mother-in-law's mother) who insisted on the company of the young exclusively as she approached ninety because she said it was the only possible direction to go. But I noted often it was really much more than that. It was, just as it began in middle age with Samuel Johnson, a desire for the continued approbation, respect, and love of youth, a sense of worth well into old age for what she had done to be appreciated by those coming after her who would be undergoing the same ancient anguish and travail on life's journey. Whittaker Chambers, who wrote the twentieth-century anticommunist masterpiece *Witness*, had such a relationship with young William F. Buckley, Jr., when he was a young journalist first out of Yale. Buckley describes how Chambers, in his midfifties, detailed the inexorable fatigue unto death in fighting, Solzhenitsyn-like, the lost cause against the creeping cancer of Western communism. When Chambers died, and news of it reached Buckley at his desk in New York, the young man bent over in tears for the first time in his life. Buckley was a necessary love for Chambers, who knew that in Buckley the anticommunist fight would be carried on.

At fifty, attending a veterans pro tennis tournament, I once heard the aging great tennis player, Pancho Gonzales, remark that the only differences between himself and young pros like Bjorn Borg or Jimmy Connors were in the legs and in the eyes. The mind, he said, could make up for the eyes by anticipating the art of the possible with his opponent, but nothing could replace the legs. The net result at fifty is the triumph of quality over quantity, a certain ability to abstract the essence of a situation without going off in all directions before finally striking on a solution. In this way the businessman at fifty seems to have an uncanny ability to put his finger right on the problem, to cut through all the nonsense and go right to the heart of the deal. As a surgeon, I can now use half the number of stitches I had to use twenty years ago and get twice as good results. The trick is knowing the crucial sutures that need to be placed and wasting no time on excess energy expenditure. It is a matter of the selection of detail, the particulars that are most important, most necessary to the occasion.

Recently, I heard a dear minister friend of mine deliver an Easter sermon that I had first heard him give when we were young, twenty-five years ago. At that time he had shown as proof of the resurrection of Christ how Our Lord remained on earth following his crucifixion for forty days prior to his ascension into heaven. He went on at great length to show how (1) he had first appeared to Mary at the tomb; (2) to Peter on the way there; (3) to the two travelers on the road to Emmaus; (4) to the scared disciples gathered in the upper room; (5) to Paul on the road to Damascus; (6) to Thomas who doubted his bleeding wounds; (7) to a multitude of 500 gathered people. With each laborious point he made, he came down on a syllogism to offer historical evidence of the resurrection of the body. It was memorable, but labored, and did not really speak to the essence of the occasion. But when I heard him the second time, he quickly disposed of such points and went to the beautiful meaning of the occasion. He admonished us for being only Easter Christians, told us that love was stronger than hate, assured us the only way to transcend ourselves was to give our life away to others, and that the example of Christ was there for everyone to see. Unlike Buddha or Muhammad or most of the other great religious leaders of the world who said, follow my teachings, Jesus alone said, follow my life example and you too will have everlasting life. I thought as I listened to my friend draw out his message how marvelously cool and assured he seemed about it. There was none of the laborious pedantry of having to prove life after death to an audience, there was only a confident middle-aged man speaking in half the number of words he had used earlier telling us you will gain your life only by giving it away and here is the example living on among you in Jesus Christ to prove it. The selection of detail, the metaphoric essence, the easy precision, the commingling of thought and feeling are the deserved joys of accomplished middle-aged man.

Similarly, the sex act itself takes on new meaning because it, too, becomes more qualitative and less a matter of selfish quantitative frenzy. Young people are certain that old people have no fun, but old people are convinced that young people have no fun. The young can't ever picture their parents making love and can't imagine their enjoying it—dried-up prunes that they are. When I married my young wife, her girlfriends, casting aside all the wisdom of the ancient Greek myths in which lusty old gods were forever descending on some maiden in the glades, advised her to get some shellac to keep it up whenever I managed a hard-on. Little did they know the joy of quality, the self-control, the consideration, the unfrenzied progress, the sustained performance that comes over a middle-aged lover and is the envy of every young man. Tell them sex is better at fifty than at fifteen for all that, and more. And it gets better with age.

For most men at fifty, the perspective on money becomes very interesting. It has been said that money is the most common source of marital disagreement, even greater than arguments over the children. And certainly man on the ascent is very conscious of and sensitive to his family's money needs. This often makes for parsimonious habits in the twenties, thirties, and forties. But these saving habits are soon broken by the circumstances of the world and the needs of adolescent and college children. In short, whatever his nature, generosity is now thrust upon him and he must give to survive—not just to those about him, but to tax deductible institutions, and to the United States Government. A man at fifty need only look about him to realize that ability does not necessarily mean prosperity, that his colleagues who are equal or superior or inferior to himself have suffered good or bad luck, as much as anything else, to account for where they are. No amount of talent or industry will neutralize a cancer in the family, a crippling automobile accident, an unfair circumstantial lawsuit brought against you that goes bad. And so man gradually comes to realize not only must he give money away almost habitually to those about him, but that the earning of it is largely a matter of chance and, hence, something of a bore. I have talked to many businessmen who say they continue in business, dealing daily with thousands of dollars, simply because they know nothing else. But it is not the money as such that is important to them, as most of us outsiders would seem to think. What the businessman is excited about is pulling off the deal, making something work. This is an exercise in his own ego appeal, not an exercise primarily in finances. Charlie O. Finley's business-tycoon excitement at owning the Oakland A's is to bring a winning team to that city. It feeds his ego and gives him a

reason to be excited about his life. Financially, he'll be the first to tell
you, the venture is a failure. He could not have done it just for
money. He wants to share his excitement and talent for baseball with
others. Unfortunately, this often leads young men to call him stingy
in his contracts, and young women to seek him out as a sugar daddy.
But they take a narrow view of the likes of Charles Finley. Sure,
there's a price tag on his affections, because as a businessman that's
all he grew up knowing. But what he really wants to do with his
money is to entertain others and add to their happiness, and maybe
feed his ego by swinging a few business deals en route. The middle-
aged man of fifty is not primarily driven by the security of money,
anymore than by the fear of failure. Money has become to him the
commodity of exchange that it really is, but one that only has meaning when integrated with the feeling it serves. He knows he can drink
but one martini at a time.

At fifty, pleasure is no longer confused with happiness. The attitude of a merchant banker dealing daily with such business tycoons
and huge money matters is beautifully described by Joseph Wechsberg in his study of the famous Hambros banking family of the City
of London:

Some people will never learn the elusive technique of conversation
during lunch in an old merchant bank. One talks about everything
except the matters one really would like to talk about—such as getting a million-pound credit. The conversation is about farming,
roses, horses, politics, families. The chairman grows roses and the
deputy chairman breeds race horses. The guest unfamiliar with the
City's strange customs doesn't know that all the time he is being
carefully scrutinized—his manners, his clothes, his speech, his sense
(or lack) of humor, his attitude and personality. The general impression will eventually decide whether he's going to be backed by a
million pounds and whether any security will be demanded. This is
the merchant banker's assessment—a mixture of experience and
flair, analysis and instinct, inherited from generations of shrewdly as-
sessing ancestors. At Hambros they like to say that merchant banking is not a concrete science but an abstract art, and during lunch the

practitioners of this art seem to work at their best. By the time the butler has served the traditional fruit cake and a fine old port, there is usually unanimity in the minds of the partners about the risk—and about the client.

The attitude of the successful money-man himself is succinctly described in this obituary, lovingly written about multimillion dollar oil tycoon, William F. Buckley, Sr.:

He never compromised on the principle with which he set out fifty years ago, independence of thought and act, and had small patience with much that went on in the increasingly penned and herded world about him. He stood against that tide when he first met it and always thereafter, believing it contrary to human needs—in the oil business as in all human affairs.

He meant to make money, and succeeded, and looked on money as a fructifying agent, not as an end. To him it was the raw material of new ventures, proving an original philosophy.

Finally, in his midfifties man begins to feel the mature love of woman in all its abundance. In his contemporaries of the opposite sex is now possible all the ripeness of mature love and understanding that only an accomplished relationship can provide. This love of a middle-aged woman can be the most fulfilling experience in a man's life. It can astound and overwhelm him again like puppy love and reach unexpected depths of intimacy and mutual understanding because it is tempered by the experience of having lived most of a life and having now to face the melancholy of fall. It was during middle age that Adlai Stevenson first met Agnes Meyer, a woman near his age. Later she would own the *Washington Post*. After his first visit to her country home in upper New York State he wrote her that his visit had "worked a miracle I somehow find it hard to explain. Never before have I dissolved so utterly with another human being. I don't understand your alchemy. . . . I can't, and have ceased to try to understand, how an older woman, a total stranger, could suddenly, without at least the normal preliminaries of acquaintance, give me both feminine understanding and masculine participation, and mental provocation and moral confidence."

It was such reassurance that inspired Stevenson to run again for the presidency in 1956, almost certainly to lose again the national war hero Dwight David Eisenhower, as he did. Stevenson observed that love was the one recurrent theme of life that seemed to remain and go on forever, while all else, including two magnificent attempts to become President of the United States failed. He reminds us all that the Statue of Liberty is a lady.

ELEVEN

THE EXCITEMENT OF THE DAY

The difficult we do today, the impossible takes a little longer.
—Motto, the United States Marines

To BE INVOLVED in science is to be involved in the excitement of the present. Science is governed by method that breeds a fascinating dynamic that floods us daily with new discoveries and involves our whole society in constant change. This change may not always be good for society, but it is good for science. To be able to splice a human gene and change the makeup of man even before he's born is a frightening social possibility, but nevertheless an exciting scientific vista. Men and women of science find themselves caught up in this thrilling dynamic, sharing each other's secrets, but still ferociously trying to get to that new discovery first. A scientist's defect is apt to be the personal defect of all of us, an inappropriate and poorly developed sensitivity to feelings. But not to know about current scientific findings is not to share in the amazing daily excitement that is going on all about us. This short chapter is a glimpse of some of those exciting advances now in progress.

Current hospital laboratory studies are sometimes classified as being "invasive" or "noninvasive." Thus, there will be an invasive lab and a noninvasive lab, with reference to how the human body is approached. Invasion includes any testing beneath the skin, usually by puncturing, such as in blood tests or needle aspiration or injections of body cavities or joints, whereas noninvasion includes respiratory tests or cardiograms or even simple observation. For example, vaginal secretion collections from sexually excited females show the presence of peculiarly odoriferous short-chain fatty acids very similar to the pheromones demonstrated in higher primates. Such studies would be considered invasive of the human volunteer female subject. On the other hand, observations of coitus in the stumptail monkey would be noninvasive of the monkey subjects. Because the stumptail has a particularly prolonged coitus, both sexes can be studied carefully with reference to orgasm. Since similar consummating body rigidity, vocalization, spasm, and facial expression occur in male and female specimens alike, this is presumptive evidence of orgasm in both these primate sexes. However, such observations are subjective, unmeasurable, and noninvasive, although perhaps no less real. You almost have to ask the stumptail female. In any event such results are not as "measurable" as they are "observable" by investigators.

Observation and measurement are methods used for most human investigation today of a noninvasive character, taking the form of psychological testing. Such testing consists primarily of data gathering, and is susceptible to all the intrinsic flaws in the questions and answers of the examiners and respondents. A large element of subjectivity is necessarily present. In recent years, experimentation in sexual differences has become more invasive in the sense that brain waves and responses have been monitored and chemical blood changes recorded. Certainly, psychology in a very real emotional sense is invasive, and recording brain waves by surface electrodes in an equally real sense may be considered noninvasive. Perhaps psychological and physiological is a better semantic division of labor, if we bear carefully in mind the two are functionally inseparable, as we look at some of the new directions of research.

In the past twenty years we know that sex has come out of the closet. It is written about, read about, and gazed upon—as always— at every street corner. The question is, is it acted upon any differently? This seems to depend largely upon socioeconomic level. The ability to experience guilt-free coitus has increased markedly in less well-off groups and at a younger age. There seems to be a lessening of middle-class morality in this regard as sociosexual activities are started at a much younger age for both boys and girls. Age of masturbation and coitus have both decreased in less well-educated groups. In college freshmen, however, the incidence of virginity among males and females is not dramatically different from that of their forebears of twenty years ago, although there is a slight increase as college students progress to becoming seniors. Interestingly, when you interrogate young men and women of both high and low economic groups you find little correlation between sexual standards and meaningful or thoughtful sexual philosophy. Rigid party-line views are not held, as they once were, by males and females about sex. It is regarded more as a natural function that may or may not have yet occurred to the person or couple involved. At higher socioeconomic levels this seems to have resulted in the same degree of participation, while at lower economic levels some greater promiscuity is apparent.

Not surprisingly, promiscuity among men and women leads to permissiveness about abortion. There is a line that can be drawn in college women from love to sex to promiscuity to permissiveness about abortion. The number of times a woman or man is "in love" relates directly to the frequency of coitus, which once begun always increases, and the more it increases the more tolerant each partner becomes of the possibility of abortion. Like so much else with young people, there is no careful forethought in most of this but rather reaction to an experience; then necessity may become the mother of invention. Even in the educated, abortion is just another mode of responding to a situation, part of the available modern armamentarium, so to speak, and not profoundly based on advice or philosophy. It just is. And for that reason it is a sad fact of modern life that love leads directly to an increased tolerance of abortion by both sexes in our society.

The rhetorical question is often asked, "Why didn't Jesus write a book?" Most of the other great religious leaders of the world did just that so that their teachings would be down clearly in black and white for all to study and learn. The answer might be that Jesus knew that such writings give people a false view of love and faith and inspiration by allowing hypocritical adherence to strict codes instead of to the spiritual dimension of living. Nowhere is this barren concept of the written regulation more sterilely apparent than in our bureaucratic attempts to secularize sexual education. The proposed new curriculum in "Education of Human Sexuality" by the State Department of Education of one of our leading states recommends that children study human intercourse in the early preschool arena by age three. By age six they are to study child molestation and sexual abuse, by age nine menstruation, conception, ejaculation, nocturnal emissions. At age twelve they take field trips to the drugstore and family-planning clinics to gather data on contraceptives and begin to feel comfortable in the process. They learn that to get an abortion or use contraceptive devices is a decision wholly up to them because, under the law, they are "emancipated minors." The thought that one could not really be emancipated and yet be minor, has not struck the organizers of such programs. It is thought more important that early teenage girls learn of pelvic examinations irrespective of the mode.

The assumption behind sex education is to protect young persons from being unwittingly put upon, emotionally or intellectually, in their sex at any time. But the effect too often is to depotentiate, hence grossly secularize, the true loving essence and desire between the young, and thereby render sex at best an acceptable, healthy, physiological exercise, and unfortunately little more. We know that virgin innocence is beautiful because sex is a kind of soulful knowledge which, once embarked upon, we never abandon. And that knowledge may be of the wonderful positive essence of ourselves or it may lead us into the dark abysmal destructive side of our nature. The sex educators would have us grow up guilt-free of all sexual promiscuity, when the core of the human being has always cried out, because of inchoate sexual misgivings, for a meaning that goes far beyond that moment in the back seat or the quick one-night stand. All of us have had such mental hangovers, most particularly the young. The upshot of this has been that we teach theory that in no way alters the genuine practice of successful youthful sex, because the sexual connection the young are always seeking is to the ideal soul, and you can't legislate feelings by cerebration. The effect of sex education has been to coat the sexuality of youth with a patina of thought without substantially altering the basic problem of their really feeling gratifying sex.

In 1976, in California, there were 142,000 abortions. In 1978, the year for which the most recent figures are now available, the number approaches 200,000. In 1977 110,000 pregnancies were recorded among teenagers between the ages of fifteen to nineteen. Of these 51,000 were abortions. This means that in this country the abortion rate now runs into the hundreds of thousands, and in countries like Japan, where abortion on demand has existed for years, the number is into the millions.

Pro and anti-abortion groups spend most of their time disputing the right to life of an unborn fetus, and the right of a woman to control the destiny of her own body. Very little time and thoughtful energy is expended on the long-term effects of abortion on the female psyche, on which psychiatrists are now at last shedding increasing light. Their findings confirm those impressions of all real, organic, practicing physicians whose odious job it has always been to actually scrape women free of supposedly unwanted pregnancies.

The psychic trauma to women is often immense and correlated to the age and maturity of the woman. The fact is that young women have often used their bodies to become pregnant for secondary gain. To have an independent income, to latch onto somebody, to feel worthwhile, to get away from home, to feel needed, to really do something, to have a sense of power, to glorify motherhood—these are some of the common reasons given by teenage girls who have become pregnant. Because of the superficiality of this analysis, the immediate effects of abortion seem to be minimal. This is all the more so if a woman can be "suctioned" when she is just a few days late for her period and, although the likely possibility of pregnancy exists, she can be left to rationalize the episode as probably just an overdue period. It is when women get older that the trouble begins, often retrospective trouble.

The menses themselves give women a sense of loss, of missed opportunity. "What a waste," she is often heard to exclaim as she grows older and knows yet another ovum has gone unattended. The process is indeed a form of death, a sloughing off, a bleeding out that women are all too familiar with. And all these feelings of loss or neglect of her naturally appointed role to cease menstruation and create a new life out of her own retained blood are exaggerated a millionfold when, once in that state of potential motherhood, she relinquishes it to the cold clinical process of abortion. Prevention is one thing, but concerted loss of a process begun so close to her natural self often requires a serious repression. Suppression, the conscious intentional exclusion from thoughts of unacceptable feelings, is often insufficient for the aborted woman. She cannot cerebrate what is so integrally dear to her nature, and hence repression, a process by which unacceptable desires or impulses are excluded from consciousness and left to operate in the unconscious unassimilated, is often the result. Repression we now know is more common than not after abortion, and we know that repression sooner or later will surface as psychic complaints. An older woman, whose eighteen-year-old son has just been killed in Vietnam, comes to me complaining that God has punished her for an abortion she had had prior to his birth twenty years earlier. A swinging international airline hostess, age thirty-two, is rescued from the railing of Golden Gate Bridge after her third abortion. A married mother, age twenty-eight, becomes asexual and goes into prolonged depression after an abortion for "economic reasons" because of her marriage and job. A twenty-four-year-old nurse, who went off quietly to New York for hers, returns unable to do her job for months, is heartsore with unmanageable nightmares. In short, the psychic trauma of abortion to women is untold and immense, whatever the mitigating circumstances. This is not to deny that clearcut indications, as in cases of rape, deformity, maternal distress, contagious disease, mongolism, do lessen the medical and maternal burden considerably by rendering conscious suppression more justifiably apparent. It is merely to point out the psychic truth that woman is nature and contains within herself, very close to her soulful self, the vehicle of carrying on this life. And any breach of that natural trust carries its price in the unconscious where, over the course of time, psychic complaints may fester and eventually become manifest.

Once again this is a difference between men and women. For men are dissociated from the internal aspects of carrying the means of reproduction within themselves, and hence abortion, while a disappointment to some men, is regarded by most from a distance. Men will not blame the death of a son in Vietnam to some age-old prior abortion, or consider going off the bridge, or become impotent, or have incapacitating nightmares. Their loss, while frequently heart-felt, is at a distance from their soul compared to a woman for whom that unborn life has been carried within her very substance. Thus man suffers for woman for her abortion, while she, intending always in good faith to control her own destiny rather than to allow its natural course, comes to suffer entirely for herself as a woman. This is manifested in man by inconvenience, frustration, while in her it is manifested as often as not by deep psychic complaints and disturbances.

Response to sexual imagery is being carefully studied in men and women with reference to the different erotic reactions to noise, reading experiences, and visual stimuli. Both sexes are highly and almost equally susceptible to all such stimuli, with several notable and helpful exceptions. Women generally are more erotically aroused by sensuous noise, such as love mood music, but most particularly love talk and tender whisperings. In the matter of erotic reading women and men show about the same response, although the response is more prolonged in women and may last "chronically" in females for up to twenty-four hours. Thus the tension built up by erotic reading in women tends to require a greater controlling effort, and this effort almost always takes on the form of avoidance. Genital activity and focus is enhanced for male and female alike, and reading erotica increases fantasy, drive, and behavior as is manifested in display, masturbation, and coitus, with the difference that for women the flavor lingers longer. With visual stimuli women are somewhat less arousable than men. But this "somewhat" is only slight, and seems to be a function of exposure time, because objective signs of arousal occur about as often in both sexes to sensuous sight stimuli. Coitus, masturbation, orgasm, and fantasy are similar for the twenty-four hours following exposure. There is increased incorporation of specific fantasy into the ensuing sex activity in both sexes. Emotional tension and instability are slightly greater in women, and avoidance reactions are also greater in women, making them more uncomfortable following visual stimuli. In men and women the image may persist as long as twenty-four hours and beyond. But with sudden exposure women may tend to react negatively or not at all. Thus, with sexy slides thrown on a screen, women will tend to abhor extremes (perversions) and men enjoy or tolerate them. When the same sexual constellation is "evolved" for women in a full-length movie, it is apt to be accepted. Similarly, males may abhor a vulgar nightclub act that women find completely acceptable, if the ambience has been properly prepared. This "slowness" on the part of the female may be cultural, because females are trained to be cautious and act with restraint in matters of sex. On the other hand it may be the reflex quickness of the male "hunter instinct" that responds, or the slow "socializing necessity" of female sexuality that's involved   whatever. The fact is men and women react *almost* to the same extent and definitely in the same direction to sexual stimuli of noise, reading, and vision.

Sex drive has been measured in terms of every imaginable parameter from far-out fantasy to frequency of daily masturbation and coitus. The conclusion is that the variability between sexual appetites is immense and highly individualized. This is especially true with woman, whose orgiastic possibilities are infinite, whereas men require a sexual latency period. As we have seen, androgen levels seem to relate in a quantitative way to female sex drive. The more the merrier. But males respond only to an optimum level of circulating androgens. Less than average is apt to slow potency somewhat, but more than average will not quantitate any increased potency as it does for the female. These sex drive findings have an important bearing on courtship and marriage.

Males with a high sex drive generally tend to put off females and slow the progress of courtship. Perhaps this is because woman's natural reluctance to acquiesce is heightened by such an onslaught, perhaps because she derives ego appeal from his unslaked omnivorous attentions, perhaps she simply knows it's there with him any time she wants it. And it is hers for the asking. The effect of a man coming on too strongly is to delay sexual progress. On the other hand, if the woman has a high sexual drive the reverse is most decidedly true, and courtship and marriage proceed at a more rapid pace. This is true whatever the sex drive potential in the male partner, namely high, medium, low, or indifferent. The sexually acquisitive female usually gets what she wants from the male who, as every barnyard reveals to us, is considerably at the mercy of her choice. The female is the keeper of the key.

The vigor of the sex drive has been shown to markedly influence our sociosexual conditioning. Couples who have a high sex drive and go quickly to sex have much less perceptual compatibility. That is, those who dive immediately into sex tend to do that at the expense of understanding both themselves and each other, not just emotionally but socially and intellectually. Thus, high sex-drive couples are apt to have a tiger by the tail, for they are apt to indulge sex indiscriminately before refining a relationship.

When it is the woman alone who possesses the high sex drive in a couple, there is little or no damage wrought to perceptual compatibility. This is also true of a low sex-drive woman. The reason for this seems to be, as previously discussed, that women place a socializing interpretation on sexuality. Her sex is geared more to a totality of existence, and whether or not her sex drive is high, it will not distort for her the total meaning of a living relationship. Her sex life is a natural part of herself, and unless she is pathologically promiscuous and using herself for gain, sex involves all of her existence. No differences in intraperceptual or interperceptual understanding will be found in couples as the result of the female's sex drive. But courtship progress for a low-drive man will progress faster than for a high-drive man with whatever woman. Courtship's progress to marriage is best, however, when sexual discrepancy between the man and woman is not great.

Men and women react differently in their sex to the events of the day, indicating again how sex to a woman is more a totality of existence, to man it is or can be something apart. Measurements of men's depressions, periods of boredom, episodes of success and failure, or introversion have little or no influence on the frequency of heterosexual performance. What such mood dispositions do seem to influence is indulgence in erotic fantasy and self-arousal, both of which markedly decreased when man is moody. But sex, especially established sex with a familiar partner, is little affected, anymore than the flights of fantasy necessary to that sex might possibly inhibit. This is not the case with woman whose working day gives her cause to feel sexy or not sexy. Sexually speaking she cannot stand outside herself and still enjoy sex as a man can at the end of a bad day. Which does not mean that she can't or won't participate. "I could fuck," a woman will be heard to say to someone she loves at the end of such a day. But she is not apt to enjoy herself for herself, as he is himself, under such trying circumstances. Women have always marveled at how men can perform "even when they don't feel good."

Brain electrical activity was first amplified and described in 1924. Although it is the basis of the new science of biofeedback, it has only been with the advent of modern technology that this field has really come into its own. Prior to 1977 there was no categorical listing in the Index Medicus for biofeedback. In the last two years over 2,500 papers have been entered in the medical literature! It is a field hot with possibilities and hope.

By definition, biofeedback is the use of mirror instruments to make a person aware of normal or abnormal body processes and bring them under voluntary control. Since changes in our physiological state are often the result of emotional reactions, biofeedback becomes a psychophysiological discipline that assesses mind-body relationships and attempts to evaluate responses to such things as stress, fear, sexual excitement, relaxation, anxiety. Since the physiological response to each of these is normally beyond our awareness, the attempt is to render these changes conscious by allowing us to see, or hear, or feel signals not normally available. In this way we may be able to develop an understanding of the interrelationship between body needs and environment, personal relations and unconscious needs, and the physiology associated with them. The underlying hope, indeed basic philosophy, of biofeedback is to teach the individual to control his own responses by returning the responsibility for those responses back upon himself through learned conditioning. To this end, certain main feedbacks have been delineated: muscle feedback, skin feedback, temperature feedback, blood pressure feedback, heart rate feedback, sex feedback, and brain wave feedback.

Using needle electrode placements in selective muscles, subjects can learn to control the firing of different muscle groups in the body. When we are tense it is primarily our muscles that are tense, so relaxation and neuromuscular control are the two most important modalities of biofeedback work. Controlling facial muscles has reduced migraine headaches. Controlling breathing muscles has reversed asthma. Similarly, back spasms, wry necks, neuralgias, stroke, and facial palsies have all benefited from feedback training. With the help of auditory reinforcement stimuli whole muscle groups, such as thigh muscles, have been rehabilitated. The affective conscious control that can be brought to bear on injured or insulted muscle groups is amazing.

Skin temperature feedback and electrodermal feedback may be our best index of autonomic (visceral or unconscious) nervous system response. The so-called galvanic skin response has been used for years in lie detector tests. Physiologically it reflects sweat gland activity (increased salt secretion) which results from excitatory or so-called sympathetic nervous system discharge. Stress thus varies skin conductance by increasing it and is readily measurable. By feeding back responses to emotional arousal one becomes aware of causal mechanisms. Phobias and anxieties have been successfully controlled, as have sweaty palms and stuttering. Skin temperature per se represents a useful window on autonomic functioning, as we have seen with sexual arousal. But fear, anger, startle, and quick orienting responses are all sympathetic discharges. A skin thermograph shows a sympathetic cooling off of the skin and cold and clammy palms. Skin temperature used along with relaxation training in tension diseases, such as high blood pressure and asthma and migraine, has been very effective.

Heat flow in the body is of course dependent upon blood flow, which is a function of the constriction of the vessels in which it is

268

being carried. The constriction in turn is a function of smooth muscle contraction controlled by the sympathetic branch of the autonomic nervous system. Blood pressure and heart rate are closely allied to the tenseness of the pipes wherein they pump. When we are excited, our heart races, our pulse increases, and the blood vessels constrict, leading to a hypertense state. Through biofeedback, significantly slower heart rate changes have been effected even in a single session, and blood pressure lowering has been equally dramatic. There is evidence to suggest that voluntary heart rate control may be developed. Even in those who have cardiac pathology with arrhythmias, a regular rhythm has been restored. A combination of relaxation technique and cardiac slowing has been most effective in the treatment of high blood pressure and in the management of cardiac anxiety attacks.

Penile-erection and vaginal-feedback techniques have been used successfully to modify sexual behavior. A strain gauge loop surrounds the penis in the male or enters the vagina in the female. In the male, tumescence is measured, in the female, vaginal flow and temperature. Both women and men have demonstrated their educability to voluntary sexual enhancement or inhibition as the occasion warrants by biofeedback techniques. Men have learned to increase erections in cases of impotence, and women to relax and contract appropriately in cases of vaginismus. Greater control over vaginal muscles during intercourse is described by women, and greater conscious potency by men.

The major and most important modality of studying biofeedback I have left till last. It is recording brain waves, or using the electroencephalogram. Brain waves are typically perceived as oscillating potentials ranging from less than 1 to up to 50 cycles per second. Frequency of these waves has been correlated with specific states in humans. For example, alpha, or relaxant affective waves, are present in meditators and practitioners of yoga. Similarly delta, theta, sigma, and beta waves have all been described, with beta waves having the most excitatory frequency (15+ cycles per second). Thus alpha training becomes important for human relaxation, and individuals can benefit from enhancing the differentiation between alpha and beta by biofeedback. It is most useful in those areas of agitation where mental relaxation or quietness is required. Some people have related the theta wavelength to our creative energy state—a state halfway beteen alpha dormancy and beta excitement where a judicious balance of seminal impulse and cerebral drive most successfully converge. Beta waves of excitement are clearly observed when the opposite sex is flashed nude on a screen. Alpha wave training has been most successful in obsessive-compulsive psychiatric states and least successful with passive-aggressive disorders. It has been used with beneficial results in chronic pain problems where shifting awareness may be indicated.

I have dwelled on the rudiments of biofeedback at some length because it is the avant garde of sex research today, promises great excitement, and is apt to lead to many new findings. For example, the skin temperature and galvanic skin response is much greater in men. This is true in amplitude only, not duration. If the same test with known answers is administered over a period of time, women continue to respond with their sympathetic nervous system long after men have "gotten the trick of it." Thus, in lie detection, men are apt to exhibit a more reliable test initially, but over a period of time would not be as reliable recorders as women, whose image persists longer. In feedback training of heart rate, no difference has been observed between the sexes in ability to slow the heart, but men do seem to be more capable of controlling the speeding up of the heart rhythm. This is equally true with auditory or visual conditioning. What is different (and this is current and choice!) is that men and women use different cognitive techniques to achieve the same slowing of the heart under different conditions. For example, under preconditions, when men and women are simply asked to concentrate and control their heart rate by slowing it, both men and women show the same alpha wave pattern in left and right brain hemispheres. That is, right-handed men and women use a similar dominant hemisphere to control heart rate under unlearned conditions. But when biofeedback learning is instituted, these same women shift to a right hemispheric or affective control mechanism of alpha waves in the less dominant half of the brain. In men the interhemispheric relationships don't change, but in women, as soon as a problem-solving element is introduced, a lateralization occurs. Asked to recite well-known lyrics or whistle a familiar tune and women immediately activate their less dominant "alpha" hemisphere. Men don't. Ask men and women to covertly activate sexuality by calling up sexual fantasy imagery or by using sexual language, and women immediately lateralize. Men don't. Though both males and females record the same subjective success to this feeling response, or to slowing the heart's rate in meditation, the cognitive mode with male and female to achieve this state is strikingly different. We now know from extensive electroencephalography that males regulate the left (dominant) side of the brain better than the right, and females the right (less dominant) better than the left. This does not mean that cognitive abilities are necessarily related to alpha control, but it does mean that the cognitive approach is different in women and men. The ability to increase alpha waves in one hemisphere in both sexes is correlated with the ability to increase alpha in the opposite hemisphere, and there is greater alpha in the less dominant hemisphere in both sexes, but this is relatively greater in the female because it is more often used by her sex in learning. Overall, females show consistently more asymmetry, more bilaterality, more flexibility, and more control of their brain waves. It is convincing proof that the thought process, the actual mode of thinking, is different in women and men. If the less dominant hemisphere is our alpha side, our more affective side, it is fair to say that women use this side of themselves much more than do men and are therefore more diffuse and more loving in their thought processes.

More emphasis has been placed recently on neurophysiological differences. In this regard there are no established gross observable differences in the brain size or configuration between the sexes. But this does not exclude the possibility that there may be organizational differences. For example, the matter of cerebral dominance may be more complete and definitive in the male. A right-handed man will have his speech centered in the left half of his brain and his visual spatial acuity in the less dominant or right side of the brain. This was thought to be equally true of women until just recently when it was shown that woman's verbal and spatial abilities are more likely to be duplicated on both sides of the brain, more dispersed as it were, and hence an insult to either side of the brain (for example, tumor, stroke, trauma, surgery) is not likely to incapacitate a woman as seriously. The clinical findings from large series of patients therefore suggest that woman uses the recessive (less dominant) side of the brain to greater advantage, or at least to greater functional advantage, than the male, whose hemispheric brain function seems to be an all-or-none type of activity for that locus of brain tissue. Again, woman is more diffused.

Biochemical differences between the two sexes have been shown by measuring the brain's electrical variation responses to stimuli such as light and sound. Across the board, women's brains are measurably more responsive in every sense tested and especially at higher levels of intensity. Thus their "evocation potential" is higher for a similar stimulus given to both male and female and this sensitivity in women renders them augmenters or possibly exaggerators of stimuli to the brain received via the nervous system. They would then become people who potentiate or increase the intensity of a reaction to a stimulus in their brain response. "Augmenters" tend to have a measurably lower enzyme content between nerve endings that ordinarily allow for smooth transmission of impulses. This enzyme is monoamine oxidase, and as we have seen is apparently suppressed by high concentrations of the estrogen in which females abound.

All kinds of speculations and inferences can be derived from such biochemical and physiological observations. Are women more sensitive to stimuli at the time of ovulation when their estrogen titre is highest? Are they more labile at menopause? Are they greater augmenters so they can more easily protect themselves, say, or to hear a baby cry at night? Can this account for why women rate life changes such as death, moving, marriage, job loss, as relatively more stressful and traumatic than men? Is this why in the very sex act itself she is so sensitive to diversions of sound and shelter? The answers are not in the scientific findings and are not likely to be, and a good scientist will always add, "much more research is needed."

Whereas the female of the species does seem to have a greater diffusion of usefulness, that is, more lateralization, between the two brain hemispheres, she also seems to have a greater control over that lateralization process than the man. Women are apparently better able to activate those brain zones needed for the task at hand, and in tests where verbal skills and nonverbal skills are the parameters, their brains turn on the hemispheres needed much more selectively and consistently than men's. This ability to turn on and shut out as if dealing with different wavelengths may make females better cognitive specialists. It may also make them better able to perform tasks that combine two modalities in a single activity, such as understanding behavior from viewing a facial expression. In may be true, therefore, that men's brains are superior at functioning with two cognitive endeavors that are not integrated, for example, running a drill press while whistling. One can't help but be impressed at how well the busy secretary or, better yet, the busy housewife is able to field so many problems of a similar and often overlapping nature and manage to selectively edit the day's ebb and flow to her everlasting credit and advantage. This fits in with such studies, as does the masculine exasperation and sense of futility when he is not able to control the cognitive area he is called upon to use with maximum intensity.

In addition to the areas of neurophysiology and anatomy, the major experimental area of hormonal influence must be mentioned. Investigators now claim it is the sex hormones themselves that act selectively on differing parts of the developing brain that render male and female neurobiologically different. They say that male and female hormones differentiate the sensory and motor processes at different rates and different times and this leads to certain nerve connections for boys and certain nerve connections for girls which, in turn, lead to varied behavior typical of the sex. As we have seen in boys, this becomes rough-and-tumble play and control of gross spatial environmental changes. In women, the emphasis is on fine movements, dexterity, and audiovisual sensitivity. Studies also support the integrated alpha brain hemispheres for female, and the dissociative alpha brain functions for male. This may lead to sex-specific abilities and characterizing man as a "manipulative animal." It may further mean that men prefer to express themselves in action, which takes little speculative imagination, to associate with their muscle endowment in childhood. It remains that women inherently prefer to receive, recall, and transmit symbols to those about her. In all of this, once again, one must allow for the tentative state of science and the bell-shaped curve of statistical variability. These are generalizations of questionable applicability in any given individual case.

Certain claims made for expectant motherhood a few years ago exemplify all the inherent weaknesses of science, and in another sense all the great virtues of science. This claim purported that there could be an 80 percent control over the sex of a conceived offspring if only certain sexual methods were pursued. The theory was that male sperms required a more alkaline vaginal tide to enhance their flow to the ovum, whereas the female-determining spermatozoa did more successfully in relatively acid states. Thus, if you wanted to conceive a boy child, the woman was encouraged to orgasm and prolonged intercourse. If a girl child was desired, intercourse should be relatively short, lacking in excessive lubrication, and even preceded by an acidic vinegar douche. It is impossible to estimate the number of people who followed this scientific dictum. There is no doubt that the initial results had some promising validity as published. But in the way of science, as the dice continued to be rolled and the data accumulated, it became obvious there was no better than a fifty-fifty chance to have male or female offspring by using this technique, and once again nature triumphed. The fact that the subsequent literature does not substantiate the original optimistic findings is most emphatically no reflection on the experimenters or their methods; instead it is just another caution about faddism in scientific methodology. We should be grateful for all scientific experimentation and the addition to our knowledge, no matter if achieved in a negative way.

Since Kinsey's report on human sexuality appeared over twenty-five years ago, there have been reams of studies on sexual behavior and performance, extending up through Masters and Johnson's recent classic publications. These studies deserve attention, but their findings need a perspective that only comes with personal experience. Among the delightful elements of love, especially nuptial love, are the little jokes late at night and all the warm laughter and intimacies shared at that time. My wife and I used to laugh that the main difference between a man and a woman was that a woman could never be a premature ejaculator. This got to be so much fun I decided to write off a question to one of medicine's leading periodicals, a sort of advice to physicians lovelorn column, and one day laughingly jotted the following on my prescription pad and sent it off:

My wife is a premature ejaculator.
Please advise.

The answer was apparently conceived in high seriousness and written with no disclaimer. The editor pointed out that it is important to make clear that women do not ejaculate. In a questionnaire circulated to an Eastern university, 70 percent of men and women in the freshman class believed females ejaculate as do males. A woman may come to orgasm with minimal stimulation. In over 600 cases only five to six such cases were found, and of these, two had no problem in their sexual fantasies. However, it could not be consciously begun and more often than not came to her as a surprise. Another patient, married to a premature ejaculator, had no problem until she had an extramarital affair. Then she realized that thirty to sixty seconds of intercourse was not satisfactory! The others would lubricate and become orgiastic immediately. As sex play continued, lubrication subsided. Their main presenting problem was dyspareunia.

The treatment plan followed was much the same as in the treatment of a male with impotence. One always hopes that men will become used to losing and regaining their erection without anxiety. These women have to be assured that the lubrication will return.

They may well even experience more than one orgasm. Obviously, the partner has to be brought into the situation.

While premature orgasm is a relatively rare entity, it does exist and must be distinguished from dyspareunia. Another rare symptom is surprise ejaculation, particularly in males under thirty years of age. And then there is the phenomenon of orgasm without a conscious pleasure component. This is very difficult to treat. Many women who feel they are not orgasmic are actually orgastic. A woman who states she "doesn't know" or is "not orgastic" can be questioned more carefully. It is estimated that one of six of the anorgastic women has been having an orgastic phenomenon for years but does not recognize it. . . .

As I say the stands now are full of this kind of sex manual information for the asking. What it really means for all of us in practical terms is at some point very soon we must return to love and relatedness. Man simply cannot live by such bread alone, nor woman. Nor both of them together. Such material cannot and will not sustain a relationship. We need something more.

The modern vistas of science, then, the studies that are really current and choice, all tend to confirm so far what we have already established about the sexes, namely, that while man and woman share many of the basic life-support systems of the body their sexuality breeds into them innate differences that govern their actions in thoughts and feeling. Most striking in this regard is the greater diffusion of the thought process in women throughout both sides of the brain, greater use of the less dominant or feeling side of our cerebral hemispheres. This gives her a more affective approach to problems, both internal and external, and also an innate ability to manage many different things at once (the switchboard operator). Her diffusion gives her a slower perceptibility in many matters of sexual stimuli, but the direction of her response is similar to the male's. Whereas females who are sexually aggressive in no way jeopardize their marital or premarital chances, the super aggressive male is often a put-off to the slower perceptibility of the female who must evolve a total social significance to her sex life. In the matter of visual, auditory, and tactile erotic stimuli, women and men are about equally disposed, with women slightly more sensitive to auditory and tactile stimuli and men more visually sensitive. In the matters of muscle control, temperature control, blood pressure control, heart rate control, and respiratory control, both men and women can be equally successful—but the cognitive mode of women again involves a more affective brain wave approach.

Women in general live closer to their feeling selves. This comes through clearly in such soul-searching depressions as are now frequently seen in our society following the trauma of abortion. The processes to a concerned male, who stands at a distance, can be a clinical tour de force. To woman, it often means that a tender and precious part of herself that she hadn't realized existed has been lost, never to be replaced, and this may leave lingering feelings that react in her adversely many years later.

Finally, perhaps most importantly, women tend to be augmenters of brain stimuli received, taking an ordinary impulse and evoking an electrically higher potential response than does a man to a similar occurrence. Just last evening, my wife and I were gazing quietly out the window of our home after dinner when suddenly a car sped down the hill careening treacherously, out of control, past a red light and crashed into a neighbor's empty car. "The driver must have had a heart attack," my wife screamed, running desperately out the door. "Probably some drunk," I said lumbering slowly after her. As it happened, another parked, driverless car had simply broken loose on a steep San Francisco hill and run down. Arm and arm, I very much calmer than she, we returned home after the incident consoling each other. Then she said, "You know the way you reacted to that, if a man had really had a heart attack, you wouldn't have reached him in time to resuscitate him." Later on that evening the phone rang and I was called out to a bad emergency. I was tempted to say to my wife, "You see, aren't you glad I saved all that energy from earlier?" But she, exhausted, was now peacefully asleep.

TWELVE

PERENNIAL
AS THE GRASS

Grow old along with me!
The best is yet to be.
　　　　—*Robert Browning*
　　　"Rabbi Ben Ezra"

IN THE SMALL TOWN of Lemoore, in Kings County, California, reside two old women, Genevieve and Eloise Reed. They are ninety-four years old and are the oldest living twins in the United States. In 1907, at age twenty-two, they were dancing stars of the Ziegfeld Follies, and thereafter sang and danced their way across America for fifteen years on stage and in the movies. To see pictures of them from that time is to see two strikingly beautiful women with gorgeous bodies and lovely accommodating faces. To see them today is to have fun with two devilish old ladies who laugh and twinkle their eyes at you as they recall those days. They wear their stockings rolled and, with canes for props as much as support, run through a few ancient routines. When asked what it is they now enjoy more than anything else in the world they are quick to reply, "Yes, we smoke and drink some and go shopping once a week. But the most fun is that we still enjoy the attention from a man." This enduring sentiment, this feeling, this chthonic force, this ineffable longing for the opposite sex unto the grave has been expressed in a beautiful modern poem by Davetta Greenberg called "I Can Count On It":

> *I will hear it on my grave*
> *tapping like anxious fingers.*
> *The hammer is real, and the siren*
> *and the soft miracle of two passions*
>
> *coming together. Tracking for years*
> *your blue veined circumference*
> *your closed peripheral eye, has brought me*
> *a shallow knowledge. I go hungry.*

Where theory and beauty and philosophy end
there is a hole in my spirit as big
as a starving belly: hunger is not
precarious. I can count on it.

When you hear this, somehow you are not really surprised. What was unquestionably the most powerful and overwhelming experience of our youth exerts the same force on us long after we are sixty and all the years beyond. Whether as we grow older the experience is fact or fiction doesn't seem to matter much. Everybody exaggerates their sex life. But the recreation and perpetuation of that powerful attraction between the sexes goes on from cradle to grave as a necessary yearning for the experience of the opposite sex and the reassurance of the missing part of ourselves. In 1960, at age sixty, on the day Jack Kennedy was elected president, Adlai Stevenson, the man whose rhetoric had prepared the nation in the ten preceding years for the likes of the young Kennedy, received this touching letter from a woman friend of his generation who had played a leading role in his volunteer organization in his political campaign.

On this day of days I can't help but write a few words from my heart. It hurts me more than I can ever express to anyone—even perhaps to you—that circumstances and timing have been such as to deny America its potentially greatest President—and to deny to my most beloved friend the opportunity to serve—and lead!—in this capacity. My emotions are mixed—just as mixed as yours . . . because you are you, and the very fact that it has not been public office, or a public forum that have made you the world figure that you are, but *you* yourself—the profoundness of your thinking, the validity of your ideas, your extraordinary prescience, and your extraordinary ability to lift hearts while you are articulating them—means that, with or without public office, you will continue to grow in stature, and leave a lasting impression on the thoughts, the morals and the ideals of this and succeeding generations.

We should not be surprised to read such a letter of love and admiration to an old defeated, yet triumphant man, a political has-been, yet a man beloved by scores of beautiful women for the rest of his life. We should not be surprised to hear that this letter from an intimate woman friend brought a tear to his eye and suffused his heart with warm reassurance and loving affection, and satisfied a need that all the politics in the world could never do. It was the whole feminine side of Stevenson crying out for love and approbation that made him touch everybody's soul in moments like this, and for the woman who wrote that wonderful letter, it was her masculine regard for him in the world that enabled her feminine self to shine through so beautifully and wholesomely.

Why do we always come back to this? Why do we always return to love and relatedness with the opposite sex no matter how weak in the bones or gone in the teeth we are? Is it simply because the alternatives are so horrendous? Or is it that there is always a part of us missing unless we acknowledge our opposite? Found buried in his posthumous papers is this magnificent answer from D. H. Lawrence that says it all:

We have our very individuality in relationship. Let us swallow this important and prickly fact. Apart from our connections with other people, we are barely individuals, we amount all of us, to next to nothing. It is in the living touch between us and other people, other lives, other phenomena that we move and have our being. Strip us of our human contacts and of our contact with the living earth and sun, and we are almost bladders of emptiness. Our individuality means nothing. A skylark that was alone on an island would be songless and meaningless, his individuality gone, running about like a mouse in the grass. But if there were one female with him, it would lift him singing into the air, and restore him his real individuality. And so with men and women. It is in relationship to one another that they have their true individuality and their distinct being: in contact, not out of contact. This is sex, if you like. But it is no more sex than sunshine on the grass is sex. It is a living contact, give and take: the great and subtle relationship of men and women, man and woman. In this and through this we become real individuals, without it, without the real contact, we remain more or less nonentities.

Man and woman have now come full circle and can face each other with the candor and understanding that only the living experience of more than half a century can give. How often it has been observed that old couples come to look and act alike, and that those old faces often take on the appearance of a newborn child, showing the same lined features of wisdom. In the end is our beginning. Yet the creative energy that resides within us is always our unconscious or female side and seems to be more durable, recurrent, and everlasting in our lives. As we age, our masculine side seems to be more brittle and begins to wane much more readily. The better-suited female of the species goes into old age with much more vigor than the male, and it is her continuing task, not to rest on her laurels, but to employ that energy in rigorous discipline and crucial experience to complete her conscious development. In this way she creates her own light to the end. Nina Schneider, at age sixty-seven, has just written her first novel. It is marvelous and fittingly titled *The Woman Who Lived In A Prologue*. It is the story of an aged woman who has completed the female life journey in all its abundance and frustration from family needs to the tyranny of housework, to the dullness and bliss of matrimonial sex, the fun and cruelty of offspring, adultery, a career, travel, shopping, the vagaries of health, and many, many, many grandchildren. She has, you would think, done and seen it all, as she says, "the entire womanly life for which I was promised I would pass into the land of the self-possessed adult." And yet this Ariadne, the obviously autobiographical heroine of the book, is not content, but pushes vigorously and creatively onward. Here is how Ariadne begins her book:

More than 5730 years from Genesis, the planet ticking like a bomb under camouflage, and here I sit poised over a throbbing eclectic [sic] typewriter, an old woman in a room that smells of wood ashes and drying immortelles (all I could rescue of my helichrysums), staring out at my garden where frost has blackened the asters and silenced the bees.

Only an optimist practiced in taking long views could see this as a setting for a prologue: hoarfrost hanging from the shrubbery like shrouded mirrors; a few wintry birds mincing on the glassy lawn. And I'm no spring chicken either. Actuarily speaking (and my late husband often did), my time is up. Yet I wake every morning to the sensation that my real life is waiting, immanent, like an embryo whose atoms are about to be assembled.

As Goethe aged he gradually became deaf and blind and repeatedly refused to do anything about it. He was mentally alert and capable of continued work if only he would have allowed his friends to help him with glasses or a hearing aid. But Goethe's message was that as a man he had already learned all that nature had intended him to learn. He said we gradually do not hear as well, or see as well, with a purpose—the blotting out of our external life, which was generally not worth it anyway. The loss of senses gave us natural reason for introspection in old age and exploration of the more important internal aspects of our souls. Goethe insisted any disruption in this process was against God's way. I recall my aging father's gleeful remark, much in the same vein. As a young lawyer he had lost many more cases than he had won before at last becoming a successful trial lawyer and judge of considerable accomplishment who remained on the bench, nearly deaf, till the day he died. "I may have been wrong," he liked to say in those days, "but I've never been in doubt." In point of fact he had already long since heard it all, a remarkable old person who had studied and knew the soul and all the gopher holes and traps along the way. And by then he was seldom wrong. It is this point that men and women must now reach together.

Our National Institute of Health has coined the term "ageism," which is not just the study of age and biological entropy, but includes our cultural attitudes and stereotypes about the process of getting old. In the past, too little regard has been directed at the normal process of aging; instead the emphasis has been on disease and dysfunction. We talk of arteriosclerosis and arthritis and heart failure as if we were all involved in a process of programmed obsolescence, when in fact there are an immense number of healthy and capable old people—some 45 million people over 60 years of age, about a quarter of our population. By the end of the century it is expected that 60 million people in this country will be over 60 years of age. This means that there is an immense amount of "gray power" around, increasingly so, the preponderance of which is active and healthy except for the normal attrition of years. For just as babies are susceptible to certain disease states, so are the middle aged, and the aged. One no more so than the other.

As women and men grow older they frequently develop a paunch. They will tell you they are eating the same way they did in college, but getting fat. And that's just the physiological point of aging. It's not that they are eating more, but that they are eating the same amount while their body metabolisms are progressively slowing. In general, the metabolic mill needs fats and carbohydrates for energy, protein for muscle building, and essential amino acids for enzyme and hormone and tissue building. It is the metabolic cycle of energy that tends to slow as we age, the turnover rate of fats and carbohydrates that allows these elements to be deposited here and there at well-known sluggish spots throughout the body. Thus it is, as we grow older, if we eat the same amount we are likely to become fat. Similarly, if we concertedly exercise as we grow old we will increase our metabolic mill and burn fat and carbohydrates and, as they say, remain toned. What we are really doing, though, is staying even with our youthful state by stressing or forcing our metabolic mill into action. The two obvious correlates to this are: (1) children are always in good shape no matter what they do; and (2) how many fat people do you know over seventy?

Since the metabolism of fats and carbohydrates is the major supply of energy to the brain, lack of this means progressive sugar and oxygen lacks in that structure and changes that are consistent with senility. At first this may be manifest in simple forgetfulness, but then may progress to gross amnesia or disorientation in time and place. Brain changes may be caused by or potentiated by changes within the arteries themselves that cause narrowing of those structures and, hence, slow circulation. This is called arteriosclerosis—literally, scarring or plaque formation in the vessels—which can sometimes be localized to one crucial vessel such as the carotid in the neck that supplies the brain, but more commonly is generalized and involves all the body arteries. Plaques in the coronary arteries are the common cause of heart attacks. The precise cause of this arteriosclerosis is unknown. It is thought it may be related to fatty acid metabolism and its cousin, cholesterol, but this is uncertain. The great blood vessel surgeon, Michael DeBakey, insists it is a congenital disease, one that those who are afflicted in middle or old age were born with as a metabolic defect. In any event, the slowing of the body energy metabolites of fats and sugars and the decreased blood supply from narrowing of our arterial blood vessels slow the internal vital functioning of the body. This is true not only for the brain, but for the heart, the intestines, the liver, and the kidneys, which being the clearing house for the degradation products of the body are perhaps the most vital organs we possess as we grow old. "Don't walk when you can run," an old man once said to me, "and void every chance you get." The kidneys may not only be subjected to inadequate blood in-flow, but inadequate urinary emptying ability because of obstructive processes (such as the male's enlarged prostate) from below. Therefore the kidney risks a double jeopardy as we age.

But if all else goes well in the aged, there is still one body system subjected to actual mechanical physical abuse that, just like the parts of your car, sooner or later wears down and out. This is our musculoskeletal system. It is our system of wear and tear—sinews, ligaments, tendons, bones—that we go banging around on every day, sustaining trauma, supporting all the other structures within. We become aware of this system more and more as we grow older. After forty everybody's back bothers him or her at one time or another. Joints creak, muscles ache, the hands and feet get cold and stiff. The tiny shock-absorbing cushions that line the joints wear out. The spine settles down. We become shorter. I was shocked to measure my own height recently and discovered I had lost three quarters of an inch in the last seven years. Old people often become Munchkins, little people, their muscles can't work the stiffened bones and so they, too, tend to atrophy. In the female, with dropoff in estrogen, the bones become demineralized; calcium is lost, making bones even more brittle than in the male, whose older hips are not fractured nearly as often as hers. She also tends as she grows older, because of her immune system, to develop more arthritic complaints, which further incapacitate movement. With loss of bone tone and muscle tone there is an accompanying loss of overlying tissue turgor, which gives way to a characteristic dry wrinkling of the skin, especially at points of constant stressful motion about the eyes, neck, hands, and major joints.

In the present meager state of the art of the physiology of aging and death, there are very few positive correlates established. It seems that we all have an intrinsic genetic clock for longevity that, interdicting disease process notwithstanding, will run its course unto the end. This genetic clock resides similarly within the chromosomal nucleus of all our cells, within each individual cell, where the "brains" of each of these tiny organisms reside that, taken together, make up the whole body. You can measure body hormones, for example, and find no constant from person to person, with the exception that cortisone does seem to remain high, the adrenal remains active, right up to the end. It is as if this gland takes over in the aged from the unreliable cyclical pituitary to become our master gland, and when our adrenals fail their reliable circadian message to the body seems to fail as well. You can do special cell studies with the electron microscope and you will find that only the connective tissues of the body, the bricks and mortar that support the more definitive cellular elements, show any characteristic changes. Our elastic tissue, for example, that allows for the expansion of skin and the distensibility of blood vessels is progrssively less apparent as we age and is replaced by rigid scar tissue. Even the microscopic criteria of a senescent cell are undescribed because they are not readily apparent. Thus we know and do have such criteria for visualizing an immature cell, and can recognize young cells of all kinds very easily. But if you view a heart cell or a blood cell of a healthy twenty-year-old beside the heart cell of a healthy but aging eighty-five-year-old there will be no discernible difference in the cells themselves. This is not to say that the aged kidney will not show pockets of scarring, evidence of focal disease, of destruction and regeneration, but is to say that the mature kidney cell is a homogeneous element indistinguishable by age alone. I have often tested pathologists by giving them unknown microscopic slides, and on the basis of cell structure alone they repeatedly strike out. To guess the age certain peripheral clues have to be used—absence of supporting tissue, blood vessel changes, regional disease processes, all manner of historical information.

These findings have led to the highly speculative unitary theory of physiological aging and the death process wherein at some point a genetic message is received by the body's viable cells, presumably in the nucleus of those cells, that informs them that the game is up. Some feel this is mediated by a neurohumoral element that is released by the nervous system and acts on tiny granules that surround each cell nucleus, called mitochondria. These transmit the message uniformly to the brain of the cell, all of which then act in body accord and death becomes generalized. The pathologist, it should be added, has no problem recognizing death when it comes under the microscope. It is only life that puzzles him.

What this comes to, as we grow older, is an amazing sense of necessary patience and endurance with the entropy process of life. The refinement of our abilities to cope as we get on is one of the great achievments of life and is filled with daily heroism. Our thoughts and feelings, which we can now more easily nurture, are in the full person an immense compensation for what becomes only the "things" of the body for which we have already lived too frenzied a life. Older people have learned for the most part that quality is much more important than quantity. I think of the aged Robert Frost at Jack Kennedy's inaugural, standing there on the Capitol steps in cold Washington in January, attempting to read his inaugural poem, which the wind ruffling the papers made it impossible for his ancient eighty-eight-year-old eyes to do. Completely unperturbed he looked at the audience and recited his "The Gift Outright" beautifully and flawlessly, a poem about the unique and magnificient birthright of America. And just today in my church, an aging visiting minister couldn't see the text from his dim pulpit light, and closing the book proceeded to recite the entire story of the prodigal son, word for word from the King James version, completely by heart. He said he had had time recently to learn it for just such occasions. What happens to both men and women if they survive the life-threatening diseases between fifty and seventy is that they develop a peculiar long-term organic immunity to such things as cancer and infection that often enables them to go on and on for many years. This gives them time for wisdom and a quiet confident kind of love. It is said that T. S. Eliot, who married his much younger secretary while he was in his seventies, was suffused with an unbelievable serenity and warmth and happiness at the end that he had not experienced throughout his earlier life.

And yet the darker view of aging persists, especially in America where adolescence is almost pathologically prolonged and the emphasis is on the NOW of youth. In our hype society, where every five years a new generation arrives (the rock groups of age fifteen are passé by age twenty), the incongruencies and burdens of the elderly are a sore thumb. The view is held that loss of memory, rigid points of view, economic dependence, offensive senility get in the way of progress and the necessary hustle of our culture. The truth is that senility begins at birth, in mind and body, and progresses in varying degrees in all of us throughout our lives. Old age is, in fact, less a problem than an opportunity for the most part. The mere fact of having survived for over fifty or sixty years is an opportunity to impart an immense wisdom to youth. There simply is no substitute for having been there and felt it for yourself. Fortunately, some countries, such as Denmark and France, and some cultures, such as the Oriental, respect and venerate the aged for just this reason and provide for them accordingly. I shall never forget the sight of Jack Kennedy, age forty-two, the new president walking arm in arm with ex-President Eisenhower at his Gettysburg farm after the terrible

Kennedy blunder at the Bay of Pigs, where we had surreptitiously attempted to invade Cuba and overthrow dictator Fidel Castro. It ended in total disgrace and disaster for Kennedy and our country. But there was the aged warrior in his seventies consoling the younger man. You had the feeling Eisenhower would no longer have found himself in such a mess, but he knew just what it felt like to be there and was probably the most reassuring person Kennedy could have sought out that day to be told, "This too shall pass."

All of us, as I have said, have trouble imagining our parents having sex, as if this darkened area was strictly the province of youth. And from this psychological vantage point arise many of the misconceptions about sex activity in the aged. Any physician who has worked in the geriatric vineyards will tell you sex is as much a part of the life of the elderly as it is of the young. When the bones stiffen and the muscles become less supple, there are physical limitations to performing in all the ninety-nine positions intricately described in Japanese pornographic woodcuts, but sex is real and everlasting to most old people however prune-faced they may appear. For older people, sex is a much more qualitative undertaking, lacking the frenzied quantitative approach of young reproductive people, particularly the male of the species. Performance in the older man is a more sustained and gradual undertaking, infinitely more pleasing to women of all ages, whose major frustration with younger excitable men is that it's often all over before it's begun. Coitus reservatus is a natural acquisition of the aging male who is now able to go on at great length to please his partner. Sometimes male orgasm is minimal or absent as men grow older, but this does not diminish his pleasure or his special increased ability to please a woman. For her part, the woman's sexual potential is maximized in her late twenties and early thirties and remains a constant, giving her a lustiness well into old age.

Above all, to maintain our sexuality, we need to maintain a sexual interest. This is not emphasized to the extent it should be, and many people are left with the impression that sex is "a natural part of life" that will arise and assert itself whenever its time has come. But it doesn't quite work that way. Sex is the easiest thing in the world to bruise and injure and hence cast aside if it is not nurtured and cared for. This means being healthily interested in sex and acknowledging and allowing that part of ourselves. When we see next to us in the pornographic movie a little old man with his hat on his lap playing Omar the tentmaker, we should smile that we are both getting our jollies, however tawdry our technique. It seems there is a four-level progression in our lives with reference to erotica which shows a typical progression with age. First is youth, which tends to attribute desirable effects to all matter of erotica such as movies or display or reading material. At middle age there is in men and women either a neutral or a negative view of the same. By late middle age we are no longer so adamantly certain of the adverse effects of erotica, and many varied and mixed reactions are found. Finally, in old age we have achieved definite categorical positive and negative opinions, as much as to say yes in one group and a resounding adamant no in the other. It takes little imagination to tell which group has kept its sexuality alive and stimulated. As they say, use it or lose it.

Long before George Burns, octogenarian, became famous for playing God and being seen about Hollywood with a different young lady every night, the Bible affirmed man's lustiness well into old age. Adam was 130 when he begot his son Seth, and lived 800 more years and had other sons and daughters. Seth was 105 when he begot Enosh, who was 90 years old when he begot Kenan. Kenan was 70 when he had Mahalalel, who was 65 when he begot Jared. Then came Enoch, Methuselah, and Camech, all of whom had children after age 150. And the famous Noah was 500 years old when his Shem, Ham, and Japheth were born.

Notwithstanding the precarious reliability of these Old Testament timetables, the point is clear that lustiness well into old age was an acknowledged part of the game. In fact, the name Benjamin is a Hebrew name that means a male offspring born in old age. Picasso, almost ninety, was making it with young girls. Henry Miller, lust writer, had a son in his eighth decade, Charlie Chaplin was involved in a paternity suit in his seventh, and Senator Strom Thurmond of South Carolina has just reproduced at eighty. Joan Miró is still going strong at eighty-six. For the ladies the track record is equally impressive. Stella Campbell, whom George Bernard Shaw called the greatest English actress at the turn of the century, married two men young enough to be her grandsons when she was at an advanced age. One of my college classmates knew Tallulah Bankhead (in the biblical sense) and vouches that her appetites were as inexhaustible and endless as her age. Tallulah was tiring out young male lovers at an age she wouldn't dare to disclose, and last year stripteaser Sally Rand, age seventy-five, packed a wild house in San Francisco doing a fan dance my father once sneaked off to see at the Chicago World's Fair in 1933.

Not only is desire apparently everlasting, but the emotional tensions that surround it—jealousy, intrigue, prejudice, passivity—also maintain their pleasurable and painful characteristics ad infinitum. The artist Gauguin, by his own admission an old man by the time he made his second and final visit to Tahiti, tells a story about tuna fishing off Papeete. He was with native Maori fishermen who began to laugh loudly and hysterically when Gauguin hauled in his first catch. Upon his insistence the natives finally explained. It seemed when the fishhook was stuck in the tuna's lower jaw, as in Gauguin's case, rather than the more usual location in the upper jaw, it meant that your *vahine* [woman] had been unfaithful while you were away fishing. "I smiled, incredulous," wrote Gauguin who was celebrated for his thirteen-year-old wives and his easy conceptualization of free and savage love. He goes on to write that he returned home immediately: "A thousand questions. Things that had occurred during the fishing. Came time to go to bed. One question was eating me up. What was the use? What good would it do? At last I asked it:

> "Have you been a good girl?"
> "Eha"
> "And was your lover today a good one?"

"Aita . . . I didn't have a lover."
"You lie. The fish spoke."

Over her face came a look I had never seen before. Her expression was prayerful. . . . Softly she closed the door and prayed out loud. . . . When she had finished praying she came up to me with resignation and said, tears in her eyes: 'You must beat me, strike me many times.' " She had indeed performed the dirty deed.

Anybody who has ever worked with the aged would not be surprised at Gauguin's old man's jealousy anymore than at the lusty, middle-aged, jealous rage of Othello as he sneaked in to kill the unfaithful Desdemona. For even Gauguin, the physiological old man, could not live up to his standards of free love for all and the unlimited bucolic paradisical life when his own ox was being gored. It is the difference between theory and practice that makes Honest Injuns of us all, whatever the chronological age. Such are the findings from commune to Camelot.

Charles McCabe, who is well into his sixties, and who is that rare breed of old-fashioned, morning-journalist friend who can manage an outstanding column in a newspaper five days a week, recently put it marvelously this way in the *San Francisco Chronicle:*

This thing, which never quite leaves us, and which can be rewarding in the memory as in fact, is just one big, fat, wonderful mystery . . .

One thing about erotic love is that it is democratic, in the exact sense. You do not have to be especially qualified, pass any exam, join any select caste, or have a certain credit rating, to be allowed into the company of those who may and do enjoy good old sex. Society does not even ask that you be good or bad to play the game, so long as you observe some pretty loose boundaries.

I have reached the age when the fires are supposed to cool, but I know I have it within me to go tearing away after some female at the drop of. . . . When I say this I don't know whether I'm boasting or making a confession, whether I'm being a dirty old man or a hopeless romantic, or a bit of each.

But the fact is there. And while I'm sort of between engagements at the minute, I do altogether hope to get entwined in the old devilment a few times more before I think of giving somebody my corneas.

Insofar as I have ever thought about what love was, during the times I was in the hands of this paradoxical fever (I say paradoxical because the fever is marvelous and the recovery quite awful) I have always regarded it as a mysterious gift, with accent on the mysterious.

I did not know what I did to deserve it. And, when I seemed able to arouse this same mysterious gift in another, I was similarly grateful. Love is one gift horse I was never tempted to look in the teeth. (Lest, among other reasons, I should start counting same teeth.)

Several years ago at a California zoo there was an old male lion called Sidney. By human reckoning Sidney was nearly a hundred years old. The problem he created for his keepers concerned his ineluctable potency and the demand for his exclusive services by the lionesses. Every time they ran a healthy young male Turk in among the ladies the lionesses simply ignored him, sat and covered their tails to wait it out for Sidney. It comes as no surprise that Sid developed a pride of lions that was one of the biggest ever in captivity, that he reproduced gleefully and regularly, and kept a variety of women constantly happy with his lovemaking. The keepers were dumbfounded, put it down to smell or something other than technique. But there is a secret in the aging male that probably even keepers don't know. It has to do with the maturity of the penis, the acquired angle of the dangle, as my kids like to say.

If you've ever noted the penile erection of a baby boy, you've seen how the little erected member points right up along his belly toward his chin. To him it looks like a one-eyed worm. This sharp upward angulation is true in all youth and young men with a hard-on, because the penis is suspended from the pubic bone by a ligamentous sling. In the way of ligaments this is tight and taut in young men and sort of props the member upward. In African Pygmies this is so pronounced in pictures one suspects them of a perpetual running hard-on. But as man grows older his ligaments loosen and become more lax, less tense, and gives the erected penis a more horizontal orientation in the aged. This directional change is very important to clitoral stimulation. The young man is more or less shoveling or scooping his way into the vagina in the missionary position, whereas the old man with the horizontal member is giving it the more natural posterior and downward thrust that pleases My Lady. Thus it comes about that the anatomically young do not as easily come to abut the clitoris, as the old man does. His old pubis and her pubis are more easily approximated because the root of the penis is not now as upright and hence allows both of them easier access to that erogenous, stimulating area for the female. Mind you, the old penis is just as hard, but the angle is different, and this gives the old boy some clitoral leverage not natural to the young. I suspect old Sidney knew some of this and put it to good advantage. My information is he was found early one Monday morning dead in the saddle with the young lioness he had been incarcerated with still urging him on. She had conceived, though, and later bore Sidney a posthumous son.

When I make my rest home rounds I'm always astounded at the sexual socialization process. You'd think that wizened-faced old anhydrous men and women wouldn't be especially particular about each other. At first it's shocking to discover that not only do they care who their roommate is, but they connive to be seated next to someone they're interested in at the card table or dinner table. And the women still insist on ribbons in their hair and decorum befitting the circumstance in their men. And their men still insist on aftershave lotion in preparation for the dance that night. Stella, who at eighty-eight suffers from arterial insufficiency to the lower extremities, nevertheless walks the halls at night and has been known to end up in strange beds. Otha presents a management problem because he prefers self-abuse to going to all those boring social functions "where everybody is trying to make out." The gamut of sexual problems is there, and the nurses on duty compile lists of such management problems, which they save for the visiting doctors who are conceived of as some sort of referees who arrive once a week to arbitrate them.

Those of us who are privileged to make these rounds experience every week the amazing pearls that drop from the aged. I am reminded again and again of Thomas Berger's wonderful book *Little Big Man* in which a journalist goes to a rest home and tapes an interview with an old man, supposedly the oldest living Indian fighter and possible survivor of Custer's last stand at the battle of the Little Big Horn. Berger's device is extremely clever because the possible senility of the storyteller acts as a disclaimer to the truth being imparted. And yet in a day and age when minority representation has just about replaced our Founding Fathers' dream of majority rule (Indian underwear—it always creeps up on you—is no longer funny), Berger has the "senile" old man tell about Indians as it was. The result is not only hilarious, but the hilarity smacks solidly of the truth. We see smallpox, smell the unmistakable odor of the campground ten miles downwind, know promiscuous Indian maidens, hear babies left to cry in the trees, live with demon rum run wild, massacres, and chieftains who care mostly about their own empty bellies. Perhaps the old boy is all wrong, of course, but if one thing is true about him, it is that he is no longer inhibited in his opinions.

What persists in old age at the rest home is a residue of truth that tends mostly to dwell on good times. Even Berger's old Indian fighter recounts his tale with joy and nostalgia for what he's experienced. One of my little old lady patients once put it this way for me—whether it was a quote or her own creation I can't say, but it is from her lips I dearly remember it. "Above all, young man, I wish you joy in the things which are fashioned for joy, and an honest sorrow in what is of its nature sorrowful." She was eighty-nine when she said this to me, and she died a few weeks later from lung cancer. What she meant, of course, was you had to experience it all in order to really have life, there was no avoiding this or that emotional experience, however distasteful, in the process of fulfillment. "Be yourself," she said to me at the end. "Especially, do not feign affection. Neither be cynical about love; for in the face of all aridity and disenchantment it is as perennial as the grass." This time I recognized the quote from the beautiful "Desiderata," the famous credo for living

296

found in Old Saint Paul's Church in Baltimore and written anonymously in 1692. It is this amazing resilience the human being has in the face of hard truth that persists to the end, and the tincture of time that heals all wounds with its remarkable balm of allowing us to enjoy the recollection of all the good things. It is Hemingway's old man in the *Old Man and the Sea*, near death and worn down from three days of fending off sharks from his tiny boat, who yet dreams of the youthful time spent on a beach in Africa when the lions came down to the water and he watched them frolic with their children on the beach. Lions playing on a beach! How beautiful an old man's dream even in the face of death.

Again and again I have faced death with old people and again and again I have made no sense for them out of those who would exhort us to "Rage, rage, against the dying of the light." It makes no sense to them, anymore than to the megalomaniacal poet of "Invictus" who declares:

> *Out of the dark that covers me*
> *Black as the pit from pole to pole*
> *I thank whatever Gods may be*
> *For my unconquerable soul!*

For one who has been charged with watching and helping people die for many years, this is definitely not the stuff of dying. The real secret to dying well is the feeling of having lived. Only those old people who somehow still feel cheated or feel they haven't experienced a full life are the ones who don't face death with courage, resignation, and welcome relief. Dying well means a lifetime that has been filled with activity, the activity of love and work and giving yourself away. This has meant, above all else, risk, I repeat risk, and a willingness to be wrong and move ahead from error. Those who have been selfish, self-indulgent, and conservers of life are often bitter at the end. Petrakis says this again in the beautiful story, "The Wooing of Ariadne," in which a Greek resistance fighter lies wounded thinking about his coming death: "I accepted the coming of death and was grateful for many things. For the gentleness and wisdom of my old grandfather, the loyalty of my companions in war, the years I sailed between the wild ports of the seven seas, and the strength that flowed to me from the Spartan earth. For one thing only did I weep when it seemed I would leave life, that I had never set ablaze the world with a burning song of passion for one woman. Women I had known, pockets of pleasure that I trembled for quick joy, but I had been denied mighty love for one woman. For that I wept."

It is hard therefore, as Jesus said, for that conserver, that self-centered or indulgent rich man to enter the kingdom of heaven. But those old people who have lived life in all its abundance, good and bad, face death in old age with open arms. They come to agree with Socrates that death is our great possession on earth, with Seneca who said death was the best invention of life, with Saint Paul who said "To die is gain." This I'm certain of, and have seen it again and again. So live. Their message is there for us and it is always the same. Live!

Years ago I spent a lot of exuberant youthful time on stage as an actor. Sometimes the applause was deafening, and to see the smiles on all those thousand faces over the footlights was an ego trip in itself. People live for just that, and just that sort of thing alone. What a fantastic approbation of YOU! But then later when you sit on the side of your bed at night and kick off your slippers you are all alone, the makeup is gone, there is no applause, suddenly an unbelievable deathly silence reigns, and it is, as Faulkner so eloquently said, the human heart against itself. The moment of truth has come. You are really you. The toothache you have ignored all day begins to throb, the cut you got at lunch on a sardine can now stings and burns, the menstrual cramps are real, the tennis elbow creaks, the nervous headache is not going away, and your loins complain. Applause will no longer make anything go away. For my part this drove me into surgery, instead of acting, where there was only the quiet metronome of the heartbeat and no applause. "You look around at the growing edifice of your life," writes the actor Peter Ustinov, "and admit to yourself that it is beautiful, but beautiful to what purpose? What and who is it for? Solitude is a necessary ingredient to the act of creation, but loneliness is very different." When I sat after surgery on my bedside and kicked off my slippers at night there was no bravo to confuse me, only the exhausted weakness my own flesh felt, only now with the goodness I had been able to render another human being, for me in that very tangible way. Now that I am older I no longer make such distinctions; I recognize you needn't only do a heart transplant to help mankind. But in the end, the complaining flesh does triumph, becomes weak, while our spirit remains demanding, forever willing and hopeful of fulfillment. We become again those Idaho school children being urged on to their psychobiological destiny by Papa Hemingway.

By now we know the signposts and roadblocks, by now we know the perils of not squarely facing our journey to the end of the night. And we feel that fullness Papa meant and how it is based on certain classic, yes primal impulses in men and women that allow them to laugh and cry and love together all along the way. We have seen them destroyed by advocacy, but never by adversity. We can look to the great love affairs of this century—the Duke and Duchess of Windsor, Kay Summersby and Dwight Eisenhower, Lillian Hellman and Dashiell Hammett, Maud Gonne and W. B. Yeats, Jacqueline Kennedy and Aristotle Onassis—to find the truth of this. But we really needn't look further than our own lives to know how our souls cry out for each other.

Every month or so I quietly drive down the magnificent coast of California to see an elderly couple both of whom have been my patients for ten years. It is one of the most remarkable experiences of my life. They each contracted the same type of rare bowel cancer at the same time. Each of them had radical surgery the same week, leaving them with colostomies and limited activity. Over the past ten years, they have had multiple hospital admissions and all manner of painful treatment together to halt their disease process from which they are both now finally dying, she perhaps more slowly than he.

In their house there is one carefully cleaned bay window, a porthole that overlooks the Pacific where nightly they share "one last drink" together and watch the golden sun sink gently into the western ocean before going off to bed. In their bedroom there is but one narrow bed which they insist on occupying, snuggled together, as they always have, until the end. I never leave them without a melancholy tear in my eye for their confidence and courage, yes, but much more for the soulful love they still share that sustains their coming death.

And this is the very beauty we are all reaching for. It is the beauty of the wholeness of our soul that needs the inevitable comfort of the male and female all wrapped up as one together in the warmth of one small bed against the night. Without acknowledging that eternal need our soul will be forever incomplete. But if we do acknowledge it, work on it, and, above all, allow the soul its fullness we will take love into the darkness of our bed each night and awaken again refreshed in the sunshine of another day. According to the great Homer it is only the gods, not us, who are immortal, "So Jove, the Olympian Lord of Thunder, went to the bed in which he always slept; and when he had got in he went to sleep, with Juno of the Golden Throne by his side."

You see, in the end even they need each other. And as for the rest of us, well, we never completely kick the habit. Woman can never completely escape herself except through her knowledge of man, and man can never realize himself except through his knowledge of woman. And taken altogether this incomparably beautiful possession finally becomes love.

REFERENCES

Chapter 1.

p. 17, William Carlos Williams, *White Mule* (New York: New Directions, 1937), pp. 1–10

pp. 21–22, Peter Ustinov, *Dear Me* (New York: Penguin Books, 1977), p. 220.

pp. 23–24, Albert Einstein, "Letter to a Child," *Princeton Alumni Weekly*, March 12, 1979, p. 17.

Chapter 2.

p. 35, T. Berry Brazelton, *Infants and Mothers* (New York: Dell, 1969), pp. 41–70.

p. 35, Jones, H. E., *Motor Performances and Growth* (Berkeley: University of California Press, 1949), pp. 1–25.

p. 37, M. Harris, *Columbia Magazine*, Summer, 1978, pp. 9–13.

p. 37, Richard E. Leakey, *Origins* (New York: E. P. Dutton, 1977), p. 237.

p. 41, Oswald Spengler, *The Decline of the West* (New York: Alfred A. Knopf, 1928), pp. 99–105.

Chapter 3.

p. 44, Spengler, *Decline of the West*, pp. 327, 328.

p. 51, Nina Schneider, *The Woman Who Lived in a Prologue*, (Boston: Houghton Mifflin, 1980), p. 245.

p. 55, William Faulkner, *The Faulkner Reader* (New York: Random House, 1956), pp. 3–4.

p. 56, William Manchester, *American Caesar* (New York: Dell, 1979), pp. 57–65.

pp. 58–59, Jolange Jacobi, *The Way of Individualization* (New York: Harcourt, Brace, 1967), p. 114.

p. 59, T. S. Eliot, "East Coker," in *Four Quartets* (New York: Harcourt, Brace, & World, 1952), page 127.

p. 59, Midge Decter, *The New Chastity and Other Arguments against Women's Liberation* (New York: Coward, McCann, Geoghegan, 1972).

p. 63, W. B. Yeats, "Among School Children," and "Leda and the Swan," in *The Collected Poems of W. B. Yeats* (New York: Macmillan, 1933), pp. 211, 212.

p. 66, D. H. Lawrence, "Phoenix," Complete Poems of D. H. Lawrence (New York: Viking Inc., 1971), p. 728.

p. 67 May Sarton, *Mrs. Stevens Hears the Mermaids Singing* (New York: W. W. Norton, 1965), p. 112.

Chapter 5.

pp. 95–96, Günter Grass, *The Flounder* (New York: Fawcett, 1978), pp. 392–94.

pp. 96–97, Schneider, *The Woman Who Lived in a Prologue*, pp. 153–54.

p. 102, Robert Penn Warren, "Brothers to Dragons," *American Poetry Review*, Jan.–Feb. 1979, p. 5.

pp. 102–3, Ernest Hemingway, *Death in the Afternoon* (New York: Charles Scribner's Sons, 1932), p. 278.

pp. 106–7, Wolfgang Lederer, *The Fear of Women* (New York: Harcourt, Brace, 1969), pp. 216–17.

p. 108, D. Goldstein et al., *The Dance-Away Lover* (New York: Ballantine, 1977), p. 15.

pp. 108–9, Herbert Gold, "War Every Morning: Meditation on a Part-Time Depression," *American Poetry Review*, Jan.–Feb., 1980, p. 43.

Chapter 7.

pp. 155–56, Grass, *The Flounder*, p. 220.

p. 161, Emily Dickinson, "My Life Closed Twice before Its

Close," *The Poems of Emily Dickinson* (Cambridge, Mass.: Harvard University Press, 1963), p. 1166.

p. 165, Manchester, *American Caesar*, p. 736.

Chapter 8.

pp. 182–83, William Faulkner, *The Hamlet* (New York: Random House, 1964), p. 95.

p. 183, W. H. Auden, "In Memory of W. B. Yeats," *The Collected Poems of W. H. Auden* (New York: Random House, 1976), p. 198.

Chapter 9.

pp. 217–18, Schneider, *The Woman Who Lived in a Prologue*, p. 282.

p. 218, Dickinson, "Surgeons Must Be Very Careful," *Poems*, p. 81.

p. 220, George Will, *Newsweek*, December 11, 1978, p. 116.

p. 221, Rainer Maria Rilke, *Selected Poems*, ed. C. F. MacIntyre (Berkeley: University of California Press, 1971), pp. 4–5.

p. 226, William Bradford, *History of Plymouth* (New York: Walter J. Black, Inc., 1948), pp. 100–101.

p. 230, George Will, *Newsweek*, February 18, 1980, p. 120.

Chapter 10.

p. 237, Virginia Woolf, quoted in *Psychology Today*, November, 1978, p. 120.

p. 238, Elio Vittorini, quoted in Schneider, *The Woman Who Lived in a Prologue*, p. 223.

pp. 239–40, Wallace Stevens, in *One Hundred Modern Poems* (New York: Mentor Books, 1949), pp. 140–41.

pp. 248–49, W. Jackson Bate, *Samuel Johnson* (New York: Harcourt Brace Jovanovich, 1975), pp. 259; 341–45.

pp. 253–54, Joseph Wechsberg, *The Merchant Bankers* (New York: Pocket Books, 1968), p. 20.

p. 254, Douglas Reed, *W.F.B. An Appreciation. Odyssey of an Oil Man* (New York: privately printed), pp. 170–71.

pp. 254–55, John Bartlow Martin, *Adlai Stevenson and the World* (Garden City: Anchor Press Doubleday, 1978), p. 115.

Chapter 12.

pp. 280–81, Davetta Greenberg, "I Can Count on It," *American Poetry Review*, March–April, 1980, p. 14.

pp. 282–83, Lawrence, quoted in *American Poetry Review*, vol. 8, no. 4, 1979, p. 37.

pp. 283–84, Schneider, *The Woman Who Lived in a Prologue*, p. 1.

pp. 292–93, Paul Gauguin, *The Writings of a Savage* (New York: Viking, 1978), pp. 100–101.

pp. 293–94, Charles McCabe, "This Thing Called...," *San Francisco Chronicle*, July 12, 1979, p. 53.

pp. 294–95, Hillinger, Charles, "What Has 4 Legs, Is 188 Years Old," *Los Angeles Times*, April 17, 1979.

pp. 297–98, Harry Mark Petrakis, *A Petrakis Reader* (Garden City: Doubleday, 1978), pp. 43–44.

pp. 298–99, Ustinov, *Dear Me*, p. 238.

ACKNOWLEDGMENTS

continued from copyright page
Differences in Development by T. Berry Brazelton, M.D. Copyright © 1969 by T. Berry Brazelton, M.D. Reprinted by permission of Delacorte Press/Seymour Lawrence.

DECTER, MIDGE. Excerpts from *The Liberated Woman* by Midge Decter. Copyright © 1972 by Midge Decter. Reprinted by permission of Coward, McCann & Geoghegan, Inc.

DICKINSON, EMILY. "My Life Closed Twice Before Its Close" and "Surgeons Must Be Very Careful" from *The Poems of Emily Dickinson*, edited by Thomas H. Johnson, Cambridge, Mass.: The Belknap Press of Harvard University Press. Copyright 1951, © 1955, 1979 by the President and Fellows of Harvard College. Reprinted by permission of the publishers and the Trustees of Amherst College.

EINSTEIN, ALBERT. Excerpt from a letter to a child, written by Albert Einstein in 1936, from the *Princeton Alumni Weekly*, March 12, 1979. Reprinted by permission of the *Princeton Alumni Weekly*.

ELIOT, T. S. Excerpt from "East Coker" from *Four Quartets* by T. S. Eliot. Reprinted by permission of Harcourt Brace Jovanovich, Inc., and Faber and Faber, Ltd.

FAULKNER, WILLIAM. Excerpt from *The Hamlet* by William Faulkner. Copyright 1940 by William Faulkner, renewed 1968 by Estelle Faulkner and Jill Faulkner Summers. Reprinted by permission of Random House, Inc. Excerpts from "Nobel Prize Address" by William Faulkner from *The Faulkner Reader*, published by Random House, Inc.

Lines from "In the Mood" by Joe Garland and Andy Razaf copyright MCMXXXIX, renewed by Shapiro, Bernstein & Co., Inc. Used by permission.

GAUGUIN, PAUL. Excerpt from *Writings of a Savage* by Paul Gauguin. Copyright English translation © 1978 by Viking Penguin Inc. Reprinted by permission of Viking Penguin Inc.

GOLD, HERBERT. Excerpt from "War Every Morning: Meditation on a Part-Time Depression" by Herbert Gold. Copyright © 1980 by Herbert Gold. Published in *The American Poetry Review*, Jan/Feb 1980. Reprinted by permission of the author and his agent, James Brown Associates, Inc.

GOLDSTEIN, DANIEL. Excerpt from *The Dance Away Lover* by Daniel Goldstein, Katherine Larner, Shirley Zuckerman and Hilary Goldstein. Published by Ballantine Books.

GRASS, GÜNTER. Excerpts from *The Flounder* by Günter Grass. Copyright © 1977 by Hermann Luchterhand Verlag, English translation by

Ralph Manheim copyright © 1978 by Harcourt Brace Jovanovich, Inc. Reprinted by permission of Harcourt Brace Jovanovich, Inc.

GREENBERG, DAVETTA. Excerpt from "I Can Count on It" by Davetta Greenberg. Copyright © 1980 by Davetta Greenberg. Published in *The American Poetry Review*, March/April 1980. Reprinted by permission of the author.

HARRIS, MARVIN. Excerpt from "Why Men Dominate Women" by Marvin Harris from *Columbia* magazine, Summer 1978. Reprinted by permission of *Columbia* magazine.

HEMINGWAY, ERNEST. Excerpt from *Death in the Afternoon* by Ernest Hemingway. Copyright 1932 by Charles Scribner's Sons; renewal copyright © 1969 by Ernest Hemingway. Reprinted by permission of Charles Scribner's Sons.

HILLINGER, CHARLES. Excerpt from "What Has 4 Legs, Is 188 Years Old" by Charles Hillinger. Published April 17, 1979 in Los Angeles *Times*. Copyright © 1979, Los Angeles *Times*. Reprinted by permission.

JACOBI, JOLANDA. Excerpt from *The Way of Individuation* by Jolanda Jacobi. Reprinted by permission of Harcourt Brace Jovanovich, Inc. Excerpt from *The Psychology of C. G. Jung* by Jolanda Jacobi. Copyright © 1962, 1968, 1973 by Jolanda Jacobi. Reprinted by permission of the Yale University Press.

JOHNSON, SAMUEL. Quote from *Samuel Johnson* by Walter Jackson Bate. Published by Harcourt Brace Jovanovich, Inc.

JONES, H. E. Excerpt from *Motor Performances and Growth* by H. E. Jones. Published by the University of California Press.

LAWRENCE, D. H. Excerpt from "Phoenix," from *The Complete Poems of D. H. Lawrence*. Copyright 1936 by Frieda Lawrence, copyright renewed © 1964 by the Estate of the late Frieda Lawrence Ravagli. Used by permission of Viking Penguin Inc., and Laurence Pollinger, LTD. Quote from *American Poetry Review*, Volume 8, No. 4, 1979. Used by permission of *American Poetry Review*.

LEAKEY, RICHARD. Excerpt reproduced by permission of the publisher, E. P. Dutton, from *Origins* by Richard E. Leakey and Roger Lewin. Copyright © Richard E. Leakey and Roger Lewin 1977.

LEDERER, WOLFGANG. Excerpt from *The Fear of Women* by Wolfgang Lederer. Copyright © 1969 by Wolfgang Lederer. Published by Harcourt Brace Jovanovich, Inc. Reprinted by permission of the author.

MCCABE, CHARLES. Excerpt from "This Thing Called . . ." by Charles

McCabe from the San Francisco *Chronicle*, July 12, 1979, copyright © San Francisco *Chronicle* 1979. Reprinted by permission.

MACINTYRE, C. F. Excerpt from *Rilke: Selected Poems* edited by C. F. MacIntyre. Copyright 1940 by C. F. MacIntyre. Reprinted by permission of University of California Press.

MANCHESTER, WILLIAM. Excerpts from *American Caesar* by William Manchester. Published by Little, Brown and Company.

MUGGERIDGE, MALCOLM. Excerpt from *The Third Testament* by Malcolm Muggeridge. Published by Little, Brown and Company.

PETRAKIS, HARRY MARK. Excerpt from "The Wooing of Ariadne" by Harry Mark Petrakis, from *A Petrakis Reader*. Copyright © 1960 by Harry Mark Petrakis. Published by Doubleday & Co., Inc. Reprinted by permission of the author.

REED, DOUGLAS. *William F. Buckley, An Appreciation—Odyssey of an Oil Man* by Douglas Reed. Copyright © William F. Buckley, Jr. Privately Printed. Reprinted by permission.

SARTON, MAY. Excerpt from *Mrs. Stevens Hears the Mermaids Singing* by May Sarton. Published by W. W. Norton and Company, Inc.

SCHNEIDER, NINA. Excerpts from *The Woman Who Lived in a Prologue* by Nina Schneider, published by Houghton Mifflin Company. Copyright © 1979 by Nina Schneider. Reprinted by permission.

SPENGLER, OSWALD. Excerpts from *The Decline of the West* by Oswald Spengler. Copyright 1928, renewed 1956 by Alfred A. Knopf, Inc. Reprinted by permission of Alfred A. Knopf, Inc.

STEVENS, WALLACE. "The Pleasures of Merely Circulating" by Wallace Stevens. Copyright 1936 by Wallace Stevens and renewed 1964 by Holly Stevens. Reprinted from *The Collected Poems of Wallace Stevens* by Wallace Stevens, by permission of Alfred A. Knopf, Inc., and Faber and Faber, Ltd.

STEVENSON, ADLAI. Quote from *Adlai Stevenson and the World* by John Bartlow Martin. Copyright © 1977 by John Bartlow Martin. Reprinted by permission of Doubleday & Company, Inc.

USTINOV, PETER. Excerpts from *Dear Me* by Peter Ustinov. Published by Little, Brown and Company.

VITTORINI, ELIO. Excerpt from *The Twilight of the Elephant* by Elio Vittorini. Copyright 1951 by Elio Vittorini. Reprinted by permission of New Directions Publishing Corporation.

WARREN, ROBERT PENN. Excerpt from *Brother to Dragons* by Robert

Penn Warren. Copyright 1953 by Robert Penn Warren. Reprinted by permission of Random House, Inc.

WECHSBERG, JOSEPH. Excerpt from *The Merchant Bankers* by Joseph Wechsberg. Published by Little, Brown and Company.

WILL, GEORGE F. Excerpt from "Visions of Sugarplums" by George F. Will from *Newsweek*, December 11, 1978. Copyright 1978 by Newsweek, Inc. All rights reserved. Reprinted by permission. Excerpt from "Armies Should Win Wars" by George F. Will from *Newsweek*, February 18, 1980. Copyright 1980 by Newsweek, Inc. All rights reserved. Reprinted by permission.

WILLIAMS, WILLIAM CARLOS. Excerpt from *White Mule* by William Carlos Williams. Copyright 1937 by New Directions. Reprinted by permission of New Directions.

WOOLF, VIRGINIA. Quote reprinted from *Psychology Today* magazine, November 1978. Copyright © 1978 Ziff-Davis Publishing Co. Reprinted by permission of Ziff-Davis Publishing Co.

YEATS, W. B. Lines from "Among School Children" and "Leda and the Swan" by W. B. Yeats are reprinted with permission of Macmillan Publishing Co., Inc., from *Collected Poems of W. B. Yeats.* Copyright 1928 by Macmillan Publishing Co., Inc., renewed 1956 by Georgie Yeats, and by permission of A. P. Watt, Ltd..

INDEX

DATE DUE